IMPROVING HEALTH AND PERFORMANCE IN THE ATHLETE

IMPROVING HEALTH AND PERFORMANCE IN THE ATHLETE

John Unitas
George Dintiman, Ed.D.

PRENTICE-HALL, INC., Englewood Cliffs, N.J.

Improving Health and Performance in the Athlete
by John Unitas and George B. Dintiman, Ed.D.

Copyright © 1979 by John Unitas and
George B. Dintiman, Ed.D.

Prentice-Hall International, Inc., London
Prentice-Hall of Australia, Pty. Ltd., Sydney
Prentice-Hall of Canada, Ltd., New Delhi
Prentice-Hall of Japan, Inc., Tokyo
Prentice-Hall of Southeast Asia Pte. Ltd., Singapore
Whitehall Books Limited, Wellington, New Zealand

10 9 8 7 6 5 4 3 2 1

Library of Congress Cataloging in Publication Data

Unitas, John,
    Improving health and performance in the athlete.

    Bibliography: p.
    1. Sports—Physiological aspects—Miscellanea.
2. Physical fitness—Miscellanea.   3. Athletes—
Health and hygiene—Miscellanea.   4. Sports—Accidents
and injuries—Miscellanea.   I. Dintiman, George B.,
joint author.   II. Title.
RC1235.U54   613.7'1   79-12459
ISBN 0-13-452607-4

To Two Great Coaches
James Max Carey and
Hubert H. Jack

Acknowledgments

The authors are indebted to numerous individuals who have assisted in the preparation and review of the manuscript. Special thanks are given to Virgil May, M.D., Orthopaedic Surgeon and University and Professional Team Physician; George Borden, University, Professional, and International Olympic Athletic Trainer; and William W. Miller, M.D., for their work with the material on Drugs, Nutrition, Prevention of Injuries, Aging and Performance.

Recognition is given to Barney Groves, Ph.D., for his contributions to the section on modern strength training and to Gilberto Rodriquez, M.D., for his expertise on allergies and athletics. The authors also express their appreciation to Mrs. Helen Unitas Gibbs, Mrs. Gladys Blough Dintiman, George Byers Dintiman, George Mitro, Steve Jacobs, Darrel Black, Stan Daley, Lester Zimmerman, and Loretta Jack for their valuable assistance.

The authors also want to thank the men at Gil's, Douglas Gibson, Chuck Williams, Tom J. Madden, and B. M. Smith for keeping us running under any conditions.

Also, a note of appreciation to Brenda and Elda who suffered through still another book; and to our champion athletes of the future, Lynne, Brian, Scott, Jennie, Brandon, Eric, and Alberto.

John Unitas
George B. Dintiman

Contents

Preface

This book fulfills a long-standing need in major sports, where misconceptions, myths, and dangerous practices still plague an area that has become an important part of the American way of life. Although athletics still contain many mysteries, there is a wealth of knowledge that should form the foundation or building blocks for training methods and practices in all sports. This book draws from all related areas—psychology, physiology, sociology, practical knowledge, expert opinion, and research—to provide answers to the questions and concerns of athletes, coaches, parents, and spectators.

The book is designed to assist the individual athlete in improving performance and reaching maximum potential in athletics through the shortest and safest possible route. It provides information for participants at all age levels, and we hope it will help bring them to the champion stage of their career. This is a question-and-answer book that provides only what we call "second-level" answers, answers that delve into the "why" and "how" and offer scientific support rather than merely citing unfounded information.

No phase of athletics is left untouched in this comprehensive approach to the massive knowledge and the many problems in the athletic world. Chapter 1 responds to the many common concerns of athletes and answers questions that are rarely asked and are even less often answered appropriately. Chapter 2 discusses the means of protecting oneself from negative environmental influences as well as preparing for optimum performance under all types of environmental conditions.

Chapters 3, 4, and 5 deal with drugs, nutrition, and weight control in athletics—each from the standpoint of maximum health protection and maximum performance.

Chapter 6 focuses upon a neglected area in athletics: that of handedness or use of the recessive (generally the left) hand. An attack for maximum development of the recessive extremities at various age levels is presented along with thorough treatment of the common concerns and misconceptions in this untapped but vital area for the potential champion.

Chapter 7 covers the spectrum of prevention of athletic injuries, to help the athlete attain a longer, healthier career by avoiding the common pitfalls.

Chapter 8 discusses the procedures, training methods, dangers, and planning essential to participation in sports at various ages, from little league football years to old age. The best and maximum ages for participation in various sports are given, as well as answers to coaches, athletes, and parents about both early and late year involvement in sports.

Chapter 9 is concerned with the special problems and practices of women in athletics. Their potential and limitations are covered in a general sense that should be helpful to women athletes in all sports activities.

Chapter 10 enters into the specific types of training programs in use in modern athletics. Each is critically evaluated with suggestions for its adaptation to your sport. The unique breakdown of training programs allows easy application to any training purpose or activity.

Chapter 11 offers a condensed version of two textbooks written by Dr. Dintiman on *Sprinting Speed: Its Improvement for Major Sports Competition,* and *How to Run Faster: A Do-It-Yourself Book for Athletes in All Sports.* No other text deals entirely with the improvement of sprinting speed. No other writing provides you with the necessary information for improving your speed of movement.

In summary, it can be stated that to the best of our knowledge there is no other book quite like this. A direct, accurate answer is provided to practically any question. Everything you ever wanted to know about becoming a champion athlete can be found in this book.

John Unitas
George B. Dintiman

1

Common Athletic Concerns

The cliché "any fool can ask more questions than a wise man can answer" is particularly applicable to athletics. There are numerous questions in the minds of athletes of all ages that need to be answered but that either are never asked or receive only a partial explanation. Fear, ignorance, and false information merely serve to retard an athlete's development, since a thorough understanding of these questions is vital to the planning of training programs, to physical development, and to the improvement of athletic skills throughout the years. Myths that retard athletic growth are both common and deeply imbedded. This chapter provides direct answers to many of these ignored and misunderstood questions. The "why" in athletics can no longer be avoided. When asked, "How does a radio work," the response that "You turn on the switch" is not an acceptable answer. Such a *first-level* answer does not delve into the internal phenomena responsible for receiving and transmitting sound waves, a knowledge of which is critical to the understanding of a radio. In this section, only *second-level* answers are provided that should result in a much greater understanding of the "why" of athletic activity.

CAN I BECOME A CHAMPION ATHLETE OR ARE CHAMPIONS BORN, NOT MADE?

Champions are products of hard work, not heredity. You do not have to be seven feet and weigh 250 pounds to become a champion athlete, nor do you need to be born with superior skill. Keep in mind that "heredity deals the cards, but environment plays the hand." Some athletes born with superior coordination and physical attributes never reach stardom, while others with only average qualities become champions. The difference is strong dedication to two broad areas: skill development for every aspect of your sport and physical development through numerous exercise programs to allow your body to perform these perfected skills with maximum power, strength, agility, endurance, and speed.

Coordination (skill in hand/eye or foot/eye movements, aerial movements or any body movements) is specific to the activity and high levels can be acquired with persistent, correct practice. You only have to watch "The Super-Stars" once to realize that not all modern-day champions are good all-around athletes. While there are exceptions like Kyle Rote, Jr., others may be poorly skilled in areas outside their specialty.

Often, the good, young athlete becomes a "jack-of-all-trades and master of none." Some even grow up to be three-sport athletes in college and still never reach champion status. Many could have become champions had they focused earlier in their careers on the one best sport for them. Becoming and remaining a champion requires total dedication to one sport year-around. This is true mainly because strength, muscular endurance, power, cardiovascular endurance, speed, agility and skill requirements vary from sport to sport. It is not possible to develop these qualities to the level needed to become a champion for more than one or two sports. The training approach to develop these areas is specific to each sport. Too much muscle bulk, for example, may be helpful to sports such as football or rugby and actually hinder performance in soccer, tennis, or distance running. This is also true for other factors. It is wise to focus by age 12–13 if your choice is an individual sport such as tennis, golf, or running, and by age 15–16 if it is a team sport such as football, basketball, baseball, soccer, field hockey, rugby, or volleyball.

Once you decide on your best potential sport, go after it with all the reading, training, and practice you can tolerate. Seek the best competition and learn to work on weaknessess until they are strengths. Master the contents of this book, learning to develop equal skill in both hands and feet, to eat the right foods, to control and alter your weight just right for your sport, to prevent disabling injuries that disrupt training, to stay in condition year-around, to develop your body to the fullest through exercise programs for your sport, and to develop your sprinting speed to its maximum potential.

Modern-day champions are hardworking, dedicated individuals. They did not develop superior skill or physical qualities in one year. For many, it meant at least two workouts every day and countless additional hours of practice time on skills over a period of 5–12 years. Those that eventually made it were the most persistent, dedicated and hard-working—not necessarily the most genetically blessed.

IS IT TRUE THAT SOME PEOPLE ARE ALLERGIC TO EXERCISE?

Yes. In a few cases, rashes do occur on the skin of the neck, upper thighs, behind earlobes, and occasionally on other parts of the body. This reaction may come about at the beginning of exercise and then disappear if exercise is continued, or it may be present after exercise. Generally, the rash does not last long and presents little health danger.

Why this happens is not well understood. It is felt that the histamines produced by exercise are not as readily destroyed in the body of an allergic person. Very gradually increased doses of histamine regulated by a physician, do build some tolerance in allergic individuals and help to improve this condition. This is not, however, a cure.

Very few people experience allergic reaction to exercise; for the large majority of the population, no reaction occurs. However, the possibility could provide a good crutch for opponents of exercise much the same way endocrine difficulty is blamed for obesity and the toilet seat is blamed for venereal disease. If allergic signs are present, avoid trunks that are extremely tight, wear clean, soft, and loose clothing for maximum ventilation, and consult your physician immediately. Some people break out in a rash just thinking about exercise; most of them will quickly sit down until either the rash or the thought disappears.

CAN ASTHMATICS EXERCISE AND ENGAGE IN SPORTS COMPETITION?

Yes. Exercise Induced Asthma (EIA) may occur in some individuals, however, requiring pre-medication before exercising. The symptoms of generalized wheezing, coughing, chest tightness, rapid shallow breathing, labored indrawing of air, and prolonged expiration last only a short time and will terminate even without medication in most cases. Athletes who experience some of these symptoms should work with their physicians and prevent their occurrence through self-administered self-medication. Don't stop exercising.

WHAT IS ATHLETE'S HEART?

The term "athlete's heart" or "sportherz" was first introduced in 1899 by a Swedish researcher who detected enlarged heart muscles among skiers and referred to the condition as a physiological enlargement. The term picked up momentum as the years went by, and today it has been mistakenly referred to as an abnormally enlarged heart muscle brought about from athletics or exercise.

Exercise does develop the heart more fully and cause it to become heavier, larger, and slower (fewer beats per minute), and to eject much more blood per beat than the untrained heart. These changes are natural and make the heart muscle much more efficient.

Keep in mind that a sound heart cannot be damaged by exercise. The few cases of death or heart damage associated with strenuous exercise have generally occurred where there was an undiagnosed heart or vessel condition.

It is also interesting to note that the heart size in champion athletes regresses after training is discontinued. The term "athlete's heart" should not be used. The changes that occur from athletics and exercises are not only known and normal, but also desirable.

WHAT IS ATHLETE'S KIDNEY?

In general, it is a mild condition characterized by the appearance of a small number of red blood cells in the urine. The disorder is common among football players, boxers, swimmers, and track and field athletes. It is apparently caused by a direct blow to the kidney area and/or forced bending.

There is no danger involved unless the condition leads to hemorrhage. Nevertheless, it is wise to contact a physician as soon as any abnormal symptoms occur and observe progress carefully. Serious kidney damage is unlikely; however, unattended damage and repetitive trauma are dangerous combinations. The malfunctioning of one kidney will end your athletic career.

HOW IS BLOOD PRESSURE MEASURED?

Blood pressure is measured by an instrument called a sphygmomano-meter and is expressed in millimeters of mercury units. A stethoscope is also used since blood pressure must be both heard and seen.

Blood pressure is merely the pressure of the blood against the inner walls of the arteries. A cuff is placed around the upper right arm just above the elbow joint while the person sits with the arm resting at heart level. The stethoscope earphone is then placed in the tester's ears and the bell placed over the person's brachial artery just above the elbow toward the inside of the arm.

The cuff is now pumped up until no sound can be heard. At this point, the tester releases the pressure slowly while observing the mercury column of the sphygmomanometer and listening. When the first pulse sound is heard, a reading on the mercury column is recorded as the *systolic pressure*. Keep in mind that the cuff is actually pumped up until the brachial artery is collapsed and no blood is permitted to pass through. A tourniquet has a similar effect. The exact pressure that then allows blood to pass through as the the cuff pressure is released is the point at which pressure against the outside and inside of the artery are the same—systolic blood pressure. This reading is always the higher one, since it represents the time when the heart is working or pumping blood.

Pressure continues to be released until the sound or beat changes and becomes muffled and almost inaudible. The mercury reading at this point is recorded as the *diastolic pressure* (lower figure, since the heart is pausing to fill up).

The difference between the systolic pressure and diastolic pressure is *pulse* pressure. Thus, an individual with a reading of 120/80 has a systolic pressure of 120, diastolic pressure of 80, and pulse pressure of 40. The diastolic reading is more important, since it represents the period when the heart is not adding to the force already present in the arteries.

WHAT IS NORMAL BLOOD PRESSURE?

Before we list some "normal ranges," it is important to note that pressure is altered by a number of factors:

1. *Age.* Blood pressure is higher in older people.
2. *Sex.* Slightly lower in women before menopause, higher thereafter.

3. *Emotion.* Increases with the slightest emotion.
4. *Posture.* Lowest in reclining position, higher in sitting position, and highest in standing and moving positions.
5. *Eating.* Systolic pressure rises after eating a large meal.
6. *Exercise.* Long-term endurance-type exercise tends to decrease pressure.
7. *Hardening of the Arteries.* With the buildup of plaque, arteries narrow and pressure increases. As an analogy, the same volume of water will place greater pressure on the inner lining of a narrow hose than of a wide one.

Normal blood pressure depends upon the individual. In general, a systolic pressure of 75–100 mm of mercury (children), 100–120 (young adults), 120–140 (older people) is within the normal range. The normal ranges of diastolic pressure is 60–80mm for children, 70–85 for young adults and 70–95 for older people. The old rule of thumb of 100 plus your age for systolic pressure should *not* be followed. It is now evident that a systolic pressure of over 140, even for a short period of time, is considered dangerous.

Consult your physician on normal pressure for you. A group of Thailand men, for example, were found to have readings of 90/60, which was perfectly normal for their style of living. Your physician will speak in terms of normal ranges and compare your pressure today with what it was in the past.

SHOULD ATHLETES GIVE BLOOD DURING THE COMPETITIVE SEASON?

No. The majority of research shows that this practice is undesirable and will decrease your performance. The performance of gymnasts, cross-country runners, wrestlers, and team sport participants was shown to be lowered and remain lowered for 5 to 18 days following donation of one pint of blood. Since competition in most sports occurs at least once weekly, there is little chance that you could recover fully in time for a contest.

Another factor is the psychological effects of blood donation upon performance. When a group of subjects were blindfolded and a needle was inserted to give the impression of blood being removed without actually withdrawing blood, performance was still decreased seven days later. Obviously, an athlete feels that giving blood causes weakness and loss of efficiency. This feeling then decreases performance.

Avoid giving blood while you are training unless it is a serious emergency. A part-time job is much more sound than the practice of "selling" your blood periodically. Give blood no more than once every six months to ensure your safety. Give to help others, not yourself. The practice of selling your blood is unsound and leads to too frequent visits to the hospital. It is not a very safe method of paying the rent.

WHAT IS THE PROPER WAY TO BREATHE DURING VIGOROUS EXERCISE?

Through your mouth. This allows air to enter and exit much faster since there is less resistance to overcome. At rest, the most efficient breathing is through the nose. Air is then warmed, moistened, and cleansed of foreign particles. However, on hot days, air does not need to be warmed and so mouth breathing actually helps to cool the body. During exercise, *nose breathing* cannot keep up with the increased demand for oxygen. To demonstrate this fact, you need only run a distance of one-fourth mile or more with your mouth shut.

Breathing is a very simple process that involves three steps: (1) gas exchange in the lungs, (2) gas transport to tissue by the blood, and (3) gas exchange between the blood and tissue. The rate of breathing is controlled by the amount of carbon dioxide in the blood rather than by the lack of oxygen. Normal breath rate varies from 12–20 per minute during rest to as high as 50–60 during exercise. As conditioning levels improve, breathing rate per minute is lowered.

In general, you will be more efficient if you leave breathing to nature. At rest, each person has a rate and depth of breathing most efficient for him or her; nature will find it. In sprinting, experts disagree as to how to breathe. Forced breathing prior to the command, "get set," and then holding the breath until the gun, is common in sprinting and swimming. This procedure is thought to improve steadiness and starting quickness. Some sprinters hold their breath throughout a 100-yard dash.

Since atmospheric oxygen is needed, exercise is one of the few times that it does not pay to keep your mouth shut.

I BECOME DIZZY WHEN PRESSING HEAVY WEIGHTS AND OCCASIONALLY ALMOST PASS OUT. WHAT CAUSES THIS?

You are not breathing correctly. In fact, you are holding your breath. You have touched upon an occurrence called the "Valsalva phenomenon." Don't let this phrase scare you, but don't take it lightly, either; it can result in death.

The Valsalva phenomenon causes a number of changes: (1) cardiac output is reduced, (2) cerebral blood vessels are constricted, causing (3) oxygen shortage and loss of consciousness. The danger occurs when you hold your breath (after hyperventilating) against a closed glottis and also contract the stomach muscles. The military press with extremely heavy weights provides an ideal setting for this occurrence.

Breath holding is dangerous! Hyperventilation before swimming underwater, for example, is related to anoxia (severe oxygen deficiency) and loss of consciousness. Underwater breath-holding contests should be avoided.

To breathe properly during weight training, inhale while the muscles are contracting and exhale while the muscles are relaxing. Loud and timed breathing does nothing more than fix the chest walls, which in turn aids shoulder and arm movement. However, do not be too concerned with controlled breathing when lifting weights. For efficiency and safety, just leave breathing adaptation to nature.

WHAT IS A HEART MURMUR?

A heart murmur is an abnormal sound caused by turbulent blood flow. The sound is caused by the speed of flow and by the currents which are due to restrictions and obstructions. The difficulty may be in an impaired valve that fails to close completely or valve orifices that are narrowed and slow the flow of blood.

In the case of valve defects, a greater load is placed on the heart, heart walls may increase in size, and tension increases inside the walls. In effect, the heart is less efficient and, in a sense, has to regurgitate blood twice.

In what is termed *functional* murmurs, no structural defect is evident to account for the abnormal sounds.

It is good to note here, do not participate in any form of strenuous athletics without a complete physical examination. Remember that exercise cannot harm a healthy heart, but it can cause serious damage to an unhealthy one.

WHAT IS CONSIDERED TO BE NORMAL HEART RATE?

The range of 50–100 beats per minute is considered normal. Most people will fall within this range. A 35–110 range is considered normal by some experts. Anyone falling outside these ranges would need to be examined carefully before he or she could be said to have an abnormal condition. Within this broad range, some reference point is needed to determine normality. Comparing your present rate with that of a year or so ago would be helpful. A rate of 100 today compared to 60 of a year ago would be abnormal.

Keep in mind that heart rate is affected by a number of factors: (1) age—high at birth, lowering steadily, and then increasing again in old age, (2) body position—lowest in a lying position, higher when seated, and highest when standing, (3) food intake—accelerated for two or three hours following a meal, (4) emotions—increased even because someone is about to or in the process of taking your pulse, (5) exercise—increased during exercise; lying or resting rate lowered as your conditioning level improves. The average resting pulse rate of the first ten finishers in the Boston Marathon several years ago was 36, (6) sex—7–8 beats per minute higher in women.

To check your rate, lie down or sit for approximately five minutes before placing the tips of the index and middle finger on the palm side of the wrist directly below the thumb. If the beat is too mild, use the carotid pulse by placing the same two fingers in the hollow of the neck. Count the beats for 15 seconds, then multiply by four. Be sure to repeat several times to check accuracy. Take the pulse in exactly the same position, under the same conditions, and at the same time of day every month.

If your exercise program is effective, heart rate per minute will slowly decline over a period of months and years.

DOES HYPNOSIS IMPROVE PERFORMANCE?

Yes. Both strength and endurance have been shown to improve while subjects were in a hypnotic trance. However, this is not a technique that can or should be used in athletics.

It appears that hypnosis helps performance by removing inhibitory influences that control the number of motor units activated and thus allowing a greater number to come into action. Suggestion and emotional excitement are also forms of hypnosis that can assist performance. Suggestion from a confident coach or even self-suggestion can favorably aid the athlete. Excitement can also cause "tying up" and poor performance; this reaction may be due to the activation of antagonistic muscles (muscles that should relax when the agonistic muscles contract) that oppose movement.

There is some indication that athletes have been hypnotized against pain to permit them to play with an injury; others have been hypnotized to win; still others have been hypnotized to aid rehabilitation from "minor" injuries, or for muscle relaxation. It would seem highly unethical and dangerous to use hypnosis to allow play with an injury.

ARE ATHLETES LESS INTELLIGENT THAN NONATHLETES?

Definitely not. They are, however, stronger, faster, and quicker, and they possess greater endurance, flexibility, power, and agility than the nonathlete. Clichés such as "strong as a bull and half as smart," "strong back and weak mind," promote this myth among the general population. An occasional athlete who reaches the masses and converses poorly also adds fuel to the fire.

When the question is approached experimentally, however, results are quite clear. High I.Q. children and gifted children display a greater interest in athletic games than the normal population. Participants in intramural sports possess a higher mean intelligence ranking than non-participants. Gifted students also have been found to have earned more varsity letters than nongifted students. Hundreds of examples of athletes who are exceptional scholars can be cited. Also, more and more professional athletes are completing degrees in medicine, law, teaching, and other professions.

There is a relationship between athletic skill and intelligence. One study did demonstrate that gifted students perform better than normal students in explosive power, sprinting speed, softball throw for distance, and basketball shooting. Among the mentally retarded, there is a clear relationship between skill and intellectual achievement.

There is no such thing as a good, dumb athlete. It takes a high degree of intelligence to perform in most sports—particularly at the college and professional levels. There are "dumb" athletes and "dumb" nonathletes. Athletics neither decreases nor increases intelligence, nor does it attract more people of low intelligence than other activities and professions. Don't bother trying to convince anyone of this fact—you won't.

DO ATHLETES LIVE LONGER THAN THE NONATHLETIC POPULATION?

Participation in athletics is thought by some to improve and maintain health and to prolong life. Others feel that life is shortened by athletics.

An early death of a famous athlete receives wide publicity and is purposely misinterpreted by opponents of exercise. This is just the type of reinforcement they need to justify inactive lives.

Numerous researchers have attempted to compare the longevity of athletes and nonathletes. All have come to the same conclusion: there is no difference between the two groups. These studies provide only part of the answer and one must consider these facts:

1. Women exercise less than men; however, they live longer.
2. Heredity, diet, and job hazards are not taken into consideration in these studies.
3. Athletes are much more physically adventurous and are more likely to die from accidents. If only natural death were used, results of similar studies might differ.
4. Athletes are more likely to gain weight when exercise stops; weight gain shortens life.
5. Athletes are more likely to attempt strenuous exercise later in life without preconditioning—a dangerous practice.

So athletes live as long as the nonathletic population. The athlete who continues daily exercise throughout life (with no interludes of inactivity) may last the longest. Unfortunately, there are no studies to support this theory. Even more unfortunate is the fact that there are so few subjects to study.

DOES MASSAGE IMPROVE PERFORMANCE?

Massage may aid performance for some individuals. It was first developed as a method of detecting pain and later recognized as a valuable tool in improving circulation (an aid to venous return of blood back to the heart), increasing blood flow to a massaged area, improving muscle tone, raising body temperature, stimulating the nervous system (massage to the head), improving skin elasticity, and encouraging perspiration and removal of toxic agents. Massage must also be directed at a specific muscle group which varies from sport to sport.

Massage is used in athletics at three time periods:

1. *Before competition*, to prepare the muscles for rigorous activity, particularly in cold weather, and to improve physical and psychological states. *Gentle* massage is preferred.
2. *During competition,* to increase the flow of blood and relax muscle groups during rest periods. *Light* massage is preferred.

3. *After competition,* to help eliminate fatigue products, relax muscle groups, and aid recovery. *Kneading* is preferred.

Massage will *not* improve muscle strength, increase endurance, or aid skill execution. Hard, systematic training remains as the only known effective technique. If you're looking for a cure-all or a shortcut to conditioning, *rub* your head and think—continue to massage your head until you return to your senses.

IS MENTAL PRACTICE HELPFUL IN LEARNING A SPORT'S SKILL?

Yes. Mental practice refers to merely thinking about the execution of a skill without any physical involvement. Thus, you might sit and seriously contemplate about the forehand drive in tennis, thinking through the entire movement. It is hypothesized that this method causes mental activity or organization that aids physical performance. Research supports this theory as indicated by improved performance, following mental practice, in bowling, handball serving, free-throw shooting, weight lifting, dart throwing, and sit-ups.

It is not as simple as it seems. You must know how to concentrate and what to think about. Also, mental practice is not a *substitute* for actual physical practice. Physical practice is more effective than mental practice; however, the use of both mental and physical practice is more effective than physical practice alone. Try it by applying mental practice just *prior to* an actual physical practice session, *with* a physical practice session, or as *homework* in your room. You can sense the muscular involvement. It is also a good substitute for worrying.

WHAT CAUSES MUSCLE SORENESS FOLLOWING EXERCISE?

You may experience one or two types of soreness: (1) general soreness that is present immediately and disappears three or four hours after exercise stops, or (2) localized soreness or lameness appearing 8 to 24 hours after exercise stops and persisting for several days. The older you are, the longer the period between exercise and muscle soreness. At age 20, it may appear within a few hours, at age 25 the following day, and not for two or three days for the 50-year-old.

The exact cause of this phenomenon is unknown, although it appears that pain occurs because the muscles are working without adequate blood supply and as a result the waste products are not removed; it is thought that the accumulation of lactic acid and acid metabolites irritate the receptor organs of pain located in the muscles. This theory may partially explain the cause of general soreness, but sheds little light on localized soreness. Localized soreness is sometimes explained as being caused by injury to muscle fibers or of the sarcolemma (gap between the fiber and the axion), which transmits current to contract the tendon; damaged tissues are then repaired, resulting in a stronger muscle that is less vulnerable. However, it is unrealistic to believe that fibers are so sensitive and weak as to be ruptured by mild or moderate exercise. A more accepted theory is that fluid builds up, causing swelling and stiffness. The fluid compresses and irritates the nerve endings and causes pain. Regardless of the cause, it hurts, will impair your performance, and is almost certain to occur if you report to the first practice in any sport in poor physical condition.

HOW IS SORENESS RELIEVED AND PREVENTED?

Soreness can generally be relieved by asking your coach to:

1. Determine which muscles are sore.
2. Consult a book on anatomy to locate the attachments of the sore muscles.
3. Hold the attachments as far apart as possible for 1½–3 minutes. Repeat twice waiting 1–2 minutes between the two repetitions. For pain in the calf, for example, place the subject in a seated position, leg extended fully, and push the toes toward the knee.
4. Perform the above every four hours until pain is relieved.

You can reduce the risk of soreness by warming up properly, avoiding bouncing-type stretching exercises, and slowly increasing your exercise effort rather than overextending yourself early in a workout or training program.

The location of muscle soreness indicates either the area of least trained muscles or the area of greatest exercise concentration. In early season, you are likely to experience some muscle soreness. Light exercise will help to remove the waste products and eliminate the pain. Do not stop exercise completely because of muscle soreness; it may reoccur when you return to vigorous training.

WHAT IS MUSCLE TONE?

The term muscle tone or *tonus* refers to the quality of firmness in a muscle. Years ago, it was thought that this firmness was due to constant contraction of a number of motor units that alternated to prevent fatigue. A more modern theory suggests that it is due to the property of elasticity of the muscle and connective tissue and the pressure in the tissue caused by body fluids. It is true, however, that some muscles are often slightly contracted even at rest.

Exercise improves the tone of skeletal muscles, with weight training bringing about the fastest improvement in a specific area. For overall improvement, activities such as running, swimming, cycling, and participating in sports offer the best approach. Poor tone in inactive people may be the cause of faulty posture, which could be improved with exercise.

Muscle tone can be measured by a precise instrument that is commonly used in the rehabilitation of injured muscles. Merely pressing various body parts will give you an indication of tone. To learn the difference between good and poor tone, press firmly on the bicep muscle (front of upper arm) and compare with a press to the stomach area.

IS RELAXATION IMPORTANT IN ATHLETICS?

Yes. The ability to relax helps to alleviate stress, tension, and fatigue, and can aid endurance and skill execution in any sport. Keep in mind that relaxation is a science in itself, with complete textbooks written on this topic. The brief comments here in no way cover its many aspects.

If there were two athletes with identical skills and conditioning levels, the one who had better mastered the art of relaxation would be the better performer. He would conserve more energy by avoiding unnecessary movements. He would give little concern to winning or playing badly. He would merely be in control, playing efficiently without mental distractions.

Relaxation allows you to use the muscles efficiently (correct number of muscle fibers activated, correct amount of force applied) and execute a skill with perfection. Tension inhibits this muscle control and causes an incorrect movement by destroying steadiness. Without a high level of conditioning, this steadiness would be replaced by tremor and uncoordinated movements.

You can help to develop relaxation by: (1) correcting faulty sitting, lying, and walking posture, (2) perfecting skill with continuous practice with "intent to improve," (3) relaxing fully during rest periods, while waiting to perform, (4) resting the eyes several times daily four or five minutes, (5) attaining a high level of conditioning, (6) practicing self-hypnosis, (7) learning to stand, sit, and walk in a relaxed manner during every inactive second of a contest.

In short, you must learn to conserve your energy and avoid tension during physical activity or competition, during the inactive periods of competition, and during completely inactive periods.

WHAT IS SECOND WIND?

In some athletes, signs of fatigue such as breathlessness, rapid pulse, and sore muscles are suddenly relieved. The load that appeared strenuous and may have caused breathlessness subsides. When this occurs, an athlete is capable of additional effort. This so-called second wind may not take place for you, or it may happen following some types of exercise and not others. In fact, some athletes complain that they never experience this sudden "freedom" from fatigue.

It is not fully understood why second wind occurs or what brings it about. The following observations may shed some light on the subject and assist you in the future:

1. It occurs earlier during violent exercise than during moderate exercise.
2. It is more likely to take place when the weather is hot, free from chilling winds, and when the performer is wearing warm sweat clothes.
3. It may come about sooner when a long, vigorous warm-up was used.

When second wind occurs, body temperature rises, arterioles relax and open, and energy is saved in supplying working muscles with oxygen. Obviously, at this point stress is relieved and you are capable of continued exercise. It may be that it happens in the following way: Fatigue products accumulate in the muscles because, until the respiratory system has time to adjust, the activity is anaerobic (performed with oxygen debt). There is, in simple terms, a lag in the chemical regulation of breathing. Eventually, respiration increases and catches up. This may be second wind. Actually, it is really the "first wind," as atmospheric air is finally being used efficiently.

Experiment in your training through use of a long warm-up, warm clothing, sweat box, or even artificial heat prior to exercise. When you find the technique that brings about this sudden relief from physical stress in your sport, use it before competition. Also, warm up properly. Most people's "second wind" is really their first: they quit much too soon even to have a second.

DOES SEXUAL INTERCOURSE HINDER PERFORMANCE?

No. At one time, scholarship agreements by some universities contained a clause against marriage, revoking the scholarship if the athlete did marry. This and numerous strict curfews imposed on athletes just prior to a contest may have helped develop this myth. Actually, sexual intercourse utilizes the approximate calories and energy expended in a 100-yard dash. Any athlete can recover from such minimum exercise in only a few hours and be relatively assured that his reserve energy stores are at their maximum. Coaches who do not favor marriage generally base their concerns on the multitude of problems, worry, and stress associated with matrimony.

There have been many coaches who practiced self-denial along with their athletes: eating at the training table, avoiding alcohol and tobacco, getting plenty of rest, and even engaging in calisthenics. *Mention has never been made of any coach giving up his sex life during the competitive season.*

DOES EXERCISE DECREASE SEXUAL ACTIVITY?

Definitely not. In fact, it is generally agreed that a physically fit individual, at any age, is more sexually active than an unfit individual. There is also a cause-effect relationship. Sexual activity will improve following the use of a daily exercise program over a substantial period of time (two or three months).

Dick Gregory, in a recent lecture to several thousand students, spoke about the true harm of tobacco: he claimed it destroys the sex organs. While this statement may be somewhat exaggerated, it is true that smoking does retard sexual activity.

The favorable effect of exercise and absence of smoking upon sexual activity may be partially psychological, associated with improved self-concept or image due to weight loss, feelings of virility, absence of tobacco breath, and a more healthy outlook on life. For the obese, exercise that brings about considerable weight loss can also help solve impotency problems that may be either physiological or psychological in nature.

Only at the beginning of a new exercise program for a previously inactive individual will tiredness retard sexual activity.

WHAT IS A STEADY STATE?

A *steady state* is a condition of homeostasis or body equilibrium, in which the internal workings are functioning efficiently to meet the demands of exercise to the point where one could continue that same activity for an indefinite period of time, provided tempo and pace are not altered.

The oxygen transport system governs when a steady state is reached. Specifically, when the atmospheric oxygen breathed in is exactly equal to exercise needs, a steady state has been reached. For joggers or runners, this may mean that they are capable of continuing at that same pace and under those same conditions for a long period of time. With more vigorous exercise, atmospheric air is insufficient to supply active muscles, so fatigue lactates build up in the muscle tissue and eventually exercise will cease or an athlete will be forced to slow down or alter his or her tempo.

SHOULD ATHLETES BE ALLOWED TO SWIM DURING THE OFF-SEASON PERIOD?

Yes. Swimming is a valuable summer activity offering considerable enjoyment and relaxation. Some individuals still harbor the misconception that swimming softens muscles and prevents the development of firmness and bulk needed for sports such as football, basketball, lacrosse, soccer, and rugby. There is absolutely no evidence to support this myth. In fact, swimming can be a valuable supplement to other conditioning programs. Vigorous swimming, using various strokes, can develop heart-lung endurance, with a portion of this improvement carrying over to other activities. On the other hand, you must admit that lazy lying in the water for long periods will contribute little to conditioning.

Swimming during the off-season or in-season period does not soften muscles; nor does it detract from strength gains acquired from other programs. If you become a "beach bum" and spend all your time walking in the sand while neglecting a summer conditioning program, there is reason for concern. You are expected to report to fall sports in top condition. Perhaps this is the real worry of coaches.

IS WARM-UP REALLY NECESSARY IN ATHLETICS?

At this point, let's say that warm-up is almost universally used by athletes in all sports for the purposes of (1) improving performance and (2) preventing muscle injury. The warm-up has been the target of researchers for the past 50 years and they have not always been in agreement. Of 37 studies reviewed, one study indicated that warm-up is harmful to performance, 12 found neither beneficial nor harmful effect, and 24 showed that performance was improved. Few cases of muscle injuries were reported when warm-up was not used. A limitation of most studies is the fact that no attempt was made to show that warm-up actually increased body temperature. Few studies used rectal temperature to demonstrate elevated temperature; those that did found warm-up *was* an aid to performance.

The theory behind warm-up is the dependency of muscle contractions upon temperature. Since increased muscle temperature improves work capacity and warm-up increases muscle temperature, it is assumed that it is a necessary practice. The amount of fluid in the knee is also increased with warm-up; oxygen intake is improved and the amount of oxygen needed for exercise is reduced following warm-up. Nerve messages also travel faster at higher temperatures. This logic is excellent, but it is not always backed by research.

Drawn from the findings of well-controlled studies that demonstrated elevated body temperature through warm-up, the following suggestions are offered:

1. Warm-up of a vigorous nature should be used for 10-15 minutes prior to activity.
2. Only a few minutes should elapse from completion of the warm-up until the start of activity.
3. More warm-up is needed in cold environment to cause the body to reach the desired temperature.
4. Warm-up will not bring about early fatigue and hinder performance.

It should also be pointed out that groups with a favorable attitude toward warm-up perform better with it, whereas groups with an unfavorable attitude do not. You also probably have a slightly greater chance of injury without warm-up. Experiment with different types and determine the best method for you and your activity.

WHAT IS THE BEST TYPE OF WARM-UP?

Warm-up methods fall into four categories:

1. *Formal.* Using the skill or act that will be used in competition: running before a 100-yard dash, or shooting and jumping before a basketball game.
2. *Informal.* General warm-up involving calisthenics or other unrelated exercises.
3. *Passive.* Applying heat to various body parts in numerous forms.
4. *Overload.* Simulating the activity for which warm-up is being used by increasing the load or resistance, such as use of weighted boots prior to a 100-yard dash or swinging two bats prior to hitting in baseball.

Each of the above methods has been shown to be helpful by some researchers. Each has also been shown to be of no value by others. Formal warm-up appears to be superior to informal procedures.

Evidence indicates that warm-up improves performance in the following circumstances:

Activity	*Type of warm-up*
1. accuracy of free-throw shooting	formal
2. arm speed	formal
3. bowling accuracy	formal
4. hitting performance in baseball	formal
5. leg strength	formal
6. passing and shooting a basketball	formal
7. speed of arm or leg movements	formal
8. swimming speed	formal, passive, informal
9. vertical jump	informal, passive
10. accuracy, velocity, and distance of throwing a ball	formal, informal, overload
11. spot running or running in place	formal

There has been no improvement noted in the following activities:

1. muscular strength	passive
2. endurance	passive, formal informal
3. performance on a bicycle ergometer	informal
4. arm speed	passive
5. 50-yard dash	formal
6. 440-yard dash	formal

As important as the *type* of warm-up is its *length*. Muscle temperature rises in 5 minutes and continues to rise for 25 to 30 minutes. With inactivity, the effects drop rapidly until, after 45 minutes, additional warm-up is needed. It would seem advisable to use 20–25 minutes of warm-up that causes perspiration and is a progressive procedure leading to all-out effort. Warm-up should end about 5 or 10 minutes before the contest begins and be initiated again just prior to the contest. Find the magic combination for you and your sport. Then stay with it.

IS IT NECESSARY TO TAPER OFF OR WARM DOWN FOLLOWING VIGOROUS EXERCISE?

Yes. This is desirable at the end of a vigorous workout. The explanation for this is quite simple. Blood returns to the heart through a system of vessels called veins. The blood is pushed along by the contraction of the heart and the "milking" action of the veins. The veins contract or squeeze and move the blood forward against the force of gravity while valves prevent the blood from backing up. If you stop suddenly, the milking action of the veins, which occurs only through muscle contraction, will stop; the blood return will drop quickly and may cause blood pooling in the legs (blood remains in the same area), leading to shock or deep breathing. The deep breathing then lowers carbon dioxide levels and muscle cramps develop. These cramps may last for 24–48 hours.

You should warm down following a long-distance run or a strenuous event such as the 440-yard dash. A general warm-down routine might consist of running 880 yards to one mile at a pace of two to three minutes per quarter-mile, each quarter-mile slower than the previous one.

If you ever suffer from the severe cramps that can occur from blood pooling, you will never omit a warm-down again. Make it a part of your general routine and avoid the problems.

WHAT ARE THE OLDEST SPORTS?

The exact date, site, and origin of some sports is unknown. Few originated in the United States, although basketball, football, volleyball, and baseball are claimed. Of these four, football was probably an outgrowth of rugby (which originated in England), baseball an offspring of cricket (also English), leaving basketball and volleyball to U.S. credit. Regardless of who deserves the credit, the United States has been a major force in the growth of practically every sport.

Archery	Developed by Neanderthal man 100,000 years ago.
Badminton	Probable place of origin is China in Pre-Christian era.
Baseball	1750's—derived from cricket. 1834—developed by Abner Doubleday at Cooperstown, New York.
Basketball	1892—James A. Naismith introduced game to a class at Springfield College. Invention of winter indoor game inspired by Luther Gulick in 1891.
Cricket	Pre-1344—believed to have originated in England.
Fencing	1410—German manuscript describing fencing as a sport. Exact origin unknown.
Football	1869—first intercollegiate game between Princeton and Rutgers. 1850's—touch football played in U.S.

Golf	Origin unknown. 1457—law passed in Scotland to prohibit golf.
Gymnastics	Originated in ancient Greece.
Handball	Origin lost in antiquity. Played in ancient Greece and Rome during Middle Ages.
Ice Hockey	1855—first game played by British Regiments. Origin unknown.
Rugby	1839–originated at Rugby College, England.
Soccer	Kickball game called "Harpastun" played in ancient Greece. 1175—played in England.
Swimming	Wall carving traced to 9000 B.C.
Tennis	1300—initiated in France.
Track and Field	776 B.C.—first Olympic games held in Greece.
Volleyball	1895—invented by William Morgan at Holyoke, Massachusetts YMCA.
Water Polo	1870—London Swimming Association began informal football in the water.
Weight Lifting	Pre-Christian era.
Weight Training	″ ″
Wrestling	Exact date, site, and origin unknown. Traced as far back as existence of civilizations of Babylonians, Egyptians, and Hindus.

WHAT IS THE MAXIMUM NUMBER OF PUSH-UPS AND SIT-UPS THAT HAVE BEEN PERFORMED?

A total of 6,006 push-ups were performed in 3 hours, 54 minutes. Another athlete completed 1,227 in 37 minutes. The sit-up record is 15,011 done in less than 6 hours.

Additional feats of strength and endurance that may interest you are listed below (from the Proceedings of the First International Symposium on the Art and Science of Coaching, Toronto, Canada, 1972):

Walking: 215 miles, nonstop, in 47 hours, 42 minutes
Running: 121 miles, 440 yards, nonstop, in 22 hours, 27 minutes
Cycling: 168 hours on a track (seven days)
Clapping: Continuous for 14 hours, 6 minutes at 140/minute
Bagpipe Playing: 50 hours
Face Slapping: 30 hours, claimed a draw
Spitting: 25 feet, 10 inches
Free-Throw Shooting: 144 in a row off one foot
Skipping: 32,089 turns without a miss in 3 hours, 10 minutes
Chinning the Bar: 106

Some of the above feats may appear impossible; however, they have been authenticated. Man's potential is far greater than most of us realize. The trick is to reach this potential in your sport and get the most out of yourself at all times. Unfortunately, a magician can't help you. Dedication, punishment, and the ability to withstand the physical pain of intense training are the successful combination.

DO FATHERS WHO ARE OR WERE ATHLETES PRODUCE MORE BABY GIRLS THAN BOYS?

No. The emphasis on baby boys, however, is greater in this group. When an athlete announces that his wife has just had a girl, the kidding begins. One person points out that the constant body heat present doing a workout results in the inability to produce a male offspring. Another blames the athletic supporter. Actually, there are male-producing sperm (androsperms) and female-producing sperm (gynosperms). No evidence is available to suggest that the sperm of athletes contains the two in any different proportion than the nonathletic male population. Masculine men are not any more likely or unlikely to produce male offspring. In fact, the sex of your child is in no way linked to masculine appearance, physical prowess, or lack of either.

Believe it or not, there has been research to determine the incidence of males and females born to fathers who are coaches. Unfortunately (for the kidders), there was no significant difference between the number of males born to coaches and to the noncoaching and nonathletic population.

There is some exciting research being conducted with regard to increasing probability of having a preferred sex. If you are interested, consult your physician for the most recent findings.

WHAT PHYSICAL DIFFERENCES EXIST BETWEEN BLACK AND WHITE ATHLETES?

This question is repeatedly asked because of the observation that black athletes are represented above their population proportion. Social and economic reasons do account for some of this high achievement; however, it must be said that there are physical differences:[1]

1. There is no significant height difference between blacks and whites.
2. The average weight of a black is from 3½ to 5½ pounds greater than the average weight of a white.

a. Skeletons of blacks are heavier than skeletons of whites.
b. A highly conditioned black possesses about 38% percent less protective fat.
3. Blacks have longer arms than whites, and the hand is also longer and wider.
4. Blacks have longer legs than whites.
5. Blacks have a shorter trunk in sitting height.
6. Blacks have a greater neck girth than whites.
7. Blacks are significantly more mesomorphic (more muscular) than whites.
8. Blacks are significantly faster in the knee-jerk or patellar tendon reflex, which may be associated with sprinting speed.
9. The vital capacity ratio for lungs is much less in blacks.[1]

The tendency to be heavier, more muscular, and possess longer legs and arms has implications for superior speed and performance in many sports. Inferior lung capacity leaves the black athletes less equipped in distance running and endurance activity. In basketball, football, boxing, sprinting, and numerous sports that have not been easily accessible to the black athlete there is reason to suspect that physical endowment provides an athletic edge. One thing is certain: the black athlete is not operating under a physical handicap. As soon as social handicaps are removed, many other sports are guaranteed to attract highly skilled black athletes.

2
Environment and Performance

Athletic performance and the function of the human body are altered by a number of environmental factors such as air pollution, altitude, clothing, field conditions, humidity, magnetic fields, noise, precipitation, radiation, and temperature. In many instances, the body requires an acclimation period, or exposure on a systematic basis, prior to all-out efforts. Ignorance in this area can and does result in loss of life each year on the athletic field or in the gymnasium. More commonly, it decreases performance, hinders conditioning improvement, and causes defeat.

This chapter discusses the possible effects of environmental factors upon performance, the dangers involved, the proper acclimation procedure necessary, and other tips that either aid performance or prevent loss of proficiency.

IS PERFORMANCE AFFECTED BY TIME CHANGES AND UNUSUAL HOURS FOR COMPETITION?

Yes. Man operates under a type of rhythmic behavior on a 24-hour basis. The physiological measurements (heart rate, body temperature, reaction to medicine, and so on) taken at 12:00 noon vary considerably from those taken at 12:00 midnight. While there is no experimental evidence to show how much physical performance is affected by competing at unaccustomed times, or by time changes when flying to a new time zone, it is safe to assume that there is an unfavorable effect.

Just as athletes need time to adjust to competition at high altitudes, they also need acclimation to different time zones and competition times. A minimum six-day acclimation period is suggested if top performance is desired. The body is extremely adaptable and will adjust; unfortunately, leaving in early morning to arrive at 8:00 or 9:00 A.M. just prior to a 2:00 P.M. game in the new time zone requires fast transition. It is too much to ask. You will be performing as an early-morning competitor, undoubtedly less efficient in spite of the fact that the sun may be shining overhead.

WHAT IS THE BEST TIME OF DAY FOR A CONTEST?

Performance is likely to be highest when competition time corresponds closely to daily practice time. Midafternoon is generally the best time for competition.

We are rhythmic creatures who are thrown out of synchronization with abrupt changes in time schedules—a normal occurrence when competing away from home.

HOW DOES HIGH ALTITUDE AFFECT ATHLETIC PERFORMANCE?

In general, performance in endurance-type activities, such as running distances of 800 meters or more, are hindered. Loss of proficiency can approach 20 percent. In Mexico City, the site of the 1968 Olympics, all times in distance runs were poorer than those performed at sea level by the same competitors. Let's examine why performance was hampered.

Man can supposedly live for prolonged periods at an altitude no greater than 18,000 feet, although some individuals have survived at heights of more than 29,000 (Mt. Everest) without supplemental oxygen. At high altitude, the density of the air is decreased, air is dry, exposure to the sun is increased, oxygen pressure is decreased, and, to add further complications, there is smog, it is colder, and winds blow harder. As a result, you are more subject to dehydration, burns from sun and wind, irritations of the eyes, nose, and lungs, and reduced oxygen supply. These differences in conditions cause numerous physiological changes and do reduce efficiency.

The situation is not entirely hopeless. The 20 percent reduction in efficiency can be reduced to as low as 10 to 12 percent through training at high altitudes for at least three to four weeks prior to competition. In fact, training for a week and then returning to sea level for a few days and then again training at high altitude has been shown to improve performance—both at sea level and at high altitudes. Olympic rules allow as much as four weeks of training at the Olympic site during the six months preceding the games.

It may also be necessary in high altitudes to change your mode of breathing in distance running, to breathe more often in swimming, and to alter your pace in the early part of a race.

WHAT IS THE IDEAL TEMPERATURE FOR HIGH-LEVEL PERFORMANCE?

The "comfort range" varies from one person to another and depends upon the type of physical activity and what temperatures you have been acclimated to. The amount of clothing worn (to preserve or dissipate heat), the amount of heat generated by activity, and the amount of acclimation time, then, determine your comfort range.

Individuals who live in tropical weather must adjust (one to two weeks) to cooler climates before performance will stabilize. The same is true for someone coming from a cooler to a warmer climate. Keep in mind that acclimation is also lost quickly unless continued exposure under training conditions takes place. Merely existing in a type of climate will not bring about acclimation and steady performance. Even individuals who live in a particular climate under sedentary conditions need a period of acclimation when training begins.

WHAT IS THE DIFFERENCE BETWEEN "RELATIVE HUMIDITY" AND "ABSOLUTE HUMIDITY"?

Relative humidity is the ratio between the moisture vapor in the air and the maximum amount of moisture vapor the air *could* hold at that temperature. Humidity and relative humidity are used as synonyms. The weather report gives the relative humidity, which is of little value to the athlete, giving no indication of skin evaporation rate or the amount of cooling from the lungs.

Absolute humidity provides more information to athletes since it indicates just the water vapor in the air and does not consider holding capacity. Needed evaporation also depends upon air movement, vapor pressure, and ambient air differences. Thus higher humidity is tolerated when there is considerable air movement. When the air is still and the humidity is high, little evaporation occurs and overheating is likely. Unfortunately, that isn't the only combination causing problems. Hot, dry weather (10–15 percent relative humidity) causes extreme sweating and loss of fluids and salts, again increasing the chances of overheating.

Check humidity levels daily during the hot months. Certain combinations of absolute humidity, temperature, air movement, activity intensity, and clothing can hamper performance and endanger health. The wrong combination coupled with a long, hard workout can result in death.

DOES A HIGH HUMIDITY CLIMATE AID LONGEVITY?

There is no evidence to suggest that high humidity either increases or decreases life span. Researchers cannot isolate humidity from ethnic, nutrition, and health habit differences. A higher incubator humidity of 65 to 90 percent has been shown to improve the survival chances of premature infants. Also, the number of calories burned at rest increases about three kilograms per minute with each 1 percent rise in humidity. As a result, you are in higher gear in a humid climate. This fact has brought about the question of longevity; however, to date no revealing evidence has been uncovered.

ISN'T HUMIDITY THE REAL LIMITING FACTOR WHEN PERFORMING IN SUMMER MONTHS?

While both temperature and humidity combine to form hazardous conditions, humidity *is* somewhat more important and must be carefully observed by both coach and athlete. With the relative humidity at 100 percent, performance is going to be affected even in a highly conditioned, heat-acclimated athlete. Unfortunately, the absolute humidity in some parts of the country often exceeds this limit.

The secret once again is acclimation. It is a dangerous practice to expose a group of athletes to unusually humid conditions that may differ drastically from their own environment.

Humidity affects the evaporation of water from the skin. This evaporation and subsequent cooling are needed to prevent overheating by maintaining a heat balance. The body simply needs help.

WHAT CAN BE DONE TO AVOID HEAT EXHAUSTION OR STROKE ON HOT, HUMID AUGUST FOOTBALL DAYS?

Most coaches and athletes are very well informed about the hazards and prevention of heat exhaustion and heat stroke. Without some control, however, the consequences are decreased performance and possibly even severe illness due to premature fatigue, heat cramps, heat exhaustion, or heat stroke. Heat stroke *is* a rare occurrence; the risk of death is higher in those who are obese, older, and nonacclimated to hot weather.

The basic problem is simply overheating. Body temperature is normally controlled by the circulatory system; however, when overburdened with supplying active muscles, it is unable to perform this task to prevent overheating. It therefore needs some external assistance.

Let's examine what you and the coach can do to reduce risk:

1. Avoid lengthy warm-up periods on hot, humid days.
2. Avoid adding to your normal intake of table salt; let taste be your guide and do not resort to the indiscriminate use of salt tablets. Eat sufficient fruits and vegetables and drink fruit juice to help maintain a mineral balance and to increase your potassium intake. Drink liquids cold to increase absorption speed from the stomach.
3. Drink water prior to and during exercise. Exercise several weeks prior to football practice under hot conditions to increase dehydration tolerance. Drinking water during practice is now an accepted method for delaying fatigue and helping prevent illness. Different athletes sweat at different rates. Some have no sweat glands at all; some lose 6–7 liters of water per day. You can't drink too much water, even though on hot days it is a good idea to try.
4. Decrease protein intake in hot weather. Protein digestion increases body heat.
5. Promote evaporation by wearing loose clothing, perforated, light-colored jerseys, and by wetting dry skin. Remove practice gear for 10 or 15 minutes on hot days to promote evaporation.
6. Check temperature and humidity, taking precaution when the temperature is 80°–90° and the humidity above 70 percent.
7. Remove wet clothing and replace. Wet clothing increases sweat and salt loss, and can lead to rapid dehydration.
8. Make accurate temperature and humidity checks with a psychrometer at 30- to 45-minute intervals, and apply the following guidelines:

Temperature	Humidity	Interpretation
Below 80°	70% or less	No precautions needed
80°–90°	70% or less	Be alert to signs of heat stress

Temperature	Humidity	Interpretation
80°–90°	70% or more	Use frequent rest periods, change wet uniforms, remove pads each 30 minutes
90°–100°	70% or less	Same as above
90°–100°	70% or more	Postpone practice or conduct short session in light clothing

Use additional precautions and slowly increase the exercise intensity of each workout until a tolerance to elevated body temperature is developed (this takes five to nine days). With time, sweat and salt loss also decreases. It is good advice to interrupt your workout each 30 minutes on hot days with rest periods and consumption of salt water (5 teaspoons of salt per gallon). Also, be alert to symptoms of heat stress such as dizziness, nausea, headache, excessive redness, and stoppage of perspiration.

Be alert to the symptoms and the precautions. The treatment for heat stroke is simply rapid cooling. Time is very important, however, and the risk of death once heat stroke occurs is high. As in so many other areas, the emphasis should be on prevention, for once the cycle is in full swing, recovery or survival chances are not good.

WHY CAN'T THE BODY LOSE HEAT TO THE ENVIRONMENT AND REMAIN COOL?

Let's quickly examine the four ways the body can lose heat to the environment:

1. *Radiation.* When body temperature is higher than that of the atmosphere (the ambient temperature), body heat loss occurs.
2. *Convection.* As a warm body loses heat, it warms the air it contacts. When this warmed air rises, cooler air moves in to take its place with those air movements (convection currents) cooling the body further.
3. *Evaporation.* The body loses heat from continuous evaporation of water from the skin into the atmosphere.
4. *Conduction.* Heat is conducted from deeper organs to the skin's surface through the blood vessels. The skin then acts as a radiation surface for heat loss to the environment.

With outside temperature of 90°F (equal to skin temperature), heat loss from convection and radiation does not take place, leaving evaporation of sweat as the only means of losing heat. Without perspiration's being converted to a gas by evaporation, the body will overheat. During hot, *humid* weather, when the outside temperature equals or exceeds skin temperature, sweat merely rolls off with no cooling. In theory, if the air is completely saturated with moisture in this kind of weather, no evaporation can take place into the air; the body would heat to 95°–108° and death would occur. This type of weather also increases the demands on the heart.

During hot, *dry* weather, regardless of the temperature, cooling does occur through evaporation which, in most cases, is sufficient to prevent overheating. Again, on some days the body needs help. It cannot adjust alone.

IS AIR CONDITIONING HELPFUL TO ATHLETES ON EXTREMELY HOT, HUMID DAYS?

Yes. Resting in an air-conditioned room while waiting to compete in a track event or tennis match, or at halftime, can help to prevent overheating and assist in returning the body to normal temperature. In fact, when rigorous activity on hot, humid days is interrupted by rest in an air-conditioned area, body temperature rise is reduced by about 75 percent.

There is one catch: the body will acclimate to heat with two to three weeks of progressively more strenuous workouts. This acclimation, so vital to spring and fall sports, may not take place if the above technique is used. The best time to use air-conditioned areas, then, is during rest intervals of an actual competition (tennis, badminton, track, football, rugby, baseball, and so forth) on a hot day.

HOW DOES IMPROPER CHOICE OF CLOTHING AFFECT BODY TEMPERATURE?

Most athletes are guilty of practicing in improper uniforms (too much or not enough clothing) at one time or another, either out of necessity or carelessness. Tradition also forces athletes to utilize clothing or uniforms unsuitable to the activity and environment. In general, improper clothing tends to either: (1) limit sweat evaporation and needed cooling on hot, humid days, or (2) fail to conserve heat on cold days. While the body will maintain heat balance under most conditions, it needs assistance on hot, humid days and on cold days. Proper dress provides this help. Without it, overheating or chilling, both of which hinder performance and provide a health hazard, are likely to occur.

Dress for the occasion. Try to impress your body and not your team-mates.

ISN'T IT TRUE THAT SOME UNIFORMS USED IN SPORTS ACTUALLY HINDER PERFORMANCE?

Yes. Tradition and resistance to change are two reasons why uniforms in many sports are not compatible with the activity. Uniforms should be evaluated in terms of:

1. Protection from injury (including sunburn)
2. Environmental suitability (warmth or coolness permitting evaporation)
3. Lightness of weight
4. Water absorption
5. Freedom of movement
6. Aesthetic qualities and fit

Numerous sports continue to use uniforms unsuited for the environment and skills of the activity. The chart below shows there is room for improvement. Slight alterations would result in improved performance and a lower incidence of injury and illness. Nurses, nuns, and airline hostesses did it—why can't the sports world? Women's tennis finally exchanged grandma's uniform for a modern style that improves movement and is more compatible with the weather.

Heel cleats on a football shoe are a perfect example. Why are they there? Do we run or cut on our heels? Do we do anything in team sports on our heels? The answer to these questions is "no." Heel cleats exist because the early shoes came out that way and no one ever challenged the decision. One high school league reduced the incidence of knee injuries by removing heel cleats; this alteration helped to prevent a locked foot in the turf when contact occurred. There is some hope. In another fifty years, basketball teams may even use mouthpieces.

ARE SYNTHETIC FIELDS HOTTER THAN GRASS FIELDS?

Yes. Studies have revealed rather large temperature differences between artificial and grass turf. Artificial turf retains heat and elevates the temperature of both the air near the turf and the shoes and feet of the player. The field will run as much as 40°F higher than air temperatures at natural grass fields. High turf readings also occur following sudden weather changes, making hazy, cloudy days a concern for coaches and

EVALUATION OF UNIFORMS

SPORT	Protecting From Injury	Environ-mental Suitability	Weight	Water Absorp-tion	Freedom of Move-ment	Aesthetics
Baseball	OK	Poor—hot	Too heavy	Too absorptive	Poor	Fair
Basketball	OK—mouth-piece desirable	OK	OK	OK	OK	OK
Football	Good	Poor	Poor	OK	Poor	OK
Gymnastics	Poor	OK	OK	OK	OK	OK
Ice Hockey	Good	OK	Too heavy	OK	Poor	OK
Racket Games: Badminton, Tennis, Handball, Squash	Not needed	OK	OK	OK	OK	OK
Rowing (Crew)	OK	OK	OK	OK	OK	OK
Rugby	Poor	Poor—hot in spring, cold in the fall	OK	Too absorptive	OK	Fair
Skiing	OK	OK	Fair	OK	Fair	OK
Soccer	Poor	Pants OK, Shirt poor	Too heavy	Too absorptive	OK	OK
Swimming, Water Polo	Not needed	OK	OK	OK	OK	OK
Team Handball	Poor	OK	OK	OK	OK	OK
Track	Not needed	OK	OK	OK	OK	OK
Volleyball	Not needed	OK	OK	OK	OK	OK
Wrestling	Poor	OK	OK	OK	OK	OK

players. Field temperatures are highest in the middle of the field and coolest at the ends. Of course the location of the field and blockage from wind and sun will produce different results.

The implication here is that higher temperatures may increase the chance of heat stroke in early season before players are acclimated to such conditions. This is a common concern on all types of surfaces and requires special care by the coach at all times. Taking into consideration all available factors, well-kept natural turf and grass are very difficult to match.

CAN ANYTHING BE DONE TO IMPROVE PERFORMANCE ON VERY COLD DAYS?

Yes. It is important to recognize, however, that both hot and cold weather may cause your efficiency to vary from 20 to 35 percent. In cold weather, the 20 to 35 percent loss is used for heat energy (to maintain proper body temperature). Athletes in football, soccer, rugby, lacrosse, ice skating, skiing, and other such sports must learn to conserve heat as much as possible if they want to perform without loss of proficiency. Here are some tips that explain the problem and offer suggestions for a higher level of performance:

1. Prevent sudden changes in temperature (chilling). This is one of the main problems in sports that involve periodic rest periods or time-outs. Use a light warm-up suit that keeps you relatively warm and also can be easily removed when the game begins. Heavy warm-up clothing will cause profuse sweating and present a barrier for passage of water vapor. The sweat then builds up on the skin and chilling occurs during rest periods. The moisture evaporates and the body loses valuable heat.
2. Use two pair of socks (layer of thin followed by wool socks) and good shoes. The hands and feet cool first and are difficult to warm.
3. Increase fat intake and reduce protein intake in your diet. Heat balance is best maintained on a high fat diet, while protein has the opposite effect.
4. Acclimate yourself by practicing in cold weather as often as possible prior to the contest. This will build up both a physiological and psychological tolerance and may improve performance.
5. Remove wet clothing as soon as possible; massage extremities to improve circulation.

6. Shiver. Shivering involves contraction of all muscle groups; it actually produces heat and increases metabolic rate two to three times the resting rate.
7. Keep moving. Activity can increase heat production 10 to 20 times that produced at rest.

It is interesting to note that obese athletes are more resistant to cold weather than thin athletes. The opposite is true for hot weather.

DO COLD SHOWERS AID PERFORMANCE?

No. They can, however, be harmful. Ice cold water that is allowed to spray over the chest area increases blood pressure (both systolic and diastolic), pulse pressure, heart rate, and decreases the amount of blood the heart pumps per minute. For a cardiac patient or someone with undiagnosed heart trouble, these changes could result in serious circulatory overload.

A warm-to-hot shower is the best choice for individuals of all ages. This provides a comfortable feeling on the skin, assists total relaxation, improves circulation, and offers no health hazard.

DO ALTERNATE HOT AND COLD BATHS AID PERFORMANCE?

No. Alternate heat and cold is effective in aiding the healing of damaged tissue; however, there is little evidence to show that performance in any sports activity is improved. In fact, it would appear that application of cold to a body part prior to activity would decrease muscle efficiency. The fad of going from a hot shower to lie in the snow in the nude will only alternately burn and freeze your behind; it will not aid performance.

WHAT IS THE BEST TYPE OF LIGHTING FOR OPTIMUM PERFORMANCE?

A clear, dry day offers the best light for safety, visual field, and mental outlook. This condition generally occurs at noon and early afternoon, before the sun descends; creating shadows and forcing you occasionally to look directly into its brightness and be momentarily blinded. Thin clouds that almost shield the sun also provide unfavorable light for sports events.

Artificial light for evening competition can provide an adequate setting for sports. Unfortunately, not all artificial light is adequate and finances often prevent proper lighting.

AREN'T THE INCREASING NOISE LEVELS IN OUR ENVIRONMENT A THREAT TO ATHLETICS?

Yes, indirectly. To date, there is no evidence of crowd noises causing the symptoms that *can* occur from high intensities of over 140 decibels: nausea, loss of balance, speech and thought impairment, increasing breathing rate, muscle vibration, and hearing loss. Even short exposure to 140 decibels or more can bring about these changes depending upon one's susceptibility or tolerance.

The maximum safe limit is approximately 85 decibels. This limit is easily exceeded, on and off the playing area, by sudden crowd noises, machinery, rock groups, and so on. It is reasonable to believe that play could be adversely affected. If present trends continue, it may be necessary to use ear plugs capable of reducing intensities by 30 decibels or more. Until then, it is good advice to avoid extremely loud noises even for a short period of time in work and recreational endeavors.

Performance in industry drops from exposure to 90 decibels of high frequency, constant noise. Research also shows that you are more apt to suffer from decreased performance due to noise if you are an emotional individual, are engaged in a stop-and-start activity requiring brief periods of concentration and relaxation (such as football), or are not performing well. Intermittent noise is worse than steady noise. Sound pressure levels also vary among individuals receiving the same noise. Researchers are experimenting with ear inserts that shut out crowd noises without greatly reducing short-range hearing.

DOES AIR POLLUTION DECREASE PERFORMANCE?

Yes, air pollution can hinder performance. First, it may cause coughing, sneezing, airway constriction, excessive mucous secretion, irritation of the eyes and throat, and numerous other disturbances that, in turn, could very easily affect performance on a given day. Second, prolonged exposure to polluted air over a number of years can cause acute infections, breath shortness, tissue destruction, respiratory illness—all of which will decrease performance.

Recently, numerous football players on several different teams in New Jersey experienced chest pains during practice session. A few collapsed during lap running and were taken to the hospital. As the number of afflicted players increased, the cause was discovered: a thick fog that prevented free air movement and kept polluted particles in the area.

Research in the area of track and field competition in polluted air supports the contention that performance is hampered. Unfortunately, the body functions best only when supplied with clean air. We can't change the body's utilization of unclean air, but we can try to change the air.

DOES WATER TEMPERATURE AFFECT SWIMMING PERFORMANCE?

Yes. Water temperature acts upon heat regulation of the body. The ideal water temperature depends upon the specific activity:

1. Learning to swim. 90°–95°F will prevent shivering and discomfort, which tend to decrease both coordination and concentration.
2. Sprint swimming. 85°–95°F, since exposure is brief.
3. Endurance swimming. 75°–80°F, since long exposure to rigorous muscular movement will produce body heat.

Unfortunately, pools have no thermostat that can quickly alter water temperatures as events change; therefore, a cooler temperature of 74°–78°F is used to protect distance swimmers. For all types of swimming, an acclimation period will aid performance.

IS SWIMMING IN POLLUTED WATER DANGEROUS?

Yes. It is possible to contract serious or even fatal illnesses from the various microorganisms and viruses present in some lakes and streams. In spite of this, it is not uncommon for swimmers to use water that is receiving millions of gallons of raw sewage daily.

Water pollution is determined by counting the number of coliform or intestinal bacteria in samples. Although these usually harmless organisms are easy to detect, accompanying microorganisms and viruses that can cause serious illness are *not*. With the coliform count at 1,000 organisms per 100 milliliters, the federal government feels that the water is approaching the danger limit. New York City permits 2,400 per 100 milliliters (*Time,* July 26, 1971).

Conjunctivitis, hepatitis, laryngitis, typhoid, cholera, and sinusitis represent some of the diseases and and conditions that can be contracted from polluted water. It must be pointed out that serious disease is a rarity even from swimming in contaminated water. Less encouraging is the fact that the 16 Virginians who died in the past 34 years from amoebic meningoencephalitis (spinal cord and brain infection) all met death as a result of swimming in one of the three fresh water lakes near Richmond.

While there is disagreement among physicians and researchers, the key factor appears to be the swallowing of the harmful organisms, and even this does not guarantee your contracting a serious ailment from polluted water. It is best to obey local health rules and avoid waters that are declared unsafe for swimmers. Make no mistake about it—polluted water can cause serious illness. If you swim with your mouth open, which is necessary in some strokes, avoid swallowing any of the water. Drink freely before you swim. This will reduce the temptation.

3

Drugs and Performance

The use of ergogenic aids (drugs) in athletics is not new. Athletes have been only slightly short of notorious in their willingness to seek fast routes to championship status. This willingness has led to use of numerous drugs that often lay unsupported claims to weight gain, unlimited energy and endurance, high levels of motivation and muscle activation, relaxation, improved strength, power, and speed, and other possible benefits. Unfortunately for the users, the controlled experiments that have been conducted do not support these claims and, more often, demonstrate a real health hazard that could culminate in death.

This chapter takes an objective look at the types of drugs that have been used in an attempt to improve performance and examines research and expert opinion concerning their value, dangers, ethics of use, and control in the athletic world.

WHAT TYPES OF DRUGS HAVE BEEN USED BY ATHLETES?

The three most common categories of drugs used in athletics are depressants (barbiturates), stimulants (amphetamines) and synthetic male sex hormones (steroids). Marijuana, heroin, cocaine and alcohol are less commonly used and rarely in an attempt to improve performance. Study the chart (pp. 40–41) and become familiar with the physical damage possible through abuse. Steroids are discussed later in this chapter.

JUST HOW ARE DRUGS SUPPOSED TO IMPROVE ATHLETIC PERFORMANCE?

Drugs alter performance through (1) a psychological effect—anticipation of assistance leads to improved performance (placebo effect), or (2) a pharmacological effect—metabolic changes.

In athletics, depressants and stimulants that act on the central nervous system are most commonly used. Depressants may aid performance by removing inhibitions and eliminating excess overexcitement. Stimulants may serve to delay or mask fatigue (physical and psychological) and allow a high degree of motivation for maximum exertion over a prolonged period of time. Steroids are thought to enhance weight and power gains over a long period of time. Depressants, stimulants, and anabolic steroids represent the three most commonly used groups of drugs in athletics. All three types are capable of destroying your athletic career and, more importantly, you.

CAN DRUGS HINDER PERFORMANCE?

Yes. People react differently to drugs of all kinds. Factors that contribute toward a negative effect and/or diminished performance include:

1. *Individual differences to medication.* Identical doses affect individuals differently: they may be toxic to one person and not to another, helpful to one and harmful to another. There is no such thing as a normal dose that will produce predictable physical, emotional, or intellectual behavior.
2. *Sensitivity to a drug.* This unknown factor can manifest itself through skin rashes, functional disturbances, and even death.
3. *Quantity consumed.* Excessive use has a toxic effect that can interrupt the function of the body systems and lead to death.

The time of day, humidity, temperature, air movement, amount of food in the stomach, fatigue, conditioning level, other medication in the system, mental outlook, and state of health are additional factors that determine the effect of any medication on the body. Too many tranquilizers will cause sluggish performance, and overuse of stimulants will cause overexcitability and loss of fine muscular movements as well as

SUMMARY OF DRUG EFFECTS

Drugs	Legal status, manufacture, and sale	Legal status, possession, and usage	Withdrawal symptoms	Physical dependence	Death by overdose	Accident proneness during use	Suicide tendencies
LSD	Felony	Misdemeanor, various state laws	No	No	No	Yes	Yes
Marijuana	Felony	Violation, misdemeanor, or felony	No	No	No	Yes	Very rare
Heroin	Felony	Felony	Vomiting, diarrhea, tremors, aches, gooseflesh, sweats, etc.	Yes	Coma, respiratory failure, shock	Yes	Yes
Barbiturates	Legal medically, felony for illegal sale	Misdemeanor, various state laws	Delirium, tremors, convulsions	Yes	Coma, respiratory failure, shock	Yes	Yes
Amphetamines	Felony for illegal sale	Misdemeanor, various state laws	Depression, apathy, muscle aches	Yes	Convulsions, coma, cerebral hemorrhage	Yes	Yes
Cocaine	Felony	Felony	No	No	Convulsions, respiratory failure	Yes	Yes
Airplane glue	No restrictions	None, or misdemeanor by city or state law	Mild	Rare	Asphyxiation, heart stoppage	Yes	Unknown
Alcohol	Various state laws for illegal stills	Sales to minors a misdemeanor; various state laws on driving, disorderly conduct	Delirium, other symptoms, tremors, convulsions	Yes	Coma, respiratory failure	Yes	Yes

From Brent Q. Hafen and Brenda Peterson, *Medicine and Drugs: Problems and Risks, Use and Abuse.* Philadelphia: Lea & Febiger, 2nd Edition, 1978. Used by permission.

Physical complications	Chromo-somal changes	Mental complications during use	Mental complications after use	Tolerance	Manner used	Abuse trend
Rare	Question-able	Panic, paranoid states, anxiety	Amotivation?, flash-backs, psychoses, paranoia, anxiety reactions, brain damage	Extremely rapid	Orally, injection	Decreas-ing
Bronchitis, conjuncti-vitis	Question-able	Rare panic or para-noid states	Amotivation?, rare psychoses, rare flashbacks	Yes	Orally, smoking	Increas-ing
Infections, hepatitis	Reported	Coma	Asocial and antisocial reactions	Yes	Injection, snorting, least effective orally	Decreas-ing
Overdose	Unknown	Intoxica-tion, acting-out behavior	Psychoses	Yes	Orally, injection	Increas-ing
Malnutri-tion, needle con-tamination	Unknown	Paranoid, assaultive	Paranoid psychoses, asocial reaction	Yes	Orally, injection, nasal and other mem-branes	Decreas-ing
Malnutri-tion, perforated nose sep-tum from sniffing	Unknown	Excited state, in-toxication	Probable brain damage, paranoid psychoses	Yes	Injection, nasal and other mem-branes	Increas-ing
Bone marrow depression, liver and kidney damage	Unknown	Excited state, in-toxication	Brain damage?	Slight	Inhalation and sniffing	Stable
Gastritis, pancreatis, cirrhosis, neuritis	Unknown	Intoxica-tion, acting-out behavior	Brain damage, psychotic reactions	Partial	Orally	Increas-ing

remove warning signs of fatigue and pain. Use of any of the three common types (stimulants, depressants, hormone steroids) over an extended period of time can lead to liver damage, kidney damage, sexual atrophy, and psychological dependence.

You can be a great athlete without drugs—and for a longer period of time. Remember that drugs produce different reactions in different people. Don't take the chance—you may be the unlucky one whose first dose is also the very last.

DON'T SOME DRUGS THAT ARE GIVEN TO SICK ATHLETES ACTUALLY AID PERFORMANCE?

Yes. This is a touchy subject. Just as service personnel frequently request penicillin for a sudden cold—symptoms that appear immediately after sexual contact—similarly, sudden illnesses just prior to an athletic contest could be staged. However, both a legitimate illness and performance can improve with drugs. Since drug use under these circumstances is therapeutic in nature, there can be no real objection.

Use of antihistamines by athletes with allergies is an example of medication that can favorably affect performance. Ailments such as colds, stomach upset, arthritis, headache, skin problems, lung-heart problems, and muscle-joint pain are also common among athletes. Medications to relieve such symptoms impose similar problems; they can, and have, affected performance favorably. It is truly a hairline distinction and represents an extremely difficult area for adequate control.

Any athlete who uses medication for anything other than therapeutic value is violating a code of ethics governing sports participation. Also, no one is immune to undesirable side effects and it therefore is sound advice to avoid any type of medication prior to an athletic contest—whether you are sick or healthy.

ONE HEARS OF DRUGS THAT CAN PRODUCE THE SUPERHUMAN ATHLETE. IS THERE ANYTHING TO SUCH RUMORS?

Most discussion centers around use of hormones. To date, use of *pituitary hormone* to produce an athletic giant has not been attempted.

Androgenic hormones, on the other hand, have been used, and claims are made for increased strength and muscle bulk when it is used in conjunction with a training program.

Thyroid hormones can cause heart irregularity and failure with prolonged use while androgenes also upset electrolyte balance and can be fatal.

Methyltestosterone does improve the performance of men over 50. Much to the disappointment of many seekers of the fountain of youth, there is no drug available that slows the aging process—methyltestosterone included.

The so-called superhuman athlete will be a product of heredity and dedicated training. Drugs would only spoil the individual and shorten his or her athletic career.

DO AMPHETAMINES IMPROVE PERFORMANCE?

Not necessarily. Amphetamines, the most common drug used in sports, are used in medicine to stimulate the central nervous system. Their use in athletics is unethical, a breach of sportsmanship that is a violation of the rules at all levels, and extremely dangerous. Use of amphetamines is hazardous because (1) doses are difficult to control, since different physiological states alter one's reaction to the drug, (2) tolerance occurs and forces you to increase the dosage for the same effect, (3) danger of addiction is present, (4) warning signs of fatigue and overstrain are unnoticed during exercise, increasing the possibility of bodily harm from overexertion, (5) vasopressor effects (elevated blood pressure) are undesirable, (6) complete circulatory collapse may occur from overexertion, and (7) heat stroke is more common to users on hot, humid days.

Results of research are conflicting. Some researchers found improvement in endurance and strength while others do not confirm these findings. Experimentation with performances in swimming, throwing weights, walking long distances, and working on a bicycle ergometer leaves room for doubt. It is only logical that drugs capable of stimulating the central nervous system will make you tense and nervous. These traits are undesirable in the performance of a complex skill such as shooting a basketball, catching a football, or hitting a baseball. Certainly, no improvement in coordination will occur; decreased coordination is more likely.

You may feel pepped-up after using an amphetamine; however, this feeling is not likely to improve your performance. The long-term effects on the internal organs can and have been fatal with continuous use. Leave the illegal use of amphetamines to the horses unless you want to bet your life.

DO BARBITURATES (DEPRESSANTS) IMPROVE PERFORMANCE?

In rare instances, depressants may help some athletes by supporting the ego centers of the brain, reducing nervousness, or by aiding sleep the night before a contest. Overuse can lead to dependence, intoxication, and sluggishness the day of the contest. It is much safer to eliminate coffee, tea, cocoa, and cola, and improve relaxation techniques than to rely on barbiturates.

DOES THE USE OF ANABOLIC STEROIDS AND OTHER HORMONES IN ATHLETICS IMPROVE PERFORMANCE?

Steroids are drugs of great potency with many side effects. Testosterone (male sex hormone) is the most commonly used in athletics, particularly by weight lifters and decathlon competitors, as a means to gain weight and increase strength. Testosterone has androgenic (producing masculine characteristics) and anabolic (increasing nitrogen retention, protein building, and muscle weight) qualities. A synthetic steroid is in use that has mostly an anabolic effect without much change in masculine characteristics.

Some studies have shown that steroids increase body weight (may be due to water retention) and strength; others have not. One thing is certain: steroids are dangerous and have been known to lead to serious liver damage, a type of growth stunt in adolescents by prematurely fusing the long bones of the body, acne, sterility, stomach bleeding and cancer.

Actual performance or skill in any sport is not affected by use of steroids. The majority of champion weight lifters use steroids. The general feeling is that the drug retards fatigue during training sessions and allows more work to be done. This additional training, the argument goes, is what provides the benefits. The only possible value may come from the increased weight and strength. The fact is that you can gain weight and strength through safe means with no possible side effects. Keep in mind that long after your athletic days are over, the liver must continue to perform.

IS THE USE OF ASPIRIN HARMFUL TO AN ATHLETE?

No. Aspirin remains as the most popular household medication for all types of pains, aches, and strain. It can be purchased plain, buffered, effervescent, candied, combined with other drugs, and in different colors. It is effective in reducing fever, cold or flu symptoms, and in minimizing pain. It does little to relieve severe pain, however.

There is no over-the-counter (non-prescription) drug in existence that surpasses aspirin as an analgesic (pain controlling), antipyretic (diminishing fever), or anti-inflammatory (reducing inflammation) agent. Acetaminophen is available for those who cannot tolerate any form of aspirin; however it costs more and is not an effective anti-inflammatory agent.

Aspirin can irritate the stomach and cause reactions such as hives, asthma, and mucous membrane swelling. Taking aspirin with food, milk, or even a full glass of water reduces chances of stomach upset. Most types no longer contain phenacetin, which may cause permanent, serious kidney damage. Others have caffeine added.

Numerous studies have been conducted to determine which type of aspirin is more effective in terms of speed of absorption, pain-killing ability, stomach irritation, and safety. There are no conclusive differences among the more popular types of aspirin. All are equally effective in the areas of concern. The main difference is price. The pain that is most difficult to remove is the one in the pocketbook. Buy the cheapest aspirin available. Also, avoid overuse. It is much more sound to have a physician analyze what may be causing the symptom of pain than to mask it with aspirin.

DOES COCAINE IMPROVE ATHLETIC PERFORMANCE?

Cocaine is highly toxic, habit forming, and extremely hazardous to health. Its derivatives, procaine and Novocain, are widely used in medicine. Cocaine stimulates the central nervous system and steps up both breathing and circulation. Its use in athletics has been directed at the postponement of fatigue by masking its symptoms in an attempt to increase muscular work and endurance, and speed up recovery following activity. As with all stimulants there is conflicting evidence concerning its effectiveness.

Cocaine first stimulates the body and then is usually followed by acute depression. No sane, ethical athlete would consider its use.

DOES DIGITALIS IMPROVE ATHLETIC PERFORMANCE?

Digitalis is both a powerful cardiac stimulant and a diuretic (causing the body to eliminate fluid) and is used in the treatment of congestive heart failure to decrease heart rate and increase stroke volume (that is, amount of blood ejected per beat).

Doses of digitalis for the normal athlete will decrease heart rate, prove toxic, and will *not* improve performance.

IS THE USE OF DIURETICS HARMFUL?

Diuretics, including caffeine, are used to eliminate excessive fluid and help relieve high blood pressure. Wrestlers use diuretics to eliminate water prior to a scheduled weigh-in; dieters use them to prevent normal water retention the first two or three weeks of a new diet.

Diuretics can disturb electrolyte and fluid balance and eventually prove fatal. Their use requires careful supervision of a physician. Heart contraction can also be altered. Misuse can lead to dehydration and overheating, blurred vision, nausea, fatigue, diarrhea, drowsiness and stomach disturbances.

Avoid use of diuretics except for therapeutic value under care of your physician.

DOES THE USE OF INSULIN AND EPINEPHRINE (ADRENALINE) IMPROVE PERFORMANCE?

No. Both of these substances are produced within the body: insulin by the pancreas to assist utilization of glucose (sugar), and epinephrine by the adrenal glands to increase metabolic rate in skeletal muscles through more rapid use of glucose. Both alter muscle metabolism. Epinephrine, secreted by the adrenal medulla, is a powerful stimulant that causes numerous changes during exercise: increased rate and force of heartbeat; increased blood pressure, metabolic rate, and oxygen consumption; dilation of small blood vessels; and vasoconstriction of certain arterioles (tiny arteries) to help increase the blood supply to active muscles. The use of either of these drugs is not recommended.

DOES METRAZOL IMPROVE ATHLETIC PERFORMANCE?

No. There are reports of its use by some European athletes as a means of improving endurance; however, there is no evidence of improved performance in mountain climbing, soccer, skiing, or cycling.

IS THE USE OF VARIOUS TYPES OF NOVOCAIN DERIVATIVES TO DEADEN PAIN ALLOWED IN ATHLETICS?

No. It is against league rules at most levels of competition to use it to "numb" an injured area in order that a player may compete. Strict enforcement of this regulation is encouraged, since Novocain has the following effects: (1) raises blood pressure and dilates peripheral vessels, and (2) masks the warning signs of pain, thus allowing activity that may result in serious permanent danger to a body part. Repeated trauma or blows to an area are also a leading cause of bursitis, which demands complete rest in severe cases.

Although most players desire to compete even while injured, such action should be allowed only if there is little danger of more serious injury, and if pain and discomfort are mild enough to permit it. Local anesthetic in the ankle, shoulder, and knee, to name a few common spots, should never be allowed by coaches, trainers, or team physicians at the high school and university levels.

ARE MUSCLE-RELAXING PILLS HARMFUL?

Not if used in moderation under the care of a physician. Muscle spasm, such as a lower back trauma, frequently occurs at the site of an injury. A muscle relaxant, administered orally, acts as a depressant (tranquilizer) and helps to decrease muscle tone and spasm. It also has a general relaxing effect and removes tension.

This type of medication should be used for therapeutic purposes only. Heavy doses can cause serious illness, sluggishness, and decreased performance.

SOME ATHLETES INHALE OXYGEN BETWEEN HALVES OR DURING A TIME-OUT OR BREAK. IS THIS HELPFUL?

No. Let's examine its value from three different aspects: (1) taken before exercise, (2) taken during recovery after exercise, and (3) taken during exercise.

Before Exercise. Some early studies indicated that oxygen breathing just prior to a 100-yard dash improved performance. Follow-up research shows that improvement is psychological and that breathing oxygen before a contest or at time-outs is of no value.

During Recovery. There is no evidence that oxygen breathing speeds up the recovery process and helps to eliminate fatigue products. Users of oxygen were found to have somewhat slower heart rates than non-users, with a difference of only one to five beats per minute.

During Exercise. If oxygen could be administered while you are running a mile or playing a game of basketball, it would be valuable. Fatigue would be delayed and performance improved.

Thus, unless oxygen can be administered while you are actually competing, it can serve merely to improve your mental state should you be convinced that it is helpful. Normal breathing at sea level will saturate the arterial blood with 95 to 98 percent oxygen. Further saturation does not take place through oxygen inhalation.

To get maximum efficiency from your respiratory system, avoid smoking, train hard, and learn to breathe correctly during competition.

SHOULD ATHLETES DRINK COFFEE AND TEA?

No. These drinks have one common ingredient: caffeine—a member of the speed, pep pill, and amphetamine group. Tea contains theophylline, and cocoa contains theobromine, both related drugs. Caffeine, theophylline, and theobromine all stimulate the nervous system, particularly, the brain. They also affect the kidney, heart, blood pressure, heart rate, digestion, and metabolism. There are still additional physiological changes:

1. Resting heart rate is increased.
2. Metabolism of body cells is increased 10 to 25 percent, accelerating the burning of food for energy and requiring more oxygen. The heart is also required to work harder.
3. Appetite is decreased.
4. Blood pressure may rise in sensitive people. Anyone with high blood pressure should avoid caffeine in any form.
5. The formation of acid-pepsin digestive juice is stimulated. Excessive amounts of acid digestive juice leads to peptic ulcers. The flavor oils in coffee also irritate the digestive tract, and may cause diarrhea. *Tannin* in tea has the opposite effect, and may cause constipation. Individuals with overactive bowels precipitated by emotional tension should avoid caffeine.
6. Arteries to the brain and head region are constricted by caffeine. This aids in relieving headaches since many headaches are caused by over-dilated arteries that stretch the small nerve fibers to the artery walls. Heavy coffee drinkers may develop headaches which are relieved after a cup of coffee. It is wise to slowly taper off to one or two cups daily to avoid this problem.
7. Morning coffee can be useful in cases of simple constipation; with other symptoms such as abdominal pain, irritable colon, diverticulosis, or diarrhea, however, coffee should be avoided.

Coffee contains the most caffeine (100–150 milligrams) whereas tea (60–70 milligrams), cola drinks (35–55 milligrams), and cocoa (50 milligrams) contain somewhat less. All three have the potential to cause health problems for some individuals.

Prior to competition or any time you have a tendency to become nervous, coffee, tea, cola, or cocoa should be avoided. It is wise for the athlete of all ages to drink coffee sparingly or not at all; no more than three cups daily and never on an empty stomach.

IS IT HARMFUL TO DRINK BEER DURING A COMPETITIVE SEASON?

Yes, it can be harmful. Before discussing its effect on performance, let's examine some of the misconceptions concerning use of alcohol.

First, alcohol is a depressant or sedative, *not* a stimulant. Although the initial one or two drinks seem to improve physical and mental functions, they are actually depressing ability in these areas one to two minutes after consumption. Typing, arithmetic problem solving, memorization, and recall are hindered. The body can oxidize and remove 1/3 ounce of alcohol per hour with no ill effects. This is the amount of alcohol in one glass of beer, 3 ounces of wine, or 1 ounce of 100 proof whiskey. For this reason, for every two drinks taken, a three-hour waiting period is suggested before driving or performing any complex task.

Second, alcohol does *not* help to warm you up on a cold day. The initial increase in warmth comes from dilation of blood vessels near the skin. Actually, heat loss is increased and you are more susceptible to chilling.

Third, alcohol is not a good source of energy although it is rapidly absorbed.

There are many other reasons why you should not drink beer or alcohol:

1. Reaction time, strength, and skill are impaired by its use. Even alcohol taken the night before will decrease performance in a contest the following day.
2. Beer is high in calories and may cause a weight problem.
3. Overuse is related to nutritional problems since a balanced diet is rarely attained.
4. Numerous serious diseases are related to overuse.
5. Alcohol consumed before a contest, such as is common practice in some countries, increases the likelihood of violence during play.

It must be said that small quantities of alcohol taken just prior to activity have been shown to aid muscular endurance slightly.

Use of alcohol in any form is very undesirable for athletes. It can only decrease your individual and team's performance and possibly lead to a serious problem. Even so-called "social" drinking on special occasions should be avoided. If you must take a drink on any occasion, do it in the privacy of your home. Being seen in public will antagonize fans, who will later blame you and the coach for poor discipline when a loss or poor performance occurs—and it will occur. Forget beer, and concentrate on being a champion.

DOES SMOKING HINDER ATHLETIC PERFORMANCE?

Yes. Research has shown that cigarette smoking (1) reduces the oxygen-carrying capacity of the blood due to carbon monoxide absorption, (2) reduces the ability of the lungs to take in and use oxygen by as much as 50 percent, (3) produces an increase in heart rate with only one cigarette from 2 to 52 beats per minute which remains for 30 to 45 minutes, (4) elevates blood pressure for 30 to 45 minutes, (5) constricts the blood vessels, (6) drops skin temperature of the hands and feet from 1 to 9 degrees Fahrenheit, (7) damages small arteries that carry blood to the lung surface for oxygenation, (8) adversely affects performance in a complex motor skill, (9) decreases altitude tolerance, making you less efficient at higher altitudes—smoking one pack per day is equivalent to living at an altitude of 8,000 feet, (10) irritates the nervous system, (11) irritates the membranes of the throat and lungs, causing a cigarette cough and greater chance of infection.

What does all this mean? In simple terms, it means that performance in endurance-type activities and team sports is decreased by smoking. Even speed is hindered in some individuals. Why? Because oxygen must be taken into the lungs, distributed to the working muscles, and carbon dioxide eliminated as efficiently as possible during exercise. If you smoke, you are operating like an untuned car: you cannot use fuel efficiently. Also, a rapid heart is less efficient since it does not have enough time to fill between beats, higher blood pressure forces the heart to pump against greater resistance, and constriction of blood vessels reduces the supply of blood to all body parts.

Use of tobacco in any form is an unwise choice in athletics. Without cigarettes, you can perform at a high pace for a longer period of time. You will feel better and live longer. Stop smoking for a season and see for yourself—you may never light up again. It is interesting to note that Arnold Palmer, who had not won a golf tournament in some time, won the Bob Hope Classic in 1971 and had finished second in a previous tournament that year. Arnold had given up both smoking and drinking the month before as New Year's resolutions.

If you don't have that kind of dedication and are willing to play at a reduced level of performance, smoke in privacy. Public display of smoking during the competitive season will bring severe criticism to both you and the coach following poor performances.

DOES SMOKING CONTRIBUTE TO CORONARY HEART DISEASE?

Yes. In fact, the evidence is shocking. There is obviously a strong relationship between cigarette smoking and heart disease. The statistics comparing the smoking and nonsmoking population are worth repeating:

1. Of 2,400 electrocardiograms of overtly healthy males, there were 50 percent more abnormalities among the smoking population.
2. Death rates from heart disease are 2.8 times as high for men and 2 times as high for women (age 45–54) who smoke one pack or more daily.
3. Death rates increase with the number of cigarettes smoked, the degree of inhalation, and the number of years one has been smoking.
4. The 40–49 age represents the time of greatest risk for the smoker.
5. Coronary death rates are only slightly higher for pipe and cigar smokers than for nonsmokers.
6. Approximately 125,000 annual preventable deaths from heart disease are attributed to smoking.
7. Male smokers are two to three times more likely to suffer a heart attack than nonsmokers.
8. If a smoker has a heart attack, he is twice as likely to survive if he has been physically active.

Let's examine how smoking leads to heart disease.

First, smoking accelerates the clotting of blood, increasing the risk of a thrombus (blood clot) in the coronary arteries.

Second, smoking thickens the walls of the arterioles and/or arteries. The more narrow the opening, the more likely a clot or obstruction will form. Also, blood pressure is elevated and the heart works harder to maintain an adequate blood flow through small arterioles.

Third, carbon monoxide decreases the oxygen-carrying capacity of the blood, forcing an extra load on the heart to provide cells with the necessary oxygen. Carbon monoxide appears also to be responsible for accelerating the arteriosclerotic process (hardening of the arteries).

Fourth, smoking results in fibrosis (loss of elasticity of the lungs) making it difficult for the heart to pump blood through the lungs.

Last, smoking causes formation of plaques or raised roughened spots upon which thrombi tend to develop.

Don't underestimate the power of tobacco. It is strong enough to cause Buerger's Disease (inflamed and clogged blood vessels) and progressively limit blood to the extremities until, in advanced cases, gangrene sets in and amputation is required. If smoking is not stopped, the disease is reactivated.

What is the answer? A study of 110,000 men indicates that non-smokers who are physically active are *nine times less likely* to have a fatal heart attack than their inactive smoking counterparts. One pack daily increases your physiological age seven to ten years. You are also likely to have a heart attack seven to ten years sooner. Use the halfway measure that counts: if you must place a cigarette in your mouth, don't light up.

IS MARIJUANA SMOKING HARMFUL FOR THE ATHLETE?

Yes. Although effects vary from one person to another, a reaction similar to that produced by alcohol occurs. The behavior of users is difficult to predict as one experiences elation as well as time, distance, and sound distortion for about four hours. Drowsiness and sleep generally occur and there is most likely no hangover or physical discomfort upon waking.

Marijuana (grass, hash, hemp, joint, Mary Jane, muggles, pot, reefers, stuff, tea, weed) releases one's inhibitions and can make you irresponsible, unpredictable, and dangerous. Though it produces no withdrawal symptoms or physical dependency, a psychological or emotional dependency is common. Also, its use may expose you to the drug scene and probable use of more dangerous drugs. Evidence suggests that for some, marijuana is a basic drug to which other agents are added. It is evident that marijuana is a dangerous, habituating, intoxicating drug that is of no value to the athlete. It does not improve performance in any activity. In fact, it is a sedative that depresses body functions and will impair physical performance. It is not a sexual stimulant and is more likely to impair performance than to enhance it. While some people feel it enhances creativity, it is now clear that whatever creative thoughts may occur during use become meaningless when the effects of use are gone.

Fine, imprisonment, removal from a team, poor health, exposure to the drug scene, emotional dependence, hallucination, impaired performance and judgment, and panic reactions are some of the by-products of use. No wise athlete would consider even one "joint."

IS THE USE OF TRANQUILIZERS BEFORE AN ATHLETIC CONTEST AN ILLEGAL, UNSPORTSMANSLIKE ACT?

Millions of tranquilizers are used by the American public prior to stressful activity as a means of "calming" oneself. In general, both a pharmacological and psychological influence help to lower the excitement level. It would seem illogical to ban their use among athletes when they are so much a part of the lives of the American people. Certainly, they are overused and abused. Millions of people also chase away the drowsiness of last night's tranquilizer with wake-up pills (stimulants). Such a practice places you on a treadmill with all exits leading to the hospital or grave. Slang terms for barbiturates include barbs, blue devils, dolls, goofers, phenies, red devils, and yellow jackets. The "sting" lasts up to four hours, except with an overdose, in which case it's very, very permanent.

SHOULD SLEEPING PILLS BE USED BY ATHLETES THE NIGHT PRIOR TO A CONTEST?

Only in rare cases. Everyone longs for the perfect sleep at one time or another and feels that a sleeping pill is the answer. Actually, broken sleep on one or two nights will not be physiologically harmful to performance, even though it could have an adverse psychological effect. The "eight hours per night" recommendation does not apply to everyone. In fact, people of all ages vary in terms of sleeping habits and needs.

Analyze your situation. Perhaps caffeine drinks (tea, coffee, cola) are causing the problem. If so, eliminate them from your diet. Home remedies such as warm baths, warm drinks, ear plugs, eye shades, music, and alcohol help only *mild* insomnia. Nonprescription pills are also of little value. They are not barbiturates and contain only small amounts of pain-killing and sedative ingredients. Prescription pills can be helpful without much chance of addiction with mild use. One and one-half grains is an effective dose for most people and causes no problem with mild use.

If you suffer from *severe* insomnia, consult your physician. It is generally caused by tension and anxiety.

WHAT IS BLOOD DOPING?

Approximately one month before an important endurance competition (distance run, soccer game, cycling), about 20 percent of the athlete's blood is drawn, the fluid removed and the red blood cells (oxygen carriers) refrigerated. One week prior to the competition, these red blood cells are reinfused into the athlete to elevate red blood cell numbers beyond the original state and improve oxygen carrying capacity.

Proponents of blood doping claim a 4 to 6 percent improvement in performance. Not all experts agree. Some argue that original loss of one pint of blood hinders training at a key time (30 days before competition) and that the athlete would perform better with no blood doping and no interruption in the training schedule. In addition, it has been found that although the blood carries more oxygen, blood is thicker and harder to pump through small arteries. This change is suspected of offsetting any possible gains acquired through increased red blood cells.

HOW CAN THE USE OF DRUGS IN ATHLETICS BE ELIMINATED?

Complete abolition may be impossible; however, we may never know for sure if some initial steps aren't taken. Perhaps a plan to eliminate use should evolve around four major points:

1. *Legislation.* At all levels of competition, making the use of drugs of any form (including alcohol) illegal. Training rules have not been enough. The use of alcohol prior to competition in some sports and countries is very much condoned. National and international sports legislation is needed.
2. *Enforcement.* Machinery to punish violators.
3. *Control.* Machinery to uncover violators through simplified testing procedures such as the test for alcohol content in the blood.
4. *Education.* Awareness of danger.

Also it behooves every coach at all levels of competition to make athletes aware of the physical, psychological, and practical consequences of drug use as an attempt to improve performance. It is the coaching profession's responsibility to be constantly alert to signs of use, to constantly discourage use in any form, and to severely discipline violators.

It is impossible to police international competition. The expense and time is tremendous. In addition, tests may not detect all drugs in the evasive user. No test exists, for example, to detect steroids after an athlete discontinues use for several weeks. By then, athletes may have been using the drug in training for several years.

Nutrition and Performance

The evidence linking nutrition to both health and athletic performance is increasing. The old cliché, "you are what you eat," is very applicable to the athlete. At any stage of an athletic career, particularly during the growth years, nutrition patterns will either contribute to or detract from performance It is the purpose of this chapter to: (1) provide insight into a proper diet, (2) dispel common nutrition myths that are both worthless and harmful, (3) examine the effects of nutrition, eating patterns, and special foods upon performance, and (4) analyze new theories.

WHAT ARE THE ESSENTIAL NUTRIENTS?

Specific components of food (nutrients) satisfy three basic body needs: (1) energy, (2) formation of new tissue and tissue repair, and (3) chemical regulation of metabolic functions.

"Water" is the most critical nutrient since the body requires a constant uninterrupted supply for energy production, temperature control, and for elimination. Inadequate water supply will decrease endurance and result in rapid fatigue.

"Minerals" are divided into two groups: those available in large amounts and those needed by the body in small amounts (trace minerals). Sodium, potassium, calcium, phosphorus, magnesium, sulfur, and chlorides fall into the first group. A minimum of 14 trace minerals must be ingested for optimum health; iron, iodine, fluorine, and zinc appear to be the most important to proper body function.

"Vitamins" (fat soluble and water soluble) serve as chemical regulators and are critical to growth and maintenance of life. In general, the 14 known vitamins are needed in small amounts, and can be obtained through a balanced diet.

"Carbohydrates, protein, and fats" are all critical to the diet of the athlete. It is important to obtain proper balance of each, reduce the percent of daily fat intake, and regulate carbohydrate and protein intake to reasonable levels. Participation in competitive athletics will not greatly increase daily protein requirements. Approximately 12 to 16 percent of total calories should come from protein. Excessive protein intake leads to the consumption of too much animal fat. In addition, protein is not stored, is quite expensive and must be replenished on a day-to-day basis. The wise athlete concentrates on a well-balanced diet from the four basic food groups rather than overemphasis on protein consumption.

WHAT ARE THE FOUR FOOD GROUPS?

No diet contains the perfect combination of nutrients; mainly because this information remains unknown. It is known, however, that all body needs can be met by simply following the basic four food plan below.

Basic Food Groups	Sources	Daily Servings Needed
1. Milk	Milk, cheese, yogurt, ice cream	adults—2 servings children—3 servings teenagers—3 servings
2. High protein	Meat, poultry, fish, nuts, grain protein, dry beans and peas	2 servings
3. Fruit and Vegetable	Dark green leafy or orange vegetables 3–4 times weekly, citrus fruit daily	4 servings
4. Grain	Whole grain, fortified and enriched grain products: bread, cereal, flour	4 servings

Most athletes do not use the basic four food groups very effectively. In fact, the typical American diet is too high in calories, too high in fats, too high in protein, too high in salts, too high in sugars, and too low in fresh fruits and vegetables and water. With careful selection and planning with the above four food groups as a guide, these problems can be eliminated.

WHAT'S WRONG WITH EATING SUGAR?

Sugar is a menace to good nutrition and contributes to dental cavities, diabetes and other degenerative diseases, and excessive weight. Sugar is everywhere—read the label on any product.

Sugar in consumed in three forms (sucrose, glucose and fructose). Annually, cane and beet sugar (sucrose) consumption exceeds 100 pounds per person; 20–25 pounds of sugar syrups (glucose and fructose) bring the total to 120–125 pounds.

Sugar intake should be decreased in infancy where children begin to show a preference for it by age 1 to 1 ½, slowly increasing their desire (some experts call it "addiction") until age 19 or 20, when it slowly decreases thereafter. Avoid these empty calories in your diet—they are not needed. Anytime you do drink or eat sugar products, rinse your mouth out immediately with water to aid in the prevention of cavities.

HOW CAN THE NEED FOR URINARY OR BOWEL EXCRETION BE ELIMINATED DURING A CONTEST?

Obviously, you should visit the toilet just prior to competition. It is also helpful to reduce protein intake in the pregame meal. Proteins are a source of fixed acids and are eliminated only through urinary excretion. Keep in mind that proteins take an extremely long time to digest and will provide no energy for competition when eaten in a pregame meal. Bulky foods, raw fruits and vegetables, whole grain products, gravy, jams, nuts, and popcorn should also be absent from your diet for one or two days before a contest.

Fluid intake should *not* be reduced, since great water loss generally occurs in both indoor and outdoor activities. Coffee and tea should be avoided since both act as diuretics and stimulate urinary activity.

DOES EXERCISE FOLLOWING A MEAL INTERFERE WITH DIGESTION?

For years, people have avoided exercise after eating, believing that it was harmful, hindered digestion, and brought on stomach cramps.

Research has uncovered some important facts in this area. Vigorous and prolonged exercise slows acid secretion and the movement of food downward toward the stomach both during exercise and for about an hour later. After this time, there is increased activity in these areas beyond the normal state. With only mild exercise, gastric motility and acid secretion actually increases. What is mild or rigorous depends upon the physical condition of the athlete.

Although digestive activity is depressed during and immediately after exercise, this slow-up is countered with high activity later. Water passes from the stomach to the small intestine more rapidly during exercise. In the final analysis (over a 12–18 hour period), exercise has little effect on the speed of digestion. However, performance could be hindered from discomfort due to overeating, a psychological feeling of lethargy, or a fullness that does not allow the diaphragm to descend completely during inspiration.

IS IT DANGEROUS TO SWIM IMMEDIATELY AFTER EATING?

No. The old wives' tale that swimming after eating will cause stomach cramps and drowning has no basis. Actually, stomach cramps are not common. Common sites of cramps are the feet and back of the lower leg, and the cause is spasm of a muscle group. This type of cramp is *not* related to the amount of food in the stomach. One researcher, after studying 30,000 swimmers, observed not one case of stomach cramps.

Keep in mind that the digestive system slows its activity as soon as any type of exercise begins, since blood is drastically needed to supply active muscles. After exercise ceases, the digestive system functions at a faster than normal pace. Light meals eaten as little as one-half hour prior to competitive swimming have no effect on performance, cramps, or nausea. Some athletes defy all guidelines for precompetition eating and still experience no ill effects.

It is wise to wait approximately 45 minutes after eating if you are a beginning swimmer and become tense and apprehensive about the water. The real killer is panic and poor judgment, in spite of the fact that so-called stomach cramps get the blame. Also, a severe cramp can indirectly cause drowning. It is unlikely, however, that eating played any part in causing the cramp.

HOW CAN MOTION SICKNESS BE PREVENTED FOR THE TRAVELING ATHLETE?

Motion sickness while in a bus, elevator, train, ship, car, or airplane does occur in some athletes. Contributing factors are rolling, rising and falling, pitching, and rotation, which interfere with the "righting reflex" of the ear. Rotational movements of the body, causing the head to move in more than one place simultaneously, are more likely to produce sickness. Fatigue, a close environment, heat, odors, eye problems, fear, and anxiety are additional factors contributing to motion sickness.

A wide variety of symptoms may be present, with nausea and vomiting most common. Prevention includes: (1) avoiding warm interiors, (2) remaining mentally active while traveling, (3) drinking ginger ale, (4) using a relaxant or drug to prevent sickness, taken 90 minutes before travel and repeated at prescribed intervals thereafter, (5) avoiding a large meal just before departure, (6) keeping fresh air circulating at all times, (7) avoiding drugs that can produce nausea, (8) selecting a seat that will be least subject to motion—center of a ship, between the wings of an aircraft, (9) assuming a reclining position with the head supported, (10) avoiding reading, and (11) avoiding alcohol consumption.

It may be advisable to keep a bag handy.

WHY DO SO MANY ATHLETES COME DOWN WITH GASTROENTERITIS WHEN THEY TRAVEL?

Gastroenteritis of travelers—tourist diarrhea, G.I.'s, Aztec two-step, San Franciscitis—is fairly common among traveling athletes. Common symptoms include vomiting, nausea, stomach cramps, diarrhea, headache, malaise, chills, and mild fever. Diarrhea, nausea and vomiting are often brought about by fear, anxiety, fatigue, and depression (common moods of traveling, competing athletes). Do not mistake nature's reaction to stress for gastroenteritis. The disease has played a part in the outcome of many athletic contests in all sports since it is near impossible to perform adequately when affected. It lasts one to three days, although some symptoms such as diarrhea may continue for seven to ten days.

The cause of gastroenteritis is unknown. The possible association of over 100 different types of viruses complicate matters. Changes in climate, pollution of water with pollens, cooking oil, alcohol, ingestion of sand, and other factors have been considered. One thing is certain: you have a 25 to 33 percent chance of being affected should you travel to a strange country or area. The disorder generally occurs during the first week of your visit.

Since the exact cause is unknown, symptomatic therapy is the best medicine available: bed rest, adequate fluid intake, bland diet, and medication through a physician (antiemetics, antispasmodics, paregoric).

HOW CAN GASTROENTERITIS BE PREVENTED?

The disease is contagious and appears to be related to poor habits of hygiene. It can and has been prevented by maintaining good personal hygiene habits, controlling environmental sanitation, using boiled water, avoiding raw green vegetables and peeling fruit, cooking meat thoroughly, serving in exceptionally clean containers and dishes protected from flies, washing hands thoroughly before eating, wiping utensils clean, drinking moderately, avoiding new foods, and avoiding ice, which is often unclean.

Young, inexperienced traveling athletes are more susceptible. The longer you remain in a new location without developing the disease, the less likely you are to do so. The more you have traveled, the less likely you are to get the disease. You will be most vulnerable when traveling to tropical areas. If you develop symptoms, see a doctor at once. Making an incorrect diagnosis yourself and treating incorrectly is dangerous.

SHOULD THE TIME OF EATING BE ALTERED DURING TRAINING?

If you participate in a vigorous sport requiring two practice sessions daily, mealtimes should be slightly altered, particularly for those who experience stomach upset, cramps, nausea, and vomiting. In early training, this may be a result of poor conditioning. It is less likely to occur if meals are properly spaced.

Adjust your hours to your practice schedule:

Morning Practice	Afternoon Practice	Evening Practice
Light breakfast 1½–2 hours before	Light lunch 1½–2 hours before	Light dinner 2–3 hours before

With only an afternoon session, a big breakfast and light lunch should be eaten. With only evening practice, a big breakfast and lunch and light dinner are desirable. When practicing at odd times, make your pre-practice meal light and at least 1½–2 hours before. Careful adherence to this schedule and proper choice of foods will reduce the risk of stomach upset, fullness (diaphram will descend fully), heat stroke, and decreased performance. On the other hand, whoever is cooking may hit the ceiling.

HOW IMPORTANT IS A PREGAME MEAL?

It *can* be very important for some athletes. Keep in mind that it is desirable to have little food in the stomach (diaphragm can then descend to maximum in inhalation), to prevent gastric disturbances during competition, and to attain carbohydrate buildup in the liver and muscles. If your pregame meal helps to accomplish these three objectives, you will experience little or no stomach discomfort or nausea and function efficiently. In terms of actual fuel for work, little is supplied from a pregame meal. The emphasis, then, is on comfort during the contest. If maximum nutritional benefits are to occur, it would be wise to begin altering your diet 48 hours before a game by following the "do's" and "don'ts" below:

Don't:
1. Eat distasteful foods.
2. Eat raw fruits and vegetables.
3. Eat spicy foods.
4. Eat whole grain products.
5. Eat gas-forming foods such as cabbage, onions, beans, gravy, jam, preserves.
6. Eat fatty foods; they prevent the stomach from emptying.
7. Eat too much protein; acidity buildup occurs.
8. Drink tea or coffee if you suffer from pregame jitters.
9. Overeat; stomach should be near empty.

Do:
1. Eat in moderation approximately 3–4 hours before the contest.
2. Eat palatable food that is easy to digest, including steak, roasted and boiled meats.
3. Eat plenty of carbohydrates such as oatmeal, toast, potatoes.
4. Drink skim milk.
5. Refrain from exercise 24–48 hours before the contest in order to build up carbohydrate stores in the liver and muscles.
6. Drink fluids in the form of bouillon or juice and 2–3 cups of water to improve hydration.

Eating before a contest is often a personal matter. Research shows that light meals eaten at various times (three hours to one-half hour before a contest) do not affect performance in sprinting, middle-distance running, the mile run, or swimming. There is also no report of stomach cramps or nausea. Short, 500-calorie meals taken one-half hour before competition also are of no help or harm. In fact, the composition and size of the meal is not nearly as important as the time it is consumed. The object is to completely fill energy reserves prior to competition.

Thus, it is the energy reserves of the body that are important to performance. Fats and protein, for example, are absorbed so slowly that they will not be helpful in supplying fuel for competition even when eaten four hours before. The only food that could possibly be of benefit is small amounts of sugar, which is absorbed in about two hours. Glucose can raise the blood sugar level rapidly and may be of assistance in a contest. For most athletes, the effect of a pregame meal is psychological, based on comfort and general feeling, but a delicious, juicy steak will not help your game any more than poached eggs and toast. In general, a pregame meal should be easily digestible, high in carbohydrates and low in sugar, protein and fat.

WHAT DIGESTIVE OFFENDERS SHOULD BE AVOIDED BEFORE AN ATHLETIC CONTEST?

The list is long. The following represent some of the more commonly consumed foods that *can* upset your digestive system:

1. Fried foods. More irritating if fried poorly, underdone, or fat-soaked.
2. Rich foods. Contain a higher percentage of fats, which digest more slowly than proteins and carbohydrates.
3. Overdone meat.
4. Cheese.
5. Cellulose covering on beans and peas. Fermentation occurs, causing gas, particularly when they are baked with fat.
6. Nuts, unless well chewed or finely ground.
7. Underdone starchy foods—hot cakes, muffins, bread.
8. Unripe fruit or raw fruit that is not thoroughly chewed.
9. Raw vegetables, unless young, tender, fresh, and well chewed.
10. Highly seasoned or spiced foods. May irritate mucous membranes.
11. Sour food.
12. Sweet food. May ferment, forming acid and gas. It draws fluid from mucous membranes on contact, and causes indigestion when eaten on an empty stomach unless water and food dilute the concentration.
13. Faulty combinations. Avoid the following combinations, each of which tax the digestive system beyond tolerance: fried pork chops

and gravy, fried potatoes, fresh biscuits, and pie; baked beans and pork, brown bread and doughnuts.

14. Avoid large quantities of cold food and drink (derange blood supply to stomach and irritate mucous causing spasmodic contraction of muscle fibers). Drink iced beverages slowly to allow warming in passing through the mouth and esophagus to avoid a thermal shock to the stomach. The effect is minimized if taken at the end of a meal.

    Chew thoroughly to break food down into a semi-liquid state. This stimulates the flow of saliva, which mixes with the food. If starches are not acted upon in the mouth, they remain starches in the stomach, where there are no juices to digest them, and fermentation results.

Not all foods affect athletes in the same way. Some can eat any food combinations at any time and perform well, others cannot. Adjust your eating habits to prevent gastric upset. If you don't have a problem, why change?

WHAT OTHER FACTORS CAUSE DIGESTIVE DISTURBANCES?

The list of causes is astronomical, and in most cases the symptom of gastric upset is treated without any concern for the underlying cause, which may be serious:

1. *Malnutrition.* Sufferers of malnutrition often have indigestion and so are further malnourished due to this vicious cycle.
2. *Overfatigue.* Another cycle of "fatigue—poor eating habits—malnutrition." Some people do not digest food properly when fatigued; rest is the cure.
3. *Illness.* Pathological condition in the digestive tract.
4. *Lack of exercise.* Daily exercise assists proper functioning of the digestive tract through adequate blood supply to this and other systems.
5. *Nervousness and tension.* Peptic ulcers are more common in tense, emotional individuals.
6. *Medicines.* Stomach stress can often be overcome by taking alkalies (sodium bicarbonate, soda mints, magnesia, Tums); thus, we can eat as we please, knowing that the medicine cabinet holds immediate relief. Medicine does not cure the cause (faulty eating habits); only when drugs are abandoned will eating habits have to change to correct this condition.

Correction of the above causes is not always easy. Medicines providing quick stomach relief should probably be avoided. Continuous stomach upset countered by the medicine chest can take its toll in a few years. The day when Alka-Seltzer will not help is never far away for chronic sufferers of indigestion.

IS A POSTGAME MEAL NECESSARY?

A postgame meal can be helpful to some and harmful to others. It depends upon your emotional postgame state. A feeling of exhaustion is normal following competition and has a tendency to take away appetite in some athletes. Until relaxation returns, liquid may be the only food desired. Actually, fluids should be taken in sufficient amounts to help restore the water balance. Some sources of quick energy such as fruit juice will help to remove the feeling of fatigue. Later in the evening or whenever desired, a larger meal is both desirable and helpful for returning the body to its normal state. Keep in mind that overstuffing may interrupt sleep and cause indigestion. Select food that is easy to digest and, unless you're pregnant, only eat for one.

ARE LIQUID MEALS AS NUTRITIOUS AND VALUABLE AS COACHES AND TRAINERS CLAIM?

Liquid meals, in the form of a 12½-ounce can of protein, fat, carbohydrates, and all known vitamins and minerals, come in chocolate, vanilla, cherry, and strawberry flavors and taste like a milk shake. Each container has approximately 400 calories or about one-ninth of a pound of fat. Examine different brands for taste, caloric content, balance, nutritional value, and shelf life before making a selection. Avoid those that include only predigested foods such as glucose, dextrins, peptides, and amino acids. Manufacturers will provide sample cans if requested.

Let's examine the claims for liquid meals. They are used basically to:

1. Maintain weight balance during the season by:
   a. increasing caloric intake with 2–6 cans daily for athletes who have a tendency to lose weight.
   b. decreasing caloric intake at mealtime for the overweight athlete with one can served after each practice (curbs appetite).
   c. controlling and helping to hold present weight.
2. Improve endurance during an athletic contest.
3. Prevent nausea and cotton mouth (dryness and discomfort) during a contest.
4. Prevent sluggishness during play.
5. Provide a pregame meal that will be burned or used during play; a solid meal is not absorbed, lies in the stomach producing no energy

during play, whereas a liquid meal is absorbed in about three hours.

6. Provide a beneficial meal replacement while traveling.
7. Provide the necessary nutrients to wrestlers while dieting to "make weight."

Liquid meals are effective for weight gaining, weight loss, or maintenance, and as a pregame meal. Research indicates that it is also reasonably effective in the other areas described above. One study even reported fewer muscle cramps and cases of game sickness with use of a liquid meal.

A liquid formula that can be made in your home vacates the stomach in about two hours (contents: ½ cup nonfat dry milk, 2–3 cups skim milk, 1 cup water, ¼ cup sugar, 1 teaspoon vanilla flavoring). This is a less expensive approach that is just as helpful and very tasty when served cold.

HOW MUCH WATER IS NEEDED DAILY?

This depends upon the individual and factors such as body weight, activity patterns, sweat loss, loss through expired air and urine, and the amount of liquid consumed through other foods and drinks. Your body contains about ten gallons of water. Loss of only 10 percent, or about one gallon, is disabling, and a 15 to 50 percent loss can cause death. A minimum of six to eight glasses (1½–2 quarts) should be consumed daily—much more for the athlete.

Drinking excessive water generally imposes no problem; water is rarely toxic and the kidneys will merely excrete it efficiently. The kidneys are also capable of conserving water when the body is deprived by excreting more highly concentrated urine. Let thirst be your guide for normal daily needs. If you are participating in a vigorous sport where sweat loss is great, thirst sensations will underestimate your needs. Water will in no way interfere with performance; drink it freely before, during, and after activity. The best time to drink water before a contest is 15 to 20 minutes. If you drink 30 minutes prior to competition, discomfort might occur from fluid passing through the kidneys and into the bladder.

ISN'T THIRST AN ADEQUATE GUIDE TO THE AMOUNT OF WATER NEEDED DURING COMPETITION OR TRAINING?

It is helpful, but not adequate. Regardless of the availability of water, most athletes will not be able to drink enough to prevent a water deficit during exercise. It has been shown that male athletes who are acclimated to the heat rarely drink more than two-thirds the fluid lost in sweat; water deficit occurs.

It seems that fluid balance can be obtained only by forcing water or taking frequent drinks prior to and during exercise, without reaching the point of discomfort. Forced drinking, even when no thirst sensation exists, should minimize upset of body homeostasis during exercise, result in more efficient performance, and delay fatigue. More than 8 liters of sweat is lost in a hard day's work in hot weather. This large amount points out the amount of water that must be consumed to prevent a deficit.

Attempt to force an extra 8–10 ounces down on each occasion. This will result in less water deficit and quicker recovery to fluid balance after exercise.

SHOULD AN ATHLETE BE PERMITTED TO DRINK WATER DURING A PRACTICE SESSION?

Definitely yes. The restriction of fluids to athletes either as a means of discipline, or because of fear of stomach cramps or decreased performance, is an archaic practice that has no scientific basis. It also leads to poor performance, early fatigue, and, occasionally, serious illness, or death from heat exhaustion or stroke.

The theory behind this practice was that (1) water produces sluggishness, (2) desire for water indicates lack of toughness, and (3) absence of water builds up a tolerance and ability to perform without it, a sign of superior conditioning. All three are false and led to a dangerous practice that only recently has fallen by the wayside. The amount of illness, death, and decreased performance over the years due to such unfounded beliefs is immeasurable; the data would be shocking.

Fluids, potassium and salt that are lost through sweating must be replaced to keep the body in balance. Loss of salt encourages fluid loss and can lead to dehydration over a period of a few days. Experiments with subjects walking on the desert show that a man can lose as much as one quart of water per hour. Obviously, fluid loss this high must be constantly replaced hour-by-hour. The same is true for the athlete on the practice field; a loss of two quarts per hour is possible in athletics. Research also shows that drinking water during exercise delays fatigue and improves endurance. Salt tablets or salty water, and commercially prepared drinks, are all helpful.

Withholding of water will not produce a tougher, more disciplined athlete. It will, however, endanger an athlete's health, bring about early fatigue, and possibly lead to dehydration, heat exhaustion, or stroke. Most coaches are aware of this fact and now permit free use (within reason) of water.

ARE WIDELY ADVERTISED SPECIAL DRINKS FOR ATHLETES REALLY VALUABLE?

Not all claims of manufacturers can be substantiated. In fact, one producer of these products has been told to tone down its advertisement. These products also come varied in terms of flavor, carbonation, sweetening, and with varying combinations and concentrations of minerals.

Let's evaluate these products from the standpoint of (1) speed of absorption, (2) nutrition or mineral-replenishing ability, and (3) thirst-quenching ability. It may also be helpful to compare their effectiveness with that of another valuable liquid that should also be used during practice and competition—water.

The main purpose of these special drinks is to replace lost fluid and minerals quickly. The water, sodium and potassium, lost through sweat and water vapor from the lungs should be replaced as rapidly as possible. Water alone will not replace these minerals. One alternative is to use commercially prepared drinks, but never full strength. These drinks are much too high in sugar and should be diluted with two times the amount of water. This diluting serves two purposes. First, it reduces sugar intake and avoids the body's release of insulin and possible reduction in quick energy sources (glucose) in the blood, and second, it increases absorption time when the sugar content is less than 3 percent (serve at 40°F or lower for the fastest absorption). The American College of Sports Medicine recommends these precise quantities for sodium and potassium: concentrations should be less than 10 milliequivalents for sodium and 5 milliequivalents for potassium.

Do these drinks satisfy thirst better than water? The answer depends upon the individual. Nevertheless, this is one of the strong selling slants of these products. Perhaps, sweetened drinks are more effective in eliminating psychological thirst. We are becoming a waterless society as soda, Kool-Aid, and other drinks capture our taste buds. In many cases, the enjoyment is short-lived and the pocketbook dies a slow, certain death.

AREN'T FRUIT JUICES JUST AS EFFECTIVE AS THESE SPECIAL DRINKS?

No, fruit juices are not as quickly absorbed and do not replace all lost minerals. They do provide energy, water, and vitamin C, with the amount of vitamin C depending upon the freshness of the juice. Recently, some physicians have suggested that large doses of vitamin C improve fitness and health. While daily ascorbic acid requirements are unknown, it is evident that the body needs larger amounts during periods of rigorous physical training. Vitamin C helps to hold cells together, aids in the formation of scar tissue in wound healing, and reduces the likelihood of bruises. Also, the majority of research indicates that large doses allow greater physical endurance, improve work output, and aid recovery. Daily doses of up to 300 mg. are needed to acquire this effect. No toxic effects will occur.

Don't throw out your supply of fruit juices. Since they are high in potassium, they are a valuable post-game drink. Frozen juices also should be diluted with 50 percent water. Don't rush out for a year's supply of vitamin C; additional evidence is needed to support most of the claims.

DOES MILK HINDER PERFORMANCE?

No. This misconception must have been spread by a bull—because that's exactly what it is. Just the same, some people do believe that milk, especially when taken before competition, will cut your wind, hinder performance, or curdle in the stomach and cause cotton mouth (dryness and discomfort).

Research clearly indicates that drinking milk or putting it on cereal has no harmful effect upon performance or training. The flow and condition of the saliva are related to perspiration, water loss, and emotions rather than to any type of food. Also, milk curdles in the stomach as a necessary part of digestion—no stomach upset occurs. In fact, milk is an alkaline and may buffer or neutralize excess acid. For the benefit of your future health however, switch to skim milk. The fat content of whole milk contains unneeded calories and cholesterol.

WHAT SPECIAL FOODS HELP TO IMPROVE ATHLETIC PERFORMANCE?

While many makers of special products voice wild claims, little evidence supports their view. Let's examine some of the more common foods eaten before or during a contest that are thought by many to aid performance:

1. *Cane sugar* (2–3 lumps) or dextrose tablets have been shown to improve times in long-distance races; however, sprinting speed is not affected. Subjects who took "placebo cubes" and only thought they were receiving sugar improved as much as 40 percent—all due to psychological factors.
2. *Salt supplements* only assist in allowing you to use your normal energy and do not improve performance. Their use in extremely hot, humid weather helps to prevent cramps, early fatigue, heat exhaustion, or heat stroke for athletes who lose more salt through sweating than they consume.
3. *Alkalies* do not improve performance in any way.
4. *Caffeine* (tea, coffee, kola nuts, cola) improves work output.
5. *Fruit juices and gelatin* do not affect performance.
6. *Special halftime foods* such as molasses, cola, enriched drinks, etc. may have some slight value.
7. *Water* is still the most rapid means of restoring body fluids to normal levels and should be taken during practice sessions and games. It helps to eliminate early fatigue and dangerous heat exhaustion and stroke.
8. *Ultraviolet rays*, though not a food, have been shown to improve sprinting speed and physical fitness, although the exact reasons for this are unknown.

Unfortunately, there is no magic food that will make you perform as a superstar. The only formula that makes any sense is still hard work and dedication in practice.

WHAT IS THE HIGH PERFORMANCE DIET?

On the day of the big contest, every athlete is hopeful of possessing a maximum amount of energy for an all-out effort. The basic fuel for athletic energy is glycogen (carbohydrates released as glucose) with the carbohydrates we eat stored as follows:

Liver glycogen . . . . 110 grams
Muscle glycogen . . . . 250 grams
Glucose in body tissue . . . . 15 grams

By eating the right foods at the right time, the High Performance Diet guarantees high glycogen reserves (tripled) for the athletic contest. Nutrition preparation for a Saturday contest requires several steps:

PHASE I (Sunday to Tuesday evening): *High Protein and Fat, Low*

Carbohydrate Intake Accompanied by Vigorous Training. On Sunday, Monday, and part of Tuesday before the contest, eat only proteins and fats (with carbohydrates limited to 100 grams or less—400 calories). During Phase I, practice efforts involving the same muscles to be used the oncoming Saturday must be exercised vigorously in intense workouts of two hours or more. By Wednesday noon, athletes will find they tire easily, which is due to glycogen depletion. This feeling is part of the diet and will have an adverse effect on performance at this stage of the seven day diet.

PHASE II (Beginning at Tuesday dinner): *High Carbohydrate, Moderate Exercise.* Adequate protein and fat intake continues along with unrestricted carbohydrate intake. Salty and high residue foods should be avoided during this period. Fruit drinks are an excellent supply of some of the carbohydrates. These drinks can be used up to the day of competition on Saturday. Phase II serves to build up glycogen stores in the liver nearly three times higher than normal build-up. This additional energy reserve has been shown to delay fatigue during long, intense periods of exercise such as cross country, marathon running, and team sports. Remember, the glycogen reserves are first depleted through two and a half days of low carbohydrate diet and highly intense exercise, followed by a high carbohydrate diet and less intense exercise up to the day of competition. Such a procedure should be limited to only important contests. Also, it is an excellent idea to try out the method during a week of a practice game or match.

Choose your foods from those listed under Phase I or Phase II from the following list:

DAILY AMOUNTS OF FOOD INTAKE IN PHASES I AND II

	PHASE I	*PHASE II*
Meat	25 oz. or more	8 oz. or less
Breads and cereals	None	Unlimited
Vegetables	3–4 servings	3–4 servings
Fruit or fruit juice	4 oz. glass	Unlimited
Desserts	Fruit (one) or un- sweetened gelatins	Unlimited, including ice cream, cookies, pastries, etc.
Beverages	Unlimited water or unsweetened sodas	Unlimited, including sodas

VITAMIN E FOUND IN WHEAT GERM OIL IS OFTEN ACCLAIMED A MIRACLE FOOD THAT CAN IMPROVE ATHLETIC PERFORMANCE AND EVEN REPAIR A DAMAGED HEART. ARE THESE CLAIMS ACCURATE?

While there is some favorable evidence available, most claims for wheat germ oil and vitamin E are greatly exaggerated. As you might suspect, most so-called "miracle" foods are not backed up by scientific research. The following findings by researchers come to light:

1. Vitamin E is related to muscular function and reproduction. Its exact purpose is not well understood, although a deficiency can cause sterility.
2. Vitamin E is widely distributed in foods—vegetable oils, wheat germ oil, and green leaves of vegetables—and it can be stored in the body.
3. Large doses of vitamin E produce no toxic effect and are apparently not harmful.
4. Vitamin E appears important to physical effort and may assist in delaying fatigue when combined with physical conditioning.
5. When intake is accompanied by exercise, improvements in middle-aged men are noted in blood pressure and electrocardiogram readings.

The unknown factors associated with wheat germ oil are commonly promoted. Some champion athletes do use wheat germ oil and feel it is helpful. According to heart specialists, its use is not considered helpful in repairing the heart after an attack, in preventing heart attacks, or as a treatment for any related disease. A great deal of research is now in progress, and it should be pointed out that there are users from all walks of life (physicians included) who are strong believers in the power of vitamin E. One jar of 500 (a four-month supply) costs over twenty dollars, which would buy a lot of nutritious food that also has vitamin E.

DO SUGAR OR GLUCOSE PILLS AID PERFORMANCE?

Sugar is rapidly absorbed and can improve performance in endurance-type contests—if taken in limited quantities—it will not aid performance in short events. It seems that the body's normal stores of glucose are sufficient for activities of short duration; however, for sports such as football, rugby, soccer, basketball, baseball, marathon running, and cycling, eating glucose prior to competition is helpful. Blood glucose levels reach a peak about one-half hour after consumption and then decline rapidly. Both honey and table sugar are digested rapidly to provide quick energy. Fruit juices are also an excellent source. Honey is not superior to other sweets, in spite of claims by some manufacturers.

On the negative side, sugar products draw fluid into the digestive tract and contribute to dehydration. On an extremely hot, humid day, this could be dangerous. It is also dangerous if you eat too much sugar at one time (an entire candy bar); the body releases insulin, starting a series of complex chemical reactions. As a result, glucose is removed from the blood and stored in the fat cells and liver. This process can leave you with less glucose for quick energy than you would have had without eating the candy. To avoid this problem, dilute fruit juices with 50 percent water, commercial drinks with two times their volume in water, and eat only small quantities of sugar (2–3 cubes, ¼ of a candy bar, a tablespoon of honey). Also, sugar absorption occurs faster than the muscles can use it; thus more frequent small amounts are probably preferable to single doses (no more than the quantities mentioned above per hour).

DO LARGE DOSES OF VITAMINS IMPROVE FITNESS AND PERFORMANCE?

No. Though it is a fact that vitamin deficiency decreases performance and that a little of something (vitamins) is good, the logic that a lot of the same thing is better is *not* true with vitamins. Vitamins administered in excess do not appear to improve athletic performance. Removing vitamin deficiencies in the following areas do:

Vitamin B_1 (thiamine): found in liver, cheese, leafy vegetables, lean meats, eggs, milk, nuts, whole grains, organ meats, pork, legumes, wheat germ, brewer's yeast

Vitamin A: found in yellow fruits and vegetables

Vitamin B_1 deficiency is common, and for some individuals a supplement should be taken to improve fitness. Appearance of highly processed foods has made the availability of thiamine dangerously low in the American diet. Enrichment and restoration of cereal products as a means of supplying this vitamin is requested in 28 states.

If you eat a balanced diet, extra vitamins may be totally unnecessary. In such cases, large doses of vitamins will be of no value, waste your money, and possibly cause illness.

IS AN OVERDOSE OF SOME VITAMINS HARMFUL?

Yes. Some vitamins are toxic and can produce some pretty nasty side effects when taken in excess:

Excess of	Effects of Toxicity	Food Sources
Vitamin A	Liver and spleen enlargement, stunted growth, headache, blurred vision, hair loss, muscle soreness after exercise, skin flaking, cracking and bleeding of lips	Dairy products, liver, green vegetables, carrots
Vitamin C	Nausea, stomach cramps, diarrhea	Citrus fruits, tomatoes, cabbage, broccoli, potatoes, peppers
Iron	Liver damage, reduced absorption of other minerals	Organ meats, rice, bran, wheat germ, wheat bran
Fluoride	Damage to skeletal tissue, allergic reaction	Trace amounts present in all foods, fluoridated water

Massive doses of vitamins can also deplete your financial stores. Eat a well balanced diet and use vitamins only when necessary, such as during a well supervised diet. The multi-million dollar vitamin industry does not need your contribution. Keep in mind that although an excess of some vitamins is not toxic, vitamins also are not stored. It is a day-by-day balanced diet that is the key to proper nutrition.

IS EXTRA POTASSIUM AND MAGNESIUM NEEDED?

Low levels of these minerals can cause chronic fatigue and muscle cramps. More and more cases of deficiencies, uncovered by a simple blood test, are being reported among athletes. Potassium and magnesium tablets are available. First, analyze your eating habits and be certain you are following the Four Food Plan. Food sources are plentiful for both potassium (fruits, vegetables, pecans, walnuts, molasses) and magnesium (almonds, beans, cashew nuts, cocoa, corn, dairy products, meat, peanuts, rice, green leafy vegetables, wheat flour). If you still suspect a deficiency, consult your physician about a blood analysis.

WHAT IS THE CONTROVERSY OVER ROUGHAGE IN THE DIET?

The recent linking of low fiber in Western diets to increases in colon cancer, diverticular and cardiovascular disease, has alarmed the American public. The research uncovered indicates that South Africans, with their high fiber diet, are relatively free of these diseases. While there is no clear-cut cause/effect relationship, and no guarantee that high fiber diets will eliminate these health problems, the argument for more fiber in the American diet is valid. Diverticuluosis or the ballooning of pockets in the digestive tract, that may collect food particles, is common in Western cultures with large numbers of the population affected to some degree. Proper fiber intake offers both prevention and treatment of this condition.

Fruits, vegetables, and whole-grain cereals are excellent sources of fiber. Some cereals would be more accurately labeled as "softage" judging from the breakdown when in contact with milk and digestive juices. There is a danger, however, in going overboard and adding large daily amounts of concentrated forms, such as whole wheat bran. Excess fiber intake decreases the transmit time of food through the digestive system with some components of the fiber binding with trace minerals and rushing them through the system without a chance for absorption. Diminished absorption of needed calcium and zinc can result from excessive fiber intake. Once again, moderation is suggested with emphasis on obtaining a balanced diet.

IS IRON DEFICIENCY COMMON IN THE AMERICAN DIET?

Yes, and it can lead to loss of strength and endurance, early fatigue during exercise, shortening of attention span, loss of visual perception, and impaired learning. Each of these consequences can result in poor sports performance. At a time in our society when the need for iron is increasing, iron intake is reduced due to the removal of iron-containing soils from the food supply and the diminished use of iron cooking utensils. While animals can secure iron from muddy water and soil ingestion, our sanitary society restricts intake to selected foods and iron supplements.

Iron needs and uses vary according to age and sex. The chart below is a summarization of these variables to allow you to determine your specific needs:

Group	Daily Needs	Daily Loss	Comments
Non-growing adult males	10 mg.	1 mg.	Little need for iron; absorbs about 10% of iron ingested
Menstruating females	18 mg.	5–45 mg.*	Great need for iron; absorbs about 20% of iron ingested
Adolescent boys and girls	18mg.		Slightly greater need than above
Pre-adolescents	4–10 mg.		

*Loss during a menstrual period.

Approximately 85 percent of daily iron intake is used to produce new hemoglobin with the remaining 15 percent used for new tissue growth or held in storage.

Adolescent girls are more apt to be iron deficient at an age when great concern exists for body figure and appearance. Consequently, food intake may be restricted leading to iron deficiency. During the menstrual period, female athletes of all ages should use an iron supplement.

Iron is absorbed from meat, fish, and poultry easier than from vegetables. Twice the volume of vegetable iron is absorbed when vegetables and meats are consumed in the same meal.

ARE MOST FOODS INFERIOR DUE TO OVERPROCESSING?

No. This is a common untruth advanced by many health food concerns. Canned and frozen foods, for example, are as nutritious as fresh foods. The FDA has good control over the procedure of processing and you can be assured that your food contains ample quantities of vitamins.

The nutritional value of high-priced so-called "health foods" can be obtained by eating a variety of ordinary foods—at much less expense.

HOW DO YOU DETECT MALNUTRITION?

Good and poor nutrition are best determined by careful analysis of weekly food intake. It is obvious that one can be suffering from malnutrition and still not be thin and that the physical signs of good and poor nutrition are somewhat more complicated than just one's weight. Eating many "foodless" foods, overdrinking, lack of rest and exercise, worry and tension are not characteristic of any one physical type. The chart below provides some guidelines for detecting individuals who are well-nourished and those who are malnourished:

ITEM	SIGNS OF PROPER NUTRITION	SIGNS OF MALNUTRITION
1. Weight	Average for height	Very thin, normal or even overweight in some cases
2. Body Fat	Less than 22% (males), 28% (females), absence of excess rolls of fat	Excess rolls of fat (overweight individual) or lacking
3. Hair	Glossy	Rough, without luster
4. Eyes	Clear, no dark circles	Dark hollows, dark circles
5. Disposition	Good	Easily irritated, hyperactive
6. Sleep	No difficulty in sleeping entire night	Interrupted sleep, difficulty in sleeping
7. Digestion/ Elimination	Good	Diarrhea, constipation and nervous indigestion
8. General energy level	Excellent	Low, lacks energy for anything but minimum activity

SHOULD SALT BE USED SPARINGLY?

Yes. The body needs approximately 2500 mg. of salt (100 mg. of sodium) daily. The typical American diet contains four to five times this amount. Some experts associate high salt intake with high blood pressure and increased risk of coronary artery disease. Salt intake should also be reduced in those who retain fluids for any reason (heart, liver or kidney disease) by avoiding cured meats (ham, bacon), luncheon meats, and sausages and using diabetic salt.

An athlete should not restrict salt intake, particularly in warm, humid weather when fluid loss from perspiration is high. In extremely hot, humid conditions, a salt supplement may be needed for some athletes.

Too much salt in the diet can cause additional problems for the athlete: while salt does help retain fluids, excess salt increases urination and draws fluid from the body, potassium loss is increased, and blood clotting is more likely. Let your taste be your guide. Food contains enough salt without added large amounts of the table variety or a supplement.

WHY IS THERE SUCH CONCERN OVER BREAKFAST CEREALS?

As one physical fitness and nutrition authority put it, "Throw away the cereal and eat the boxes." Until recently, this was good advice.

Cereal manufacturers realize that children, not parents, choose the brand. Therefore, sales are more dependent upon catchy names (peanut butter smacks, strawberry balls, chocolate squares), prizes inside the packages, games on the outside, items to be purchased with box tops, colorful boxes and taste—everything but nutrition.

Read the contents carefully. There are some very good-tasting, nutritious cereals available. Some provide nearly 100 percent of daily vitamin and mineral needs with one serving. Some provide nothing more than pleasant taste and sugar. Be particularly alert to the presence of vitamin B, since a deficiency is common in highly processed foods and so thiamine is dangerously low in our diet.

WHAT ABOUT PRESWEETENED CEREALS?

As the results of Robert B. Choate's investigation indicate, about 60 dry cereals on the market are nearly worthless in nutrition. The addition of sugar does not change this fact. Presweetened cerals that have sugar as their leading ingredient (up to 70 percent or 13 to 14 percent more than a chocolate candy bar) are still grossly lacking as a good source of nutrition.

Sales charts show that low-calorie cereals (with little nutritional value) remain at the top of the list. The Choate study still has not had full impact on the American public in spite of the fact that numerous vitamin-enriched cereals are now on the market. Concerning sugar, the cereal industry indicates that about 90 percent of the cereal eaters use sugar anyway—presweetening merely controls the amount. If you want empty calories and foodless foods, drink water—at least it's free.

IS IT DESIRABLE TO EAT TWO OR THREE EGGS DAILY FOR BREAKFAST?

No. Protein can come from many other sources, such as meat, fish, poultry, milk, and cheese. Eggs should be only one source and should be consumed in moderation, about three or four weekly. The growing evidence linking high blood cholesterol to heart diseases also makes egg eating undesirable. Raw eggs in milk or other drinks should be avoided completely since bacterial contamination and food poisoning are much more probable. Add a little variety to your morning by altering the breakfast menu.

Weight Control and Performance

Proper weight control is vital to a healthy existence, a longer life free from degenerative diseases, including premature heart attacks, and optimum performance in athletic competition. For the athlete who wants to lose, gain, or merely maintain weight, it is a critical area that is greatly abused, often to the point of endangering health and hindering performance.

Basic principles of weight control must be followed if positive results are to take place safely and without detracting from performance. This chapter covers all aspects of weight control and attempts to separate fact from fiction by establishing basic principles that can be applied to most diet control problems and concerns of the athlete.

WHAT ARE SOME OF THE COMMON CAUSES OF OBESITY?

Overeating and inactivity remain as the two most common causes of obesity. Activity can do much to offset weight gain and regulate overweight tendencies. Weight gain of genetically obese mice, for example, is drastically reduced by treadmill exercise. In humans, a group of Harvard University students, forced to double their daily caloric intake from 3,500 to 7,000, suffered no weight increase when involved in vigorous exercise.

Social, genetic, and psychological factors may also result in overeating and obesity. In only a small percentage of cases are glandular and other physiological disorders related to weight problems, although many obese people blame these areas. Let's be honest: obesity due to glandular disorders is almost as rare as venereal disease acquired from a toilet seat. Sedentary living and excessive eating are the two greatest perpetuates of obesity—both can be controlled.

Some research also indicates that obese people are responsive to *external* signals (pleasant surroundings, smell, sight, taste, time of day, emotions) rather than *internal* signals (hunger) that key people of normal weight to eat. Whereas emotional disturbances generally cause obese people to eat, individuals of normal weight decrease food intake. It is theorized that if an obese person could be changed from an "external" to an "internal" eater, weight loss would be easy and permanent. To date, there is no evidence that this is being done.

ARE WEIGHT CHARTS THE BEST METHOD OF DETERMINING ONE'S WEIGHT STATUS?

No. Charts are grossly inadequate and should be used only as a *guide* to desirable weight. The major pitfalls are:

1. It is possible to be within the range of suggested weight and still be overweight.
2. It is possible to be classified as overweight or obese (10 or 20 percent above suggested ranges) when you are at a desirable weight and possess little fatty tissue. Among thick-muscled athletes with low body fat, this is a common finding.
3. After age 20, some charts allow you to gain weight with age, suggesting that it is fine to be fat at age 30, 40, or 50. Actually weight should decrease with age. If you weigh the same now as you did 20 years ago, you are probably overweight. Loss of muscle mass from earlier years is now made up by an increased proportion of fatty tissue. Ideally, you should be 5 to 10 pounds lighter at age 50 than your ideal weight at age 25.
4. The three categories of small, medium, and large frame encourage cheating. We have yet to meet anyone who took their recommended weight from the small or medium frame range; yet, everyone in this world cannot possibly have a large frame. A woman's frame is generally small until she checks a weight chart. Men rarely consider themselves anything but large.
5. The key to obesity is not total body weight, but total body fat. Weight charts do not reveal the presence of fat.

There are several more accurate methods of determining body composition. Most of these fall under the areas of skinfold fat measures, underwater weighing, and anthropometric measures. Skinfold measures are the most practical for home use. Since one-half of all fat lies just under the skin, using fat calipers or pinching the skin between the thumb and index finger can identify fat tissue. A deep pinch in the midsection that measures more than one inch indicates excessive fat in this area. Fat calipers precisely measuring in millimeters the back of the upper arm and the supra-iliac can accurately predict the percentage of total body fat.

Scales and weight charts give only your weight and suggested range. Calipers and pinching show you just how much useless fat your body contains.

CAN YOU DESCRIBE A METHOD OF DETERMINING ONE'S BODY FAT?

Yes. If you do not have fat calipers, borrow any type calipers that measure the thickness of wood or metal. Next, have someone pinch and measure you in two areas:

1. *Tricep.* Stand erect with arms hanging to sides. Partner takes a deep pinch (between thumb and index finger) on the back of the upper arm, halfway between the shoulder and elbow. You can now flex your arm and relax again to assure partner that he or she is pinching fat only and not muscle mass. The calipers are now placed 1/16 inch below the pinch.
2. *Supra-iliac.* Grasp the skin just above the crest of the right ilium (side of body about halfway between hip bone and underarm area). Lift the fold at a slight angle to the vertical along the normal fold line. Place the calipers 1/16 inch under the fold.

The norm chart below for college age men and women is in millimeters of fat (1 inch equals 25 mm, 1/16 inch equals 1.5 mm). Convert your readings accordingly.

	UPPER ARM		SUPRA-ILIAC	
Classification	Men	Women	Men	Women
Thin	1.0–7.0	1.0–10.0	1.0–10.0	1.0–13.0
Average	7.1–10.0	10.1–20.0	11.1–20.0	13.1–23.0
Plump	10.1–18.0	20.1–30.0	20.1–28.0	23.1–31.0
Obese	18.1 up	30.1 up	28.1 up	31.1 up

In general, average or thin readings in these two areas suggest that you possess a low percentage of body fat. If you fall in the plump and obese classifications in both areas, a diet and exercise program are strongly suggested—and fast.

AVERAGE WEIGHT RANGE OF SCHOOLBOYS

Range includes 10% below and 20% above average weight as given in Baldwin-Wood Weight-Height-Age Table

Height in inch.	AGE NEAREST BIRTHDAY													
	5 years	6 years	7 years	8 years	9 years	10 years	11 years	12 years	13 years	14 years	15 years	16 years	17 years	18 years
38	31-41	31-41												
39	31-42	31-42												
40	32-43	32-43												
41	34-46	34-46	34-46											
42	35-47	35-47	35-47	35-47										
43	37-49	37-49	37-49	37-49										
44	40-53	40-53	40-53	40-53										
45	41-54	41-55	41-55	41-55	41-55									
46	42-56	43-58	43-58	43-58	43-58	43-58								
47	44-59	45-60	45-60	45-60	45-60	45-60								
48		47-62	48-64	48-64	48-64	48-64								
49		49-66	49-66	49-66	49-66	49-66	49-66							
50		51-68	52-70	52-70	52-70	52-70	52-70	52-70						
51			55-73	55-73	55-73	55-73	55-73	55-73						
52			57-76	58-77	58-77	58-77	58-77	58-77	58-77					
53			59-79	60-80	60-80	60-80	60-80	61-82	61-82					
54				63-84	63-84	63-84	63-84	64-85	64-85	65-89				
55				65-86	65-86	66-88	66-88	67-89	67-89	67-89				
56				67-90	68-91	69-92	69-92	69-92	70-94	70-94				
57					71-95	72-96	73-97	73-97	74-98	75-100	72-96			
58					75-100	76-101	76-102	76-102	76-102	77-103	75-100			
59						78-104	79-106	80-107	80-107	81-108	78-104	81-108		
60						82-109	83-110	83-110	84-112	85-113	85-114	85-115		
61							85-114	86-115	87-116	89-119	90-120	93-124	95-127	
62							90-120	91-121	92-122	93-124	94-125	96-128	100-133	104-139
63							94-126	95-127	96-128	97-130	99-132	102-136	106-142	111-148
64								98-131	100-133	102-136	103-138	105-140	109-145	113-151
65								103-137	105-140	106-142	108-144	110-146	114-152	118-157
66									107-143	110-146	112-150	115-154	119-158	122-163
67									112-149	115-154	117-156	121-161	122-163	125-167
68										121-161	121-161	123-164	127-169	129-172
69										123-164	125-167	129-172	131-175	134-179
70										129-172	130-173	130-174	133-178	136-181
71										133-178	135-180	136-181	137-182	139-185
72											138-184	139-186	140-187	142-190
73											141-188	144-192	146-194	148-197

Height in inch.	AGE NEAREST BIRTHDAY													
	5 years	6 years	7 years	8 years	9 years	10 years	11 years	12 years	13 years	14 years	15 years	16 years	17 years	18 years
38	30-40	30-40												
39	31-41	31-41												
40	32-43	32-43	32-43											
41	33-44	33-44	33-44											
42	35-47	35-47	35-47											
43	37-49	37-49	37-49	37-49										
44	38-50	38-50	38-50	38-50										
45	40-54	40-54	40-54	40-54	40-54									
46	42-56	42-56	42-56	43-58	43-58									
47	44-59	45-60	45-60	45-60	45-60	45-60								
48		47-62	47-62	47-62	47-62	48-64	48-64							
49		49-65	49-65	49-66	49-66	50-67	50-67							
50		50-67	50-67	51-68	52-70	53-71	55-73	56-74						
51			53-71	54-72	55-73	55-73	57-76	58-78						
52			57-76	58-77	58-77	58-77	58-78	60-80						
53			59-79	60-80	60-80	61-82	61-82	62-83	64-85					
54				61-83	63-84	63-84	64-85	64-85	66-88					
55				65-86	67-89	67-89	67-90	67-90	69-92	70-94				
56					68-91	70-94	70-94	71-95	73-97	75-100				
57					72-96	74-98	74-98	74-98	76-101	79-106	83-110			
58						76-101	77-103	77-103	79-106	84-112	86-115			
59						78-104	81-108	81-108	83-110	86-115	90-120	91-121		
60						82-109	85-114	85-114	87-116	91-121	94-126	93-124		
61							89-119	90-120	91-121	94-126	97-130	97-130	94-125	
62							94-125	94-126	95-127	98-131	102-136	101-134	98-131	
63								99-132	99-132	101-134	104-139	103-138	102-136	100-133
64								103-137	103-138	104-139	107-143	105-140	105-140	104-139
65								106-142	108-144	109-145	110-146	108-144	107-143	106-142
66									112-149	112-149	112-150	111-148	110-146	108-144
67									115-154	117-156	118-157	115-154	112-150	111-148
68									118-157	120-160	121-162	120-160	116-155	113-151
69										121-162	123-164	122-163	120-160	117-156
70											124-166	124-166	124-166	121-162
71										122-163	124-166	126-168	126-168	124-166
72										124-166	126-168	128-170	128-170	128-170
73													130-173	130-174
74														

DESIRABLE WEIGHTS FOR MEN AND WOMEN (AGES 25 AND OVER)

| Height in Shoes | WEIGHT IN INDOOR CLOTHING, POUNDS | | |
	Small Frame	Medium Frame	Large Frame
Men			
5' 2"	112-120	118-129	126-141
3"	115-123	121-133	129-144
4"	118-126	124-136	132-148
5"	121-129	127-139	135-152
6"	124-133	130-143	138-156
7"	128-137	134-147	142-161
8"	132-141	138-152	147-166
9"	136-145	142-156	151-170
10"	140-150	146-160	155-174
11"	144-154	150-165	159-179
6' 0"	148-158	154-170	164-184
1"	152-162	158-175	168-189
2"	156-167	162-180	173-194
3"	160-171	167-185	178-199
4"	164-175	172-190	182-204
Women			
4'10"	92-98	96-107	104-119
11"	94-101	98-110	106-122
5' 0"	96-104	101-113	109-125
1"	99-107	104-116	112-128
2"	102-110	107-119	115-131
3"	105-113	110-122	118-134
4"	108-116	113-126	121-138
5"	111-119	116-130	125-142
6"	114-123	120-135	129-146
7"	118-127	124-139	133-150
8"	122-131	128-143	137-154
9"	126-135	132-147	141-158
10"	130-140	136-151	145-163
11"	134-144	140-155	149-168
6' 0"	138-148	144-159	153-173

From Metropolitan Life Insurance Company, *Statistical Bulletin*, 40:3. November–December 1959. Reprinted by permission.

HOW CAN I BE CERTAIN THAT MY DAILY FOOD INTAKE IS NOT EXCESSIVE?

Weigh yourself—at exactly the same time of day and under the same conditions (preferably in the morning upon rising). When the total daily caloric intake is equal to energy expenditure and calories lost in excreta, a caloric balance has been attained and no weight loss or gain will occur. When you eat more calories than you use, these excess calories are stored as fat. With the accumulation of approximately 3,500 excess calories, one pound of fat is stored. Remember, the body is extremely thrifty. Every unused calorie is stored as fat. Often, a change to an alternate food or drink will cause weight loss. An individual who drinks three glasses of milk daily (165 calories per 8-ounce glass), for example, takes in nearly one pound of fat per week (3,465 calories). A change to skim milk (85 calories per glass) results in a weight reduction of one-half pound weekly or two pounds monthly.

Unused calories are not only placed into a fat bank, they also cannot be withdrawn at a moment's notice. Only after weeks of deprivation and suffering can they be removed. To top it off, you have to carry the bank around with you until a withdrawal is made.

HOW MANY CALORIES DO ATHLETES OF VARIOUS AGES NEED?

An accurate answer depends upon an individual's weight, age, sex, and activity patterns. Certainly, if no weight gain or loss occurs, you are consuming enough calories.

The Recommended Daily Dietary Allowances below, for the moderately active person, were established by the National Academy of Sciences and provide a close estimate of needs for most individuals:

AGE Years	WEIGHT Pounds	HEIGHT Inches	CALORIES
BOYS			
10-12	77	55	2500
12-14	95	59	2700
14-18	130	67	3000
18-22	147	69	2800

AGE Years	WEIGHT Pounds	HEIGHT Inches	CALORIES
GIRLS			
10-12	77	56	2250
12-14	97	61	2300
14-16	114	62	2400
16-18	119	63	2300
18-22	128	64	2000

Another method to estimate your specific caloric needs (for male and females, all ages) is to use the formula:

Desirable weight × Calories per pound = Calories per day

Determine your number of calories per pound as selected from the chart below and take desirable weight from a weight chart.

APPROXIMATE NUMBER OF CALORIES NEEDED DAILY PER POUND OF BODY WEIGHT

AGE RANGES	7-10	11-14	15-22	23-35	36-50	51-75
MALES:						
Very Active	21-22	23-24	25-27	23-24	21-22	19-20
Moderately Active	16-17	18-19	20-23	18-19	16-17	14-15
Sedentary	11-12	13-14	15-18	13-14	11-12	10-11
FEMALES:						
Very Active	21-22	22-23	20-21	20-21	18-19	17-18
Moderately Active	16-17	18-19	16-18	16-17	14-15	12-13
Sedentary	11-12	13-14	11-12	11-12	9-10	8-9

HOW MUCH TIME IS NEEDED TO LOSE 25 POUNDS?

As a general rule, weight loss should not exceed 3–4 pounds weekly. Also, a physician should be consulted when the desired weight loss exceeds 5 percent of body weight. A return to an obese or overweight state tends to occur within a time period proportional to that spent losing a specific amount of weight. Reducing over an extended period of time (minimum of three months) is preferred and generally results in the acquisition of sensible eating habits which are more likely to be continued in the future. Rapid weight loss, through fasting and other crash programs, can be dangerous and often results in a rapid return to old eating habits and an overweight condition. The extended period of time also involves the pleasant personal adjustment to clothes and new positive self-image so vital to weight control. Slow, controlled weight loss, then, has the advantages of safety, permanency, and little or no loss of power for the athlete. Don't try to take it off any faster than you put it on.

One interesting study emphasizes the importance of eating habits. A litter of 4 mice (where there was plenty of food for all) was compared to a litter of 22 (small quantities of food for each). At weaning, the mice from the smaller litter were heavier and appeared healthier. Large amounts of food were then made available to all 26 mice in both litters. The 4 mice, accustomed to heavy eating, continued to eat large quantities while the other 22 ate only small quantities. The 4 obese mice all died early, had been less active, and possessed signs of heart disease. Human behavior is similar, so the need to establish good eating habits early in life is obvious.

IS RAPID WEIGHT LOSS TO MAKE A WEIGHT CLASS IN WRESTLING DANGEROUS?

It can be dangerous for some athletes. Most coaches feel that the ideal procedure is to have wrestlers lose enough weight to enter the lowest possible weight class without any loss of strength or endurance. This means that weight loss must occur over a long period of time (minimum of three months).

It is common practice to lose weight just prior to an official weighing-in by refraining from food and water, alternating exercise in heavy clothes with time in a heated cabinet (sweat box), and taking diuretic pills to cause fluid loss. Loss of up to 5 percent of body weight by this method generally produces no harmful effects, although performance is hindered and cardiovascular stress is present in some athletes. The majority of this weight is regained after weighing in with a good meal and plenty of fluids. A 5 percent weight loss is considered the maximum that should be allowed for the nonobese growing athlete. This amount is often lost during an afternoon football game.

Rapid weight loss exceeding 5 percent of body weight is dangerous; it causes changes in water metabolism and in kidney and circulatory functions. An athlete who is not overweight should not attempt to lose large amounts of weight. The safe limit for this type of individual may be less than 5 percent. The practice of keeping body weight very low during the growth years in order to make a weight class is dangerous and should be disallowed. Be extremely careful. While making a lower weight class may improve your chances of winning a match, it will lessen your chances of staying healthy. With permanent damage to a major organ due to insensible weight loss, you really lose.

HOW CAN I CONTROL HUNGER BETWEEN MEALS AND AVOID OVEREATING AT MEALTIME?

Eating regular meals and small helpings is an excellent start. This is preferred to crash diets that make between-meal time a nightmare.

As for controlling hunger, there are only two approaches: (1) keeping the stomach relatively full, or (2) raising the body's blood sugar level. Both are effective. Try several of the following suggestions:

1. Keep busy at work.
2. Increase your fluid intake both between meals and at mealtime.
3. Eat small amounts of candy such as one chocolate square about 20 to 30 minutes before meals (this raises the blood sugar level and gives the sensation of not being hungry). If you eat too much candy, the body releases insulin causing a dip in blood sugar level within a few hours and the accompanying hunger sensation.
4. Eat slowly to allow the blood sugar level to elevate before completing your meal (a meal should take 20 to 30 minutes). This will reduce the temptation to overeat or have dessert.
5. Eat bulky foods between and at mealtime: lettuce, carrots, apples, celery, fresh fruits.
6. Take numerous coffee breaks during the day. Do not use cream or sugar. Drink diet soda and other sugar-free beverages.

Dieting while competing in any sport can be dangerous. Consult your doctor. His knowledge and guidance will make any diet more effective and reduce the risk to you.

Young children 2 to 4 years old have a built-in mechanism that tells them to stop eating—and they stop. Then Mom steps in and says how shameful: "with all those children in Europe starving." Soon the mechanism is overruled by conditioning and no longer works. We still can't understand how the food gets from the plate to Europe without spoiling.

DO SACCHARIN AND OTHER CALORIE-FREE SWEETENERS ELIMINATE HUNGER?

No. To eliminate hunger you must raise the blood sugar level (this requires sugar or carbohydrates) or fill the stomach. Sugar-free drinks do temporarily aid in reducing hunger by filling the stomach and giving the sensation of fullness for a short time. Such drinks are valuable to a diet, and three or four 10-ounce bottles daily are likely to cause no harm.

On the negative side, it must be said that the controversy is not over. Large doses of saccharin have been shown to cause cancer in mice. As a result of these findings, a warning has been added to the label of all products containing saccharin. Since it is unlikely that any human would ingest such large quantities and since the evidence is not conclusive, saccharin has not been taken off the market.

AFTER DIETING FOR TWO WEEKS MY WEIGHT HAS DROPPED ONLY ONE POUND. WHAT AM I DOING WRONG?

Stay with it. You are experiencing a temporary retention of water (1–4 weeks) which obscures the actual measurable weight loss that occurs in early stages of dieting (vacated fat cells fill with water). This temporary water retention can be discouraging and cause the scales to record only moderate weight loss even when strict dieting has been employed. However, actual weight loss has occurred and will be more vividly noticed in terms of reduced pounds following this period. Do not discontinue your diet before this phenomenon passes.

Some sound diets requiring the consumption of large quantities of water avoid this reaction (increasing water consumption results in the elimination of water and actually counteracts this tendency). A more accurate measure of weight loss during the initial stages of diet is the reduction of adipose tissue in fatty body areas. Mere observation and pinching of fatty tissue will reveal benefits even in early stages.

WHAT IS A SO-CALLED STATE OF "KETOSIS" AND HOW DOES IT HELP WEIGHT LOSS?

When an individual decreases carbohydrate intake (most diets are high in protein and low in carbohydrates), blood glucose is elevated. When the renal threshold of approximately 170 milligrams of sugar per 100 milliliters of blood is attained, glycosuria appears (condition in which sugar or glucose is excreted in the urine), and polyuria (excessive urine secretion) and thirst develop. Stored fat is now made available for energy causing a greatly increased production of ketone bodies by the liver. This process is "ketosis" and is very conducive to easy weight loss.

A 24 to 48 hour fast will cause the urine to show ketones. The idea is to keep an obese individual in a state of ketosis through a high-protein/no-carbohydrate diet coupled with exercise. Carbohydrates cause the obese individual to release excess amounts of insulin, which drive the carbohydrates into the fatty tissue cells and also inhibit the release of fat from the cells. While in a state of ketosis, insulin production is decreased and fat vacates fat cells more freely.

IS IT TRUE THAT EXERCISE MERELY INCREASES ONE'S APPETITE AND DOES NOT PRODUCE WEIGHT LOSS?

No. In fact, exercise alone is recommended when desired poundage to be reduced is only minimum and, although a slower approach, this represents a much more sound, less risky method of weight reduction. Weight control is best achieved through both exercise and diet over a substantial period of time. Fat and excess poundage will be reduced by endurance programs such as distance running (one mile or more), cycling, swimming, running in place, and by endurance activities (basketball, handball, tennis, rugby, soccer, lacrosse, wrestling, and so on) much more rapidly than any other means. A combination of both endurance running and *mild* diet (calories should be reduced no more than 15 to 20 percent when diet is combined with exercise) will produce faster weight loss. An increase in appetite is thus controlled through diet and the caloric expenditure due to exercise is *not* offset by increased eating.

CAN I LOSE WEIGHT WITHOUT EXERCISE?

Yes; however, it is more difficult. In most cases, maintaining or attaining normal weight for individuals with the tendency to gain generally necessitates both diet control and exercise. It is obvious that a much greater number of calories can be eaten by the active individual without subsequent weight gain. Mere diet alone represents a truly difficult undertaking; however, the task is far from impossible, with hundreds of Weight Watchers clubs providing benefits to thousands of members without the benefit of exercise.

Obese people have been shown to expend less energy during exercise than people of normal weight. Some overweight individuals do *not* have a high food intake; they are merely inactive. The value of exercise far exceeds mere contribution to weight control. There is no doubt that exercise is a much needed addition to a diet for reasons of weight loss, improved muscle tone, and conditioning level.

Finally, it must be said that there is a difference between weight loss in terms of pounds and fatty tissue loss in terms of inches. A diet without exercise can result in about 30 percent fatty tissue loss and 70 percent lean muscle loss. With exercise and diet combined, this ratio can be reversed. It is undesirable to lose lean muscle mass when inches of fat remain. Muscle mass is useful tissue that is vital to movement and body function—fat is not. If you want to lose weight, make it fat.

ACCORDING TO SOME ENERGY EXPENDITURE TABLES, VERY FEW CALORIES ARE USED THROUGH EXERCISE. ARE THESE TABLES ACCURATE?

Energy expenditure tables such as that shown below have several limitations and must be interpreted accordingly: (1) tables are computed for an individual of average height and weight (male: 5-foot-8, 150 pounds; female: 5-foot-4, 125 pounds) and must be proportionally increased or decreased with deviations from this weight norm, (2) tables fail to include duration peaks where the expenditure may reach 1,600–2,000 calories per hour, and (3) tables fail to consider the fact that metabolic rate (amount of calories expended at rest) is increased through exercise and remains elevated 40–50 calories per hour for as long as six to eight hours after cessation of activity.

ENERGY COST OF COMMON ACTIVITIES

Activity	Approximate calories per hour	Activity	Approximate calories per hour
Rest (basal metabolism)	70	Walking slowly (2.6 mph)	200
Sitting at rest	100	Volleyball	210
Hand sewing	105	Carpentry, metal working	240
Bricklaying (6 per min.)	105	Dancing (fox trot)	266
Dressing and undressing	118	Archery	268
Singing	122	Gymnastics	270
Typewriting rapidly	140	Golf	290
Ironing (5-lb. iron)	144	Walking (3.75 mph)	300
Dishwashing	144	Badminton	396
Sweeping	169	Cycling (9.4 mph)	408
Driving car	170	Horseback riding (gallop)	441
Shoemaking	180	Tennis (singles)	450

ENERGY COST OF COMMON ACTIVITIES (continued)

Activity	Approximate calories per hour	Activity	Approximate calories per hour
Sawing wood	480	Ice hockey	930
Swimming	500	Walking (up stairs)	1100
Fencing	539	Running:	
Field hockey	546	11.4 mph	1300
Basketball	564	13.2 mph	2330
Skiing	791	14.8 mph	2880
Handball/squash	864	15.8 mph	3910
Wrestling	791	17.2 mph	4740
Football	900	18.6 mph	7790

The chart does not include the 200 to 350 additional calories that will be burned immediately following exercise for five to eight hours due to increased metabolic rate.

Let's apply these shortcomings to a male individual weighing 200 pounds who has run at a 6 minute per mile pace for 30 minutes. According to the chart, he has expended only 500 calories or about 1/7 of a pound of fat (3,500 calories = 1 pound of fat). Adjusting this for metabolic rate changes and for his extra weight we find:

	CHART: 150-pound man	ACTUAL: 200-pound man
6 min./mile pace for 30 minutes	500 calories	625 calories
Metabolic rate changes (40–50 per hour for 6–8 hours)	—	400
TOTAL	500 calories	1,025 calories (almost ⅓ pound of fat)

The actual energy expenditure in this example, then, is more than two times that shown in the chart. Adjust your estimates accordingly when you count caloric expenditure.

Weight loss without exercise is an unwise choice. Exercise is *the* most valuable means of controlling weight. The secret is to exercise daily as opposed to one all-out effort each month. A daily expenditure of 1,025 calories can result in loss of 2 pounds weekly, 8 pounds monthly, and 96 pounds in a year. That's a lot of pizza and beer.

IS EXERCISING ON AN EMPTY STOMACH HARMFUL?

No. In fact, this practice can help you lose fatty tissue. If the body has no energy-producing foods (carbohydrates) to draw upon for fuel during exercise, it must resort to fat supply. The result is a reduction in adipose or fatty tissue in the areas of greatest concentration. Obviously, if you exercise in the morning before breakfast and have not eaten since the previous evening, the only available fuel will be fatty tissue. On the other hand, when the body can utilize energy-producing foods for energy, no loss of fatty tissue occurs. If your carbohydrate diet is high, you will burn a greater proportion of carbohydrates with exercise. If intake is low, you will metabolize a greater amount of fat through exercise.

One disadvantage of performing on an empty stomach is the fact that the blood sugar level is rather low, and headache and dizziness may occur. A more sound approach, when loss of fatty tissue is desired, is to cut down on carbohydrate intake and increase protein consumption. Similar results are attained without the appearance of symptoms which tend to be psychologically distressing and discourage exercise.

WHAT EXERCISES WILL REMOVE THE FAT FROM THE STOMACH AREA?

Welcome to the club. There are millions of male and female athletes and nonathletes of all ages who are unable to remove the excess fat from the stomach and sides. Even some highly conditioned athletes maintain small deposits of fat in these areas.

For most of us, this excess fat can be removed. The remedy, however, requires hard work. We wish we could suggest a pill, taken thrice weekly before retiring to the TV chair, that would bring about all these physiological changes while you ate potato chips. Unfortunately, the only answer is calisthenics—a frightful word to many individuals, since this type of exercise has been grossly misused. The purposes of a calisthenic program directed at the abdominal area are to create what is termed "definition" and to bring out the lines of musculature in the abdominal area by removing fat and increasing the size of the abdominal muscles. The following suggestions will help you begin your program:

1. Measure your waist area carefully before the program starts. Also, borrow some inexpensive calipers and take skinfold measures on both sides and in the stomach area. If no calipers are available, merely take a deep pinch in these areas and

measure the distance between the index finger and thumb. Record this data and compare after several months of exercise.

2. "Definition" can be acquired only through a high number of repetitions. You should attempt a minimum of 100 repetitions daily. Doing fewer repetitions and adding weight behind the head will not produce the same effect; abdominal strength will improve faster, but loss of fatty tissue and definition will not.

3. Use several different exercises:

   a. *Sit-ups.* Bend legs slightly so that you can place a fist between your knees and floor. Lock hands behind the neck and sit up, touching opposite elbow to opposite knee. This exercise will assist both the spare tire and the handlebar.

   b. *Rowing exercise.* Lie flat on your back, then bring your knees up tight against the chest as you sit up.

   c. *Side bender.* Stand at a position of attention with the hands interlocked behind your neck. Bending at the trunk only, move the upper body to the right as far as possible, return to the starting position and repeat to the left side to complete one repetition.

   d. *Stomach curls.* While lying on your back, raise your head in an attempt to touch your chest with your chin.

   e. *Jack knife.* While lying on your back, bring both feet (knees straight) into the air as you attempt a sit-up. Touch your feet with both hands to form a "V" with the body trunk.

   f. *Isometric stomach contraction.* While sitting in a chair or automobile, contract your stomach muscles vigorously and hold it for 8–10 seconds. Rest 30 seconds and repeat, continuing every 30 seconds for five contractions. Add two seconds to your holding time every three days, working up to 20–25 seconds. You will be surprised with the results by the time you reach 25 seconds (three weeks.)

Remember, you must progress toward a minimum of 100 repetitions for each exercise. We suggest that you alternate using the sit-up one day and the rowing exercises the next; use the side bender, stomach curls, jack knife and isometric contractions daily.

Combine these exercises with reduced calories and your regular exercise program. The exercises will improve muscle tone and the calories will get rid of the fat in areas of greatest concentration. It won't happen overnight. Plan to stay with the program for three to four months.

WHY DOES WEIGHT CONTROL BECOME MORE DIFFICULT WITH AGE?

This is mainly a result of inactivity, more time and money for fancy dining, and the fact that metabolic rates decrease as one ages. By the time you are 70 years old, you need about 15 percent fewer calories than you needed at age 20. As the years go by, eat less, exercise more, and dine at home. When dining out, leave some calories on the plate.

WHERE IS FAT MOST LIKELY TO FORM ON THE BODY?

Several things determine where fat finally settles in the individual who eats more calories than are burned:

(1) sex—women have a higher ratio of fat to body weight and tend to deposit fat on the upper leg, buttocks, arms, and stomach, while men are most vulnerable in the stomach area, (2) heredity—general body type of an individual leaves him or her somewhat more vulnerable in certain areas, (3) endocrine secretion, and (4) exercise habits.

We have been taught for years that a muscle group that is not used will atrophy or decrease in size. No muscle group is less used among the American public than the stomach; yet, no atrophy occurs. In fact, the more the stomach is neglected, the larger it gets. Excess food that is not burned must settle as fat somewhere and it generally forms in an area where musculature is rarely stimulated. The upper leg and buttocks of men are generally firm and free from fatty tissue; women, on the other hand, generally do not engage in vigorous muscle work involving these areas and, consequently, tend to build up fat.

Your best protection from fat buildup is sensible eating habits and regular exercise. Keep in mind that fat deposits are a lot easier and more fun to put on than to remove. Furthermore, the excess weight and the miles of new network of capillaries to feed this new tissue place excess strain on the circulatory system. Since the heart and the arteries supplying it seem to be the first to go as age increases, it seems a shame to hurry their destruction.

WILL DIET CAUSE SKIN WRINKLING OR UGLY FOLDS WHERE FAT IS ELIMINATED?

Since young people have an elastic skin, this is rarely a problem for the under-30 age group. For older individuals, wrinkles and folds do occur, but they will, depending upon age and the amount of weight loss, disappear over a substantial period of time. Slow weight loss over a long period of time is less apt to result in this type of condition.

Several factors, then, determine the extent of wrinkles and folds that will appear:

1. *Speed of weight loss.* A minimum of three to six months is recommended when attempting to remove more than 5 percent of body weight.
2. *Age.* The older the individual, the more prone to wrinkles and less resilient is the skin.
3. *Amount of weight to be lost.* 50, 75, 100, 150, and 200 pound reductions can result in such ugly appearance in the stomach area that surgery may be needed to remove excess skin.
4. *Exercise.* Daily activity is needed to maintain muscle tone, increase fatty tissue loss, and decrease lean muscle loss.

The basic problem is that skin is stretched and it remains stretched after weight loss, so it just does not fit the body—much the same way a baby's skin appears at birth.

IS IT POSSIBLE TO AVOID GAINING WEIGHT WHEN SMOKING IS STOPPED?

Yes. Smoking does curb the appetite somewhat. Even more, it provides activity for the hands and takes time—time that might be spent in nervous eating. Contrary to popular opinion, smokers are also snackers and are heavier than the nonsmoking population. When they quit smoking, extra eating fills the gap. Therefore you should be alert to nervous eating when you stop smoking.

This is also a good time to overhaul your body further: begin a mild exercise program after consultation with your physician. Without exercise and diet control at this critical time, you may never see your shoes again.

DOES ALCOHOL STIMULATE THE APPETITE?

Only indirectly. Since alcohol is a depressant, it encourages relaxation, and relaxation improves appetite, so you might say that it is helpful. Alcohol contains calories (200–225 per ounce, about 125 per 12-ounce can of beer) and can cause a weight problem without stimulating the appetite. It is not unusual to consume four to six beers at one sitting.

Such a feat adds about 750 calories; five such sittings adds one pound of ugly, hard-to-remove fat. The body doesn't care whether alcohol or increased appetite gets the blame.

SHOULD FAT BE COMPLETELY EXCLUDED FROM THE DIET?

No. Fat plays a vital part in digestion and in transportation of vitamins, and is the main fuel of some muscle fibers in most muscle groups. Also, it would be nearly impossible to eliminate fats from the diet. Meat is far from pure protein and is often tenderized with fat (marbelization) to improve taste. Unless one resorts to artificial foods, fats cannot be avoided.

Fat is the highest concentration of energy or calories and should be avoided *in excess*. *Life* magazine recently carried a pictorial on the amount of fat in the American diet. Photos removed everything from common dishes except the fat, to demonstrate its prevalence. The photos are short of shocking, with fat content approaching an average of 35 to 40 percent—far too high.

Up to 65 percent of caloric intake should come from carbohydrates, 10 to 15 percent from protein, and the remaining percentage from fats.

In terms of performance, energy derived from fats is less economical than energy drawn from carbohydrates and proteins. About 10 to 12 percent more oxygen is needed to utilize energy supplied from fats. Both your long-term health and athletic performance will improve if fat intake is reduced—only a magician could completely eliminate it.

IS IT HELPFUL TO HAVE SOME DEGREE OF FAT ON THE BODY?

Yes. Athletes in contact sports should try to keep their weight slightly higher than normal, not to become one piece of lean meat. Fat deposits around the kidneys and other major organs offer needed protection from hard blows that could prove serious. Fat is not all bad; when the ratio of fat and muscle mass is normal, fat has a vital role in providing both insulation and protection.

SHOULD CARBOHYDRATES BE ELIMINATED FROM THE DIET?

Restricted, yes; eliminated, no. For one thing, exercise will draw from available carbohydrate supply for energy; if the supply is limited, the body must resort to fat for fuel, and the result is a loss of fatty tissue. Also, the brain needs a constant supply of glucose (obtained from sugar and carbohydrates). This need is so essential that the body has a built-in mechanism to convert protein to carbohydrates when the supply is absent.

Cut down on your carbohydrate intake (bread, sugar, cereal products, potatoes, and the like) but do not completely avoid these foods. Athletes need to include carbohydrates in their diet to provide ample energy for exercise.

On the other hand, there is also evidence suggesting the need for a high carbohydrate diet, particularly 24 to 48 hours before competition. Subjects were shown to have a slight increase in muscular efficiency after consuming a high carbohydrate diet (see High Performance Diet). Some experts suggest that about 50 percent of food calories should be carbohydrates for athletes in vigorous training (40 percent is normal). This would not apply to the overweight athlete, though.

SHOULD ADULTS DRINK WHOLE MILK?

The American male, the overweight female, and anyone who is vulnerable to atherosclerosis (that includes practically all of us) would be wise to drink skim milk. Resorting to skim milk eliminates damaging saturated fats and calories. In fact, if you drink four 8-ounce glasses of milk daily, a switch to skim milk will save you up to 320 calories daily, 9,600 calories monthly, which represents more than 2½ pounds of fat per month.

There is some justification for placing children on skim milk, since cholesterol buildup begins early in life, as do weight problems and the start of atherosclerosis. After an initial acclimation period of one or two months, whole milk will taste like cream and be unpleasant to you. Keep in mind also that although fortified skim milk has approximately 40 percent more calories than plain skim milk, it is probably the wiser choice for children. You don't need the fat in whole milk; you consume enough in meat and other dairy products.

ARE SWEETS IMPORTANT IN OUR DIET?

No. Most individuals get enough sugar in natural foods and do not need "empty calories" that only serve to destroy appetite and intake of important foods. A common mistake of mothers is to reward children with candy, immediately establishing the fallacy that sweets are better than other food. This reward procedure associates warmth and love with an undesirable food—a link that remains throughout life. Since food and emotion are associated in the child's mind, it would be far better to establish an association between good foods and reward.

Small amounts of candy do elevate blood sugar level and curb appetite. It therefore can be used to the benefit of dieters who want to control hunger sensations. But as an important source of energy, fuel, and cell building, or as an aid to the function of systems, candy rates low. It also can form an eating habit that will help keep you fat in the future.

IS IT TRUE THAT THE MAJOR PART OF EXCESSIVE WEIGHT IS WATER?

No. Do not restrict your water intake in any way. Water is essential to the proper function of every body system. Drinking water immediately before an exercise session, during, or immediately after will have no effect upon weight loss.

Large quantities of water act as a diuretic and will help you to lose your fluids rather than retain them. Retention of fluids is common while dieting, since water remains in the spaces freed by the disappearance of fat. This fluid generally remains for two or three weeks and often obscures actual weight loss.

The majority (about 80 percent) of excessive weight is *fat,* not water. If fat individuals would replace between-meal eating with water, there would never be any misunderstanding.

IS THERE ANY QUICK, SAFE METHOD OF REMOVING FAT FROM THE BODY?

Definitely not. The large majority of gimmick approaches involving a special apparatus or single food are of questionable value. *Vibrators* result in little caloric expenditure and do not cause weight loss. *Spot reducing* has little scientific basis, since research indicates that the greatest weight loss occurs in the area of highest fat deposits regardless of the body area or part exercised. *Steam baths* merely remove body fluids and do not significantly affect weight loss. A steam bath simply does not burn up many calories; lying in the snow would be more beneficial.

Surgery has proved successful both in removing fat deposits in the stomach area and removing a portion of the stomach. These are drastic approaches, however, and are performed only under unusual circumstances when obesity is a serious threat to health. With no change in eating habits or exercise patterns, the physician will have to keep the knife sharp—the patient will return.

Save your money, consult a physician, and implement a sound program of diet and exercise based on your individual characteristics. There is no "crash" approach to weight loss that is effective, lasting, and safe.

DO WAIST BELTS CAUSE WEIGHT LOSS?

No. Wearing a heavy weight around the waist throughout the day will burn up a few extra calories; however, the effect is negligible. The size of the waistline and muscle tone remain about the same after prolonged use.

Do not become a victim of wild advertising claims. In May 1971 the Federal Trade Commission prohibited the company marketing the Tone-o-matic weighted belt from falsely claiming that it is an effective substitute for exercise in reducing weight and waist size. This censor came after many months of radio, television, and printed advertisements. Furthermore, the Federal Trade Commission also indicates that the belt could physically injure some users.

There is no fast, easy method of losing weight and stomach fat. The only belt that may be valuable is one that you place around your head and over your mouth—immediately after eating your first helping.

CAN YOU LOSE WEIGHT FROM INFLATABLE CLOTHING AND BODY WRAPS?

No. Immediately after you remove the material, your waistline is smaller due to a shifting in fluids from one place to another. By the time you get home and drink a glass or two of water, you'll be back to normal—except for your pocketbook, where the loss was much more than water.

WHAT ABOUT MASSAGE?

Massage burns very few calories and does not cause fluid loss. It is relaxing and can slightly aid muscle tone and improve circulation. Meanwhile, the masseur himself may lose a few pounds while you rest. And to top it off, he gets paid for it.

DO LAXATIVES HELP TO LOSE WEIGHT?

No. They are no more effective than the Roman practice of forced vomiting after a gluttonous meal to allow continuous eating and socializing. Laxatives have a similar effect; however, they are a more dangerous practice and can cause gastrointestinal trouble. You need adequate fluid intake and nutrients while dieting. A laxative, taken on a regular basis, can prevent you from obtaining either, and cause dehydration and undernourishment. Be sensible. It is better to be fat than to be sick. It is impossible to defecate away unwanted pounds.

ARE WEIGHT-REDUCING PILLS HARMFUL?

Yes. Without careful supervision by a physician, the use of numerous drugs and drug combinations has been shown to be extremely harmful and sometimes fatal. The various drugs (prescription and patent medicine) employed to lose weight generally attempt to cause loss through (1) increasing metabolic rate or the rate at which the body burns up calories while at rest, (2) curbing the appetite by providing a feeling of "fullness," or (3) causing fluid loss. Amphetamines and diuretics are the two most commonly used diet pills. Amphetamines toy with the thyroid gland, cause nervousness, speed up metabolism, and require increasingly strong doses as the body builds up a tolerance; diuretics result in rapid fluid loss. Both are a dangerous attempt at weight control.

Consult your physician before starting any type of diet, and certainly before ever using any drug for weight loss. Crash dieting with pills can destroy your health and cause permanent damage to vital organs.

WHEN IS THE BEST TIME TO START A DIET?

Begin as soon as you notice weight gain of 5 percent or fat folds in a body area. Controlled eating after splurges occur (eating out, parties) can prevent the need for a diet. The longer you allow excess weight to accumulate, the more difficult it is to remove.

There are other factors to weigh also before deciding to initiate a diet. Consider starting your diet:

1. At the onset of your vacation. You will save money and avoid additional weight gain during a relaxed time when everyone has a tendency to overeat.
2. After the November-December holiday season when temptation is reduced. Or, if you really are well disciplined, begin *during* the holiday season—you are certain to avoid 3–5 excess pounds.

3. After "cold and virus" season. The winter months are particularly troublesome due to flu epidemics and colds; avoid adding fuel to the fire with lowered resistance.
4. When finances are particularly low in your household. Chances of eating out and stocking "foodless" high-calorie foods are minimized.
5. After finishing an organized sport such as softball, basketball, or rugby. Since the decrease in activity will not be followed by a decrease in appetite, this is a dangerous period requiring a change in eating habits.

If in doubt, start this minute. If you are obese and not just overweight, start a diet immediately in consultation with your physician.

CAN I LOSE WEIGHT WITH ONE-FOOD DIETS?

Nowadays more and more dieters turn to the one-food diets (grapefruit, buttermilk, egg, poultry, fish, vegetable, fruit, juice, bananas and milk, yogurt, rice). Usually, they do this without checking with their doctor.

Actually, such diets can be pretty risky. The pitfalls are: (1) you may not get the necessary daily nutriments when you eat only one kind of food, (2) you may not drink enough water, thus depriving your body of fluid for proper functioning of the systems, (3) your resistance may be lowered, leaving you susceptible to disease or infection, (4) diets of this nature are usually short-term and don't help you change your eating habits. After you stop dieting, you just gain weight again.

Losing weight is a very serious business. But it can be fun, too. Ask anyone who's acquired a slimmer waistline or a flatter stomach. The fun, of course, comes as you see weight peel off.

You can do it! Others have done it.

ARE PROTEIN DIETS THAT ALLOW UNRESTRICTED CONSUMPTION EFFECTIVE?

No. The fact still remains that approximately 3,500 calories equal one pound of fat. Every calorie that is not burned up through activity is stored as fat. It doesn't matter in what form the calories are taken (proteins, carbohydrates, fats), it only matters how many are not used. A steak or fish diet has no advantage over any other diet and will not work unless caloric intake is reduced. Also, meat is not fat free, even when trimmed perfectly. The only possible value of such a diet is that it becomes difficult to consume enough of one food to consume excessive calories. It also is nearly impossible to secure the necessary daily nutrients for daily activity.

Protein is an essential part of an athlete's diet and should comprise about 12 to 15 percent of daily food intake. For the growing athlete, higher quantities may be needed during training periods. This is also true for athletes training to improve muscle mass. In extremely hot weather, a reduction in protein intake assists in the prevention of over-heating and possible heat stroke and exhaustion.

IS IT TRUE THAT LIQUID PROTEIN DIETS ARE DANGEROUS?

Yes. Liquid protein diets, a near starvation approach to weight loss, have been implicated in more than 30 deaths, and over 100 reported cases of illness (*Parent's Magazine*, March 1978). A dieter may be deprived of essential amino acids, vitamins and minerals, including potassium deficiency which can lead to heart irregularities and sudden death. Nausea, vomiting, diarrhea (from the liquid form), constipation (from the powdered form), muscle cramps, dizziness and fainting and blackouts are some of the side effects. In addition, low calorie, protein diets are dangerous for infants; children; pregnant or nursing women; those with kidney, liver, heart, blood vessel or metabolic diseases; and those under medication for numerous disorders. The FDA has pro-posed that all protein supplements carry this warning label: WARNING: *Very low calorie, protein diets may cause serious illness or death. Do not use for weight reduction or maintenance without medical supervision. Do not use for any purpose without medical advice if you are taking medication. Not for use by infants, children, or pregnant or nursing women.* They are also an unwise choice for athletes.

DESCRIBE A 1,000 CALORIE DIET.

In this diet, you must merely consume less than 1,000 calories daily. Look at a calorie chart, select any foods you desire, and stay within 1,000 calories. It is also necessary to consume eight glasses of water daily and take vitamin supplements.

While this diet is not as effective as the Quick Weight-Loss Diet (see page 104), it will remove pounds at the rate of about two or three weekly. Since you will probably eat carbohydrates, protein, and fats, loss of fatty tissue will also not be as great. Nonetheless, 1,000 calories is few enough to force the body to resort to fat supplies for energy and cause weight and fatty tissue loss. One thing you are apt to discover: 1,000 is not very many calories:

Brazil nuts (1 cup):	905 calories
Peanuts (roasted, 1 cup):	840 calories
Macaroni and cheese (2 cups):	950 calories
Beer (8 cans):	1,000 calories

One piece of pie or cake, ice cream, or a milk shake can destroy your 1,000-calorie day.

CAN YOU DESCRIBE THE STILLMAN QUICK WEIGHT LOSS DIET?

The Doctor's Quick Weight Loss Diet[2], often referred to as the "Water Diet" because of the strict requirement to drink eight 10-ounce glasses of water daily, has become one of America's favorite choices. Again, one should be cautioned to consult a physician before attempting such a diet. The diet is extremely simple to remember and follow:

1. A multiple vitamin is consumed daily.
2. Eight 10-ounce glasses of water must be consumed daily in addition to other calorie free fluids.
3. Carbohydrates are prohibited.
4. Foods that can be eaten include chicken (no skin), lean meat, fish (broiled), hard boiled eggs, cottage cheese, coffee and tea without milk or sugar. No vegetables are permitted.

Obviously, Dr. Stillman has developed a highly restrictive protein diet. He recommends skipping the diet on weekends and returning again on Monday and thereafter any time during the year when one gains five pounds.

Low carbohydrate diets (Stillman's Quick Weight Loss Diet) have been around for a long time. According to the Food and Nutrition Council of the American Medical Association, these diets can be dangerous. Some of the pitfalls pointed out are the possibility of extreme fatigue; tendency to fainting, headache, nausea and vomiting; danger of the high cholesterol content (high fat) of and concern about "ketosis" described earlier; and a loss of calcium from the bones with demineralization of the spine. Low carbohydrate diets tend to shed pounds rapidly since dieters can satisfy their hunger even though they eat less. Serious medical concerns, however, seem to make such an approach an unwise choice.

IS THE ATKINS HIGH FAT DIET A WISE CHOICE?

No. This high fat diet has been under attack since it first appeared in the best selling book, *Diet Revolution*. A tremendous advertising blitz, a best selling book, and documented examples of actual weight loss have been too much for the American public to resist. Consequently, thousands of people have resorted to what appears as an easy, rapid and safe approach to weight loss. While the diet may produce rapid weight loss, it is far from safe. The high fat intake raises cholesterol levels and is therefore dangerous to older individuals and those suffering from diagnosed or undiagnosed heart disease. The diet is so unbalanced and limited in carbohydrates that it is difficult to follow and unlikely to maintain weight loss through a permanent change in eating habits; and the dangers of ketosis (discussed previously) are also present.

WHAT IS THE HEART ATTACK PREVENTION DIET?

The heart attack diet is one low in saturated (animal) fats, based on the theory that high cholesterol is related to heart attacks and strokes and that a low cholesterol level reduces the incidence of heart disease.

Americans do eat a fat content of 45 to 50 percent, which is too high. A lower fat diet beginning at birth would appear more desirable. The heart attack diet can be initiated at any age to lower cholesterol levels.

The diet has to be one of the most restrictive in existence. It has two objectives: (1) to limit cholesterol intake, and (2) to make unsaturated fats (fats from corn oil, cottonseed oil and safflower oil) twice as plentiful in the diet as saturated fats. Substitution of unsaturated for saturated fats will substantially reduce total blood serum cholesterol.

The restrictive foods include:

1. Bacon, salt pork, spareribs, frankfurters, sausage, cold cuts, canned meats, and organ meats (kidney, liver, etc.).
2. Meat fat.
3. Whole milk, canned milk, cream, ice cream, cheese, buttermilk, sour cream, yogurt (made from whole milk).
4. Ordinary margarine, shortening, lard, chicken fat, olive oil, coconut, chocolate.
5. Muffins, biscuits, corn bread, cakes, pies, doughnuts, rolls, pastries, etc.
6. Puddings, custards, whipped cream.
7. French fries, potato chips, fried fish, creamed soups and dishes, frozen and packaged food, crackers.
8. Candy—chocolate, butter, cream, fudge, commercial popcorn.

You also must reduce and control intake in some areas:

1. Two–three eggs per week only.
2. Four tablespoons of unsaturated oils daily are required.
3. No more than 3-ounce servings of lean meat—only four meat meals a week.
4. Poultry, seafood, or veal must be eaten at ten other meals (lunch and dinner).
5. One pint (maximum) of skim milk daily.

Before you throw away the book or shoot yourself, let's see what foods you can eat. You may eat unlimited quantities of cereal, bread, rice, macaroni, and other flour and grain products. Baked products can be eaten if made from unsaturated oils.

If you like starchy foods, and have a bookkeeper's skill in planning a weekly menu, this diet may be just for you. A modified version involves cutting down on saturated fats and cholesterol—avoiding rich foods, purchasing low-fat and nonfat milk, varying protein sources to cut down on beef and pork by substituting fish and veal, using oil instead of fats, and eliminating pastry. Cholesterol levels will not be greatly reduced but risks may be cut somewhat. The right time to start is at birth. Proper eating habits are formed and no sacrifice is evident. Ten years could be added to your life.

DO BABIES AND YOUNG CHILDREN EAT TOO MUCH?

Yes, and this causes numerous difficulties in later life. Let's examine the process in more detail.

1. *Eating habits formed in infancy carry over to later life.* A fat infant becomes a fat adult with a stopover as a fat teenager.
2. *Fat cells are formed early in life and may increase in both size and number until puberty.* Although research is inconclusive, it appears that diet decreases only the *size* of fat cells, not the *number*. With a large number of fat cells formed, return to an overweight condition is much easier. This explains why adults who were heavy babies have difficulty keeping their weight down. These extra cells also may affect metabolism and result in the need for fewer calories to maintain normal weight than is true for someone who has always maintained normal weight.
3. *Atherosclerosis (plaque build-up inside the coronary arteries) may start in early life.* There is increasing evidence that vessel damage begins in infancy and is directly related to the amount and type of food eaten.

There is little danger that your child will be malnourished, particularly if you let the child decide when to stop eating each meal. Forcing him or her to "clean" the plate is a mistake. Forcing your child to overeat, making sweets plentiful and using them as a reward, and placing emphasis on the "fat baby" will only shorten life span, encourage premature heart disease, form undesirable eating habits that will be continued throughout life, and destine your child to a life of restricted eating due to a high number of fat cells formed in early life. A lean child with a great deal of energy and vitality is far healthier and far more likely to be healthy in later life. There is no stage of life when excess fat is desirable. Start your children off right and avoid overstuffing. If you destroy their mechanism to "push up" from the table when they feel full, they are certain to need plenty of real push-ups in the adult years to control their weight.

IS FASTING USEFUL IN LOSING WEIGHT?

There is some evidence that a 24- to 48-hour fast at the beginning of a diet breaks down an undesirable chemical balance and paves the way for more rapid weight loss. Long-term fasting should be attempted only in a hospital under close supervision. This approach is used in various clinics for the extremely obese individual. It is best to avoid reducing caloric intake below the metabolic rate (amount of calories required in a 24-hour period while at rest, but not sleeping). This figure varies from approximately 1,200 to 2,000, depending upon the individual.

Fast only under the supervision of a physician. It is also wise to use a food supplement in the form of a multiple vitamin. Even wiser is an attempt to eat sensibly, thus avoiding an obese condition and the need for fasting.

ISN'T "CONTROLLED" FASTING AN EFFECTIVE DIET METHOD?

Yes, it can be one of the quickest ways to lose weight, provided all solid foods are eliminated, water intake is plentiful (eight to ten glasses daily), a vitamin supplement is used, and fasting continues for only a short time (two to five days). It is quite unlikely that fasting under these conditions will be harmful. After the first 18 to 24 hours, hunger pangs and the desire to eat will also diminish.

A variation of the above is to fast one or two days each week and eat normally on the other five days. It is quite unlikely that you will gorge yourself on eating days and offset the effects of fasting. There are also semi-starvation diets that might fit your temperament better.

The disadvantages of fasting are that eating habits may not change, so that when the diet ends, you will return to the same foods that made you overweight. Also, inadequate fluid consumption can be dangerous even for a healthy individual. On the other hand, fasting builds will power and provides clear evidence that you can lose weight and that the cause of your overweight condition was not a glandular problem or metabolic imbalance, but being a gluttonous eater.

CAN YOU DESCRIBE A FASTING AND SEMI-FASTING OR SEMI-STARVATION DIET?

Stillman, in his book, *The Doctor's Quick Weight Loss Diet,* lists nearly a hundred diets to allow people to choose something compatible with their temperament, taste, and will power. Below is a simple fasting and semi-starvation diet:

One- to two-day fasting diet	*Semi-starvation diet (350 calories)*
No solid food	Breakfast: 1 hard boiled egg, 8 ounces of skim milk
Minimum of 8 glasses of water	Lunch: 3½ ounces tossed leafy salad with non-caloric dressing
Black coffee and tea without sugar	Dinner: 3 ounces lean meat, 3½ ounces tossed leafy salad
Noncaloric beverages	Minimum of 8 glasses of water; unlimited black coffee, tea, non-caloric beverages
Vitamin-mineral tablets	Vitamin-mineral tablets

Fasting diets will result in a weight loss of 3 to 5 pounds a day; 4 to 6 pounds can be lost in three days with a semi-starvation diet.

WILL EATING ONLY ONE OR TWO MEALS DAILY HELP ONE TO LOSE WEIGHT?

No. It is nearly impossible for most people to skip a meal and lose weight. Their hunger becomes so intense at the next scheduled meal that more calories are consumed than would have been eaten in two meals. It also is difficult to get the necessary daily vitamin requirements with one or two meals daily. Breakfast is the most commonly missed meal. After approximately twelve hours without food, it is the one meal that is absolutely necessary in your diet. Research indicates that late morning fatigue is likely if breakfast is missed. Missing the noon meal is the next most common and also represents a poor attempt at weight reduction. A ten-hour period of activity without food is too long and will result in tremendous overeating at the evening meal.

Do not skip a meal. Eat less quantity at each, or eat six meals per day instead of three, consuming even smaller portions at each. This approach has been shown to result in more weight loss than the three-meals-per day approach.

CAN YOU DESCRIBE A SOUND, SAFE DIET?

Choosing a diet from hundreds appearing in newspapers, magazines and books is no easy task. As a general rule, all "fad" diets and gimmick approaches should be avoided. Keep in mind that calories do count and the amount of weight loss will be determined by the difference between the number of calories you eat and those you expend through exercise:

Caloric deficits daily (minus calories from reduced food intake and exercise expenditure—3500 = 1 lb. fat)	Approximate weekly weight loss
250 calories	½ lb.
500 calories	1 lb.
750 calories	1½ lbs.
1000 calories	2 lbs.
1250 calories	2½ lbs.
1500 calories	3 lbs.

Greater weight loss than 3 lbs. weekly is not recommended from reduced calories alone since daily caloric intake should not be less than 1200–1800 calories.

For a safe, sound, effective diet, consider these suggestions:

1. Decide exactly how much you would like to weigh. Determine the number of calories you must eat to maintain this desired weight from one of the charts on p. 86. Count calories carefully and eat only this number daily. Weight loss will occur with reduced calories regardless of the diet's percentage of carbohydrates, fats and proteins.
   a. Eat from the four basic food groups utilizing three meals a day. Choose the foods from each group that you enjoy and can continue to eat over a period of several months.
   b. Drink a minimum of 6 glasses of water daily.

c. Take one multiple vitamin per day.
d. Combine dieting with mild exercise in an activity you enjoy and will engage in daily for a minimum of 30 minutes.
e. Gear your program for a weight loss of 2 to 4 pounds weekly and plan to stay with it for a minimum of 45 days.
f. Make your evening meal your light meal, consuming less than 30 percent of your daily calories at this time. Research suggests that those who eat a big traditional evening meal do not lose as much weight as those who eat lightly. In fact, 4 to 5 light meals (total calories must conform to your desired weight) will produce the greatest weight loss.
g. Do not skip a meal.

Consult your physician, get out your calorie counter, and begin with any diet that conforms to the suggestions above.

WHAT CAN I DO TO GAIN WEIGHT?

Obviously, you must take in more calories each day than your body needs for energy. Remember that the body is thrifty and will store all calories that are not needed. On the other hand, if food energy is not available, the body will resort to fat supply for energy and you will lose weight.

Although most underweight people have normal metabolism, they are generally jumpy and tense, causing energy to dissipate rapidly. On the favorable side, a thin person uses fewer calories to exercise than a heavy person. The only real solution, then, is to greatly increase your daily food intake. If this occurs with no increase in activity patterns and if there is no existing medical condition affecting metabolism, you will gain weight.

Have patience. It is often very difficult to gain weight. Do not expect instant results. The following suggestions will help make your weight-gaining program a success:

1. Undergo a thorough physical examination in an attempt to uncover medical reasons for being underweight.
2. Maintain accurate records of the calories consumed over a period of six to ten days. Compare your daily intake to the needs for someone of your weight and activity patterns. You are probably not eating enough.
3. Increase your food consumption by eating more high-calorie foods, larger portions, seconds, and snacks. Become familiar with the high-calorie foods to your liking and eat them daily.

4. Plan your diet around familiar foods and avoid foods (even high-calorie) that you detest.

5. Avoid too many between-meal snacks. Remember, carbohydrates will elevate the blood sugar level and give the sensation of not being hungry. Thus, snacks can destroy appetite for meals, when consumption should be high.

6. Avoid drinking with meals. This will allow you to consume more food before feeling full.

7. Cut down on bulky foods such as lettuce, carrots, apples, celery, and fresh fruits.

8. Always eat dessert, a second helping whenever possible.

9. Add a fourth meal just before bedtime; however, do not overeat and cause discomfort and difficulty in sleeping.

10. Get proper rest, increasing sleeping time to ten hours and using afternoon naps to conserve energy.

11. Continue exercising to maintain proper muscle tone. Reduce exercise volume, if possible, particularly in the off-season period. Since an athlete's desire to gain weight is coupled with the need for increased bulk or muscle mass, exercise such as weight training or other strength training programs is absolutely necessary.

Handedness and Performance

There are certain advantages to being both left- and right-handed in athletics. None of these advantages is nearly as important as learning how to use *both* hands and feet with near equal skill. Yet few athletes at any level have achieved this feat in spite of the fact that such mastery is possible with only average exposure to the recessive limbs. It is the purpose of this chapter to examine carefully all concepts involved in the development of the recessive limb, to discuss factors such as the degree of handedness, determination of handedness, misconceptions that have retarded recessive limb improvement in athletics, and to offer recommendations for immediate changes in both physical education and athletic programs.

WHAT DETERMINES WHETHER A CHILD IS LEFT- OR RIGHT-HANDED?

Theories on the acquisition of left- or right-hand dominance are wide and varied, ranging from the logical to the absurd. All share one common bond: lack of scientific support. In 1871 Carlyle hypothesized that the heart (left side of body) had to be protected in warfare by turning it away from the enemy and providing coverage with a shield while the right hand engaged in battle. Plato pointed out that the child held the mother's neck with one arm and was free to grasp objects with the other. Left-handedness has been said to be a result of emotional negativism by an unwanted child. Since the right side of the body is slightly heavier than the left (approximately 1 pound) due to internal structure, it has also been stated that the center of gravity would be different for left-handed individuals. Additional beliefs include the idea that one side of the brain is better developed than the other and consequently the opposite side becomes dominant. (It is true that the nerve trunks leading from the brain are crossed before leaving the cranial cavity, with the left side controlling the right side of the body and vice versa. Therefore, right eye and foot dominance usually accompany right-handedness.) Still others contend that handedness is inherited and unalterably determined at birth.

The most logical theory is that handedness is inherited, subject to environmental influences greatly favoring right-side dominance. Children can be trained away from left-handedness and even alternate use of both sides (legs and arms) until about age four. Although handedness does appear flexible in the very young, natural handedness and corresponding cerebral dominance are established by school age. Observe the child and identify his or her dominant hand or foot. After dominance is established, teach the child to use both equally well.

I WANT TO DEVELOP MY RECESSIVE HAND BUT I HAVE BEEN TOLD THAT THIS COULD CAUSE STUTTERING AND MENTAL CONFUSION. IS THIS TRUE?

After age 10, no. Let's examine this and other common misconceptions: (1) ambidexterity will cause mental confusion, (2) concentration and training in the use of the dominant side results in "cross training" to the recessive side, in both skill and physical development, (3) left-handed athletes are inferior in skill to right-handed athletes, (4) improved recessive hand/leg skill decreases skill level in the dominant limbs, and (5) the recessive side cannot be developed to a high degree.

Ambidexterity and mental confusion. The theory that development of the recessive limb results in confusion, stuttering, hesitation, and blocking of movements is greatly misinterpreted and not strongly supported. Any harmful effects that may occur could be a result of the child's being made to feel inferior or peculiar for using the left hand.

There is at present no evidence indicating that recessive-hand training and attempts to encourage ambidexterity result in mental confusion of any kind.

Cross training. Only a very small amount of the strength and skill acquired in one limb is carried over to the other. It is evident that the dominant side is much more highly skilled and developed than the recessive side. You cannot develop your left hand by using your right hand. The only sound approach for any athlete is to concentrate on the recessive side, giving it "equal exposure" in all practice sessions.

The inferior sides. Years ago, researchers actually tried to "cure" left-handedness by converting people to right-hand dominance. Parents tend to want their children to be right-handed. The words "sinister," "gauche" and others, unlike "lefty," have carried unpleasant connotations for the left-dominant individual. As one would strongly suspect there is no difference in the intelligence of left- or right-dominant subjects. We may be a right-handed society, but there is no inherently inferior side. Both left and right dominance have definite advantages in various sports and activities. Cross laterals tend to be somewhat less skilled than a dominant left or right individual. A left-handed athlete is no less fluid in executing sports skills than a right-handed athlete. Any "clumsiness" that may be apparent results from the lack of refined use, skill and development of the recessive limb, regardless of its side, and it is here that we, in physical education and athletics should devote much needed attention.

Effects of recessive-side training upon dominant-side skill. Regardless of how much you concentrate on your recessive limb, it will not decrease skill in the dominant limb. That is, unless you fail to give the dominant side equal time and totally neglect it.

Possibility of recessive-side development. Approximate ambidexterity in a wide variety of skills and activities can be attained. Many children have been found to be socially right-dominant and physiologically left-dominant, with social dominance a conditioned or learned occurrence and physiological dominance a preferential choice aside from conditioning and order of response. Thus, it is entirely possible that some individuals are performing athletic skills right-handed who are inherently ambidextrous or left-handed. For these groups of individuals, acquiring approximate ambidexterity should be quicker.

There is not one good excuse to suggest that any athlete should avoid recessive-limb training. Development is easier at early ages and, if training continues over a five- to ten-year period, results are fantastic. If you are already 15 years old, you've lost a lot of precious time. Change your routine today. Sports are one place where it is better not to know your left from your right.

WHY ARE SO FEW ATHLETES ABLE TO USE BOTH HANDS AND FEET EQUALLY WELL?

The answer is simple. Neglect! Most people are familiar with the story of the highly trained athlete who mimicked the moves of a three-year-old child for an entire day and, after only several hours, was no longer physically able to continue. This interesting study revealed the intensity of childhood play. It would be even more interesting to merely *observe* a child or adult for an entire day. A careful recorder would note some revealing, yet sad, information. Approximately 95 percent or more of daily routines, from grooming to carrying books and briefcases, from eating to standing and sitting, all routines and play activity, would be performed with the dominant side. These movements become reflexes. Compounded by 5, 10, 20, 30, or 40 years, it is no wonder that the recessive limbs are atrophied in size and able to perform only simple gross motor movements, that posture imbalance occurs, that the recessive limbs (left in most cases) are nearly useless extremities in modern-day athletics, weakening both individual and team play, that the dominant side of the body can be identified by its larger proportions, that society has produced a mass one-sidedness with the majority of individuals "half physically educated."

Textbooks in physical education, with the exception of those in the area of kinesiology and analysis of movement, fail even to mention handedness or ambidexterity, let alone stress its importance. Our present system of physical education fails to expose the recessive limb to near equal training, and the majority of programs entirely overlook the aspect of becoming "physically educated." Even adequate recessive-limb skill in basketball, soccer, or volleyball at the senior high school, college, or professional level is far from commonplace. Switch hitting and base running in baseball; rebounding, dribbling, passing, shooting defense stance, receiving, movement without the ball in basketball; similar skills in field hockey; all strokes in handball; cradling, throwing, receiving in lacrosse; braking and using poles in skiing; kicking and trapping in soccer; receiving, lateral passing, blocking, ball carrying, straight-arm use in football and rugby; passing, serving, spiking, blocking, net retrieving in volleyball—these and many other athletic movements require performance with either side and necessitate specific training that should be initiated in elementary school physical education and continued through the college years.

Why recessive-limb training has been neglected is not clear. Let's not waste time crying and progress to an approach to remedy this oversight.

SHOULD I STRIVE FOR 100 PERCENT EQUAL PROFICIENCY WITH BOTH HANDS?

This is an excellent goal; however, after age 13–15, it is somewhat unrealistic. Listed below are the different degrees of handedness.

Ambidexterity. The ambidextrous individual may use both left and right extremities with equal ability.

Approximate ambidexterity. The ability to perform sports skills with the recessive limb nearly as effectively as with the dominant limb.

Ambisinisterness. The ambisinister individual is equally awkward with either hand. These individuals are able to master the separate parts of a skill after some time but are not able to blend the parts into the smooth movement.

Slightly handedness. The slightly handed individual prefers one hand over the other in detailed movement, but can readily use the other hand for most activities.

Natural right-handedness or left-handedness. The naturally right- or left-handed individual prefers the dominant hand for the most difficult skills.

Unreconstructable recessive handedness. This heading includes those who exhibit language difficulties when forced to use the recessive hand exclusively for detailed movements.

To achieve perfect ambidexterity with equal facility in both hands may be impractical. Strive for approximate ambidexterity with a planned approach, giving daily exposure to your recessive hand in various skills. It is possible to develop left-handed dribbling level to that of a Bob Cousy or Pete Marovich. Quarterbacks or baseball pitchers who throw equally well with both hands do exist. In fact, you can develop your left hand to a surprisingly high level with the correct approach.

WHAT DOES RESEARCH SAY ABOUT RECESSIVE-LIMB DEVELOPMENT?

The following represents a summary of findings:

1. The recessive hand is educable and should be a part of the training in most sports.

2. Throwing accuracy (softball and paddle ball ability) of the recessive hand improves following a brief training period.
3. Soccer kicking accuracy of the recessive leg improves following a brief training period.
4. Basketball dribbling ability in the recessive hand improves following a ten-session training period.
5. Basketball shooting ability in the recessive hand improves following a ten-session training period.
6. Recessive-side training can help prevent lateral deviations of the spine such as pelvic tilt, compensatory curvatures, and drop shoulder.
7. Eight-year old children increased significantly in recessive-arm distance throwing, in target accuracy (both arms), and on an index of symmetry following a one-year training period. Not the slightest indication of mental deterioration or confusion was noted in the group training for ambidexterity.
8. Throwing and kicking skill appears specific to the limb.

Once a commitment is made, improvement is easy. The secret is to engage in physical education activities that encourage equal exposure of both hands and feet. First grade is the time to begin these efforts.

CAN YOU SUGGEST ANY SPECIFIC DRILLS OR ROUTINES TO IMPROVE THE LEFT HAND FOR BASKETBALL?

Yes. Select from the list below and devote a minimum of 15 minutes daily during the basketball season and 30–45 minutes daily in the off-season. In the off-season period, it is very important that you (1) shoot, dribble, and pass with your left hand in all informal halfcourt games, (2) use the left hand in all warm-up routines regardless of who is observing, (3) work on basic moves that you perform poorly with the left hand, (4) avoid working on your strength areas—this takes up valuable time and results in little improvement, (5) practice left-hand work with "intent to improve" by analyzing each shot, knowing where missed shots hit, and considering hand position, release, and so on, and (6) be strict and never skip a left-hand training session. With repeated use, including a minimum of 100 to 200 shots daily and continuous dribbling and ball-handling drills, the left hand will respond.

All drills can force recessive hand training by merely inserting the dominant hand in your pocket or belt.

GENERAL
1. Encourage informal halfcourt competition before and after practice for a minimum of ten minutes.

2. Utilize a five-minute full court scrimmage three times weekly with arms inserted in your pocket or belt.
3. Alter scrimmage to include only recessive-hand passing.
4. Alter pre-practice warm-up drills to recessive-hand use only.
5. Insert recessive-hand training in drills not requiring special time such as dummy scrimmages for explanation of new plays, set plays, out-of-bounds plays, informal play, etc.
6. Assign specific drills to players during the off-season.
7. Encourage the principle of equal recessive-hand time or exposure in physical education classes and daily routines (carrying books and objects, brushing teeth, combing hair, eating, lifting, reaching) that will aid recessive-hand development with no ill effects on the dominant hand.
8. Use recessive-hand volleyball and water polo basketball for practice diversion during the preseason period.
9. Discuss the importance of bilateral development with players.
10. Pretest the first practice day to stimulate interest and to compare to post-test scores later in the season.
11. Establish a "recessive-hand award" trophy to the highest post-test score and/or player making the greatest recessive-hand improvement.

DRIBBLING-BALL HANDLING
1. Blindfold dribbling, moving to commands: forward, backward, left, or right.
2. Rotate ball rapidly around body and legs, changing direction each 30 seconds.
3. Perform a 6-inch dribble between and around the legs.
4. Recessive-hand tipping drills with small ring and backboard.
5. Stand 3 feet from wall and execute continuous tipping with recessive hand.
6. Stationary dribble, dribbling ball as fast and hard as possible.
7. Squeeze a rubber ball with recessive hand in free time to improve grip.
8. Finger exercises: spread fingers and thumb of recessive hand as far apart as possible; repeat in sets of ten.
9. Dribble around court endlines with recessive hand, at varying speeds.
10. Dribble at three-quarter speed with strong hand, change over to weak hand, and control three dribbles at full speed.
11. Dribble on bottom row of bleachers while looking straight ahead.
12. Practice all offensive moves from recessive side with the recessive side.

SHOOTING
1. Blindfolded free-throw shooting with the recessive hand.
2. Self-evaluation: analyze shooting style and prepare list of errors.
3. Repetitive shooting: in a position 15 feet to left (or right, for left-handers) of basket, 40–50 shots are taken in rapid fashion as a manager supplies the balls.
4. Mental practice: shoot from ten marked spots with intent to improve.
5. Use single elimination one-half court one-on-one or two-on-two tournaments using only the recessive hand.
6. Homework: assign 50–500 shots to be taken daily with recessive hand on the player's own time.
7. Giant step. Stand directly in front of the basket, taking one large step back if shot is successful. First player to reach top of free-throw circle is declared the winner.
8. Hold daily five-minute scrimmage between two teams; keep win-loss record.

With approximately one hour daily during the off-season, you can report to practice twice as strong. A player who can use both hands equally well is like one who speaks two languages—he is worth two people.

WHAT ABOUT THE IMPROVEMENT OF THE RECESSIVE FOOT?

A good rugby and soccer player must kick equally well with both feet. There are times in both of these sports when the left foot *must* be used. It is impossible, for example, for a soccer player who retrieves a ball facing the left sideline to kick the ball upfield with his right foot. It is unsound practice to be sprinting to the left in rugby and then kick the ball with the right foot.

All of the information discussed in this chapter applies to recessive foot training. No improvement occurs if you continually use the dominant foot in all situations. A rugby or soccer team with only a few ambidextrous kickers is also easily defeated. Strive to become a complete player. No player is complete who can use only one foot. The only acceptable excuse for such play is if the other is missing.

7
Injury Prevention and Performance

The hours of lost practice and game time due to injuries is costly to both individual and team performance. Injuries often curtail individual development to championship level by preventing progressive conditioning and skill training at various stages of one's athletic career. Many common injuries *can* and *are* being prevented by the wise coach and athlete. It is the purpose of this chapter to shed some light on injury prevention in major sports. No attempt is made to canvass the multitude of possible injuries, nor to suggest treatment procedures. On the other hand, the probability of certain types of injuries common to your activity or sport can be reduced by implementation of some of the preventive suggestions in this chapter.

WHAT GENERAL PRECAUTIONS SHOULD BE TAKEN TO REDUCE THE RISK OF INJURY IN MAJOR SPORTS?

Practically all studies indicate a higher rate of injury in late game or practice competition when the muscles enter a state of general fatigue. This fatigue causes a reduced blood supply to muscles; fibers become devitalized and easily torn, leaving an individual susceptible to injury.

Fatigue also reduces movement efficiency and performance (other muscles are activated in an attempt to rest fatigued muscles, and the result is loss of coordination). Thus, an athlete becomes an easier target in contact sports and may place himself or herself in a mechanically unsound position when contact occurs.

These basic principles apply to all preventive conditioning programs:

1. During the off-season, exercises should be used that strengthen injury-prone areas such as the ankle, knee, shoulder, and neck.
2. Weight training should be performed after practice to ensure full recovery prior to the practice session the following day. Training prior to practice may weaken muscular support through decreased strength and leave one more susceptible to injury.
3. Exercises should be used that are similar to those in the sport for which you are training.
4. Following a substantial training period (preseason or postseason) one vigorous weight-training workout weekly should be used to maintain strength. If a maintenance in-season approach is used, the session should be held following the Wednesday or midweek practice session.
5. Train hard. A high level of cardiovascular conditioning should be maintained. High-level conditioning and proper execution of skills are your best protection against injuries.

ARE SOME ATHLETES INJURY PRONE?

Yes. This is more common among teenage athletes who are passing through the "clumsy" stage of their growth pattern. They may be more prone to injury because of physical and mental factors as well as immaturity, lack of skill and conditioning, fear, poor eyesight, poor attitude, a low pain threshold, and other factors.

Prevention or cure should be based upon conditioning, including weight training, adequate nutrition, skill development, exposure within one's skill and physical abilities, analysis of fears, and a general de-emphasis of the frequency and severity of injuries.

IS IT TRUE THAT SOME EXERCISES USED BY COACHES ARE ACTUALLY HARMFUL?

Yes. Some exercises that have been used for the past 50 years very definitely weaken healthy body parts or aggravate an already weakened condition. Let's examine a few of these:

Full squats, squat jumps, duck walk (death walk), or similar movements that force you to rest your buttocks on your ankles and then bounce or walk in this position can weaken the knee structure, particular ligament strength. It may be absurd to believe, as an early researcher pointed out, that "the knee is not for bending"; however, one thing is certain: it cannot stand the strain of forceful bouncing to a full squat position. Since evidence against the full squat has come to light, many teams claim that they have never used the exercise. If only millions of knees could talk, the truth would be known.

Straight leg sit-ups, leg lifts with knees straight, leg lifts touching toes in midair, rocking on stomach, or similar movements also victimize the lower back area and will aggravate a lower back condition. Some physicians feel that the back is better off left alone and does not need exercise to throw off a delicate balance of muscle structure.

Many exercises have been handed down through the years. Many have never been analyzed to determine which muscles they activate and just how they affect body structure and function. Choose each exercise with care and avoid the specific exercises described above and any others that place severe stress on the knee or lower back.

ARE PROFESSIONAL FOOTBALL INJURIES ON THE RISE?

No. They have always been high. Several injuries recently have received tremendous publicity and tend to accent the problem. A survey by Dr. James Nicholas, team physician of the New York Jets, reveals the following information:

1. *Offensive players.* A significant injury occurs every 113 plays and a major injury every 360 plays.
2. *Defensive players.* A significant injury occurs every 153 plays and a major injury every 368 plays.
3. *Special Teams* (kickoff, punt coverage, and return). A significant injury occurs every 41 plays and a major injury every 103 plays.

Significant injuries are classified as those that force a player to miss two consecutive games, and a major injury is one causing an operation or absence from eight consecutive games. With 120 plays in one game, you can see that a major injury occurs about once every three games for offensive and defensive players and once a game for special teams.

Injuries make a difference in professional football, with about 15–16 plaguing each team in a season. When they involve quarterbacks, running backs, linemen or any key player, the results are disastrous for the team.

Just why injuries are so common is unknown. It certainly is true that protective equipment is steadily improving and far superior to that of five years ago. Also, physical examinations and conditioning programs (off- and in-season) are more rigorous than ever. On the other hand, players are heavier, quicker, faster, and more motivated than ever before. Spearhead and gang tackling are also causative factors. Artificial turf and use of heel cleats on regular turf are two additional factors that are responsible for some injuries. One of the biggest factors is the emphasis on the "extra inch." This leads to use of the headgear as a weapon, gang tackling, and high-speed cracking on a partially stopped, often helpless runner.

The answer to curbing injuries is not easily provided. It will take a number of rule changes.

IS ARTIFICIAL TURF DANGEROUS?

The problem has not been thoroughly investigated thus far, although efforts are underway. More and more teams are purchasing this expensive material for football fields. Companies are pushing untested fields of various composition as being maintenance-free and less likely to cause injury. Both claims are being refuted at this time.

Some types of artificial turf appear to reduce injury to the knees if they are watered down prior to use. Players complain that the artificial turf causes painful, lasting skin abrasions from only mild friction and are less than happy to play on it. The heel cleat is definitely related to knee injury. Special shoes used on artificial turf do use a shorter bar-type heel cleat that will not easily dig into the turf and lock. This should prove helpful in the knee category.

Artificial turf has numerous advantages, as revealed by Lashbrook:[1]

1. More and different types of activities can be held on artificial turf.
2. More football games can be held in one season.
3. Maintenance costs are considerably below that of grass fields.
4. Knee injuries appear to be somewhat reduced; however, evidence is far from conclusive on this.

Disadvantages include a high initial cost for installation, traction problems under certain weather conditions, burns, and the higher temperature of synthetic turf.

The test is yet to come. One thing is certain: artificial turf has not made a significant impact in reducing injuries to date. About a five-year career is still all the average professional football player can expect. With a little bad luck, it's a lot shorter, and the next 30 or 40 years after play are also a lot more painful.

DOES THE USE OF A WHIRLPOOL BATH JUST BEFORE A CONTEST HINDER PERFORMANCE?

Since an athlete emerges from the whirlpool bath somewhat light-headed and weak, it has been assumed that he or she has been drained of energy and will now fatigue rapidly. Luckily, not everyone has accepted this logic without scientific investigation. Research on the effects of whirlpool treatment upon strength and endurance has uncovered the following information:

1. Grip strength actually increased following a 10-minute treatment with submersion to the neck.
2. Strength and endurance of the leg decreased slightly following a 20-minute period in the whirlpool with the water at 104°F. When the water temperature was raised to 110°, a greater decrease was noted. With a two-hour rest period following treatment and preceding the strength-endurance test, no decrease was noted.

It is recommended, then, that a whirlpool treatment be given at least two hours before a practice session and three hours before a game. Also, the athletes should be reassured that the treatment will not leave them weak and decrepit and will not affect their play in the game. Often, this feeling of weakness, with no physiological weakness present, carries over and does hinder performance.

Do not misuse the whirlpool bath. It is helpful in the treatment of injuries that will respond to gentle massage and heat. Your trainer or doctor will advise you on its use.

AREN'T SWIMMING POOLS ACTUALLY HELPFUL IN THE REHABILITATION OF AN ATHLETIC INJURY?

Yes. People have turned to water to relieve soreness and pain since the beginning of time. Hydrotherapy (whirlpool baths) was developed from this knowledge and is nothing more than a sophisticated form of the earlier attempts of people in rivers, lakes, and oceans.

Actually, a swimming pool has some advantages over a whirlpool bath, since free movement of the injured part, regardless of its location, is permitted. Waist-deep water makes any exercise a resistance activity, slows the movement to protect the area from violent contraction, and allows full range of motion without pain. Such exercise for athletes who are unable to practice also prevents deconditioning, acting as a maintenance program until recovery occurs. The greatest advantage, however, appears to be that painless exercise is permitted that could not otherwise take place at a particular stage of recovery. In fact, an athlete can often begin swimming therapy the day following an injury.

Sample underwater exercises include: (1) running in chest-deep water, pumping legs vigorously, (2) repeating exercise 1, lifting knees to hip level, (3) repeating exercise 1, using the sprinting motion, and (4) working the injured extremity to full range of motion. Rehabilitation training programs in water should be carefully controlled in terms of the number of sprints, speed of movement, distance, and the rest interval between each sprint to ensure heart-lung strength gains.

CAN ANYTHING BE DONE TO PREVENT ANKLE SPRAINS?

Yes. Ankle injuries are the most common athletic mishap. Like the knee, the ankle structure is not strong enough to handle the demands of major sports since it is rather poorly supported by muscles and ligaments that often yield, stretch, and tear from high-speed cutting and contact.

About 75 to 85 percent of all ankle injuries are inversion sprains. That is, the outer edge of the foot turns inward such as is common with the "plant" food when cutting.

Here are some tips that will help prevent future ankle injuries:

1. Be certain that shoes are properly fitted and laced at all times.
2. Tape weak ankles before any type of workout. Tape should be placed in such a way as to pull from the outer part of the leg to the inside to build up a wall against inward turning. Cloth ankle wraps may help also.
3. Use some ankle exercises during season and in the off-season period.
    a. rotation of the foot.
    b. marble exercise: raise marbles from the floor with the toes.
    c. towel exercise: stand at edge of a towel, contract the toes slowly to bunch the towel into a ball.
    d. weight training: heel raise with iron boots to invert and evert the foot.

The typical injury involves the "soft tissue" and may strain, stretch, or tear the ligament. Swelling occurs around the bump on the outside of the ankle. Severe swelling and inability to apply body weight after 24 hours of rest is an indication an Xray is needed. The Xray will detect a fracture; it will not reveal soft tissue damage. If an ankle injury occurs, proper treatment involves immediate use of ice, pressure (towel wrapped around the ice pack), and elevation of the injured part. Discontinue activity immediately and use crutches for 24 to 48 hours until swelling and pain disappear. Ligament damage may require a cast or, if torn, surgery.

IS IT POSSIBLE TO PREVENT ATHLETE'S FOOT IN ATHLETICS?

Yes, it is possible, although it is far from easy. Among swimmers, athlete's foot (tinea pedis dermatophytosis) reaches epidemic stages, with 30–50 percent infected. Apparently cleanliness, foot powder, and frequent changes of socks still do not prevent recurrence among some swimmers.

Athlete's foot is caused by a fungus and is also often accompanied by an associated bacterial infection. Symptoms include itching, redness, and a form of rash on the soles, on toes, and between the toes. The exact cause and cure are unknown; however, control is possible. Preventive measures and treatment are similar:

1. Daily change of socks.
2. Use of tincture of benzoin and powder.
3. Use of a fungicide.
4. Careful drying of the feet and between the toe areas after a shower.
5. Use of dusting powder in athletic and street shoes to keep them dry.
6. Ask your druggist to prepare a 30 percent aluminum chloride solution and apply twice daily.

In spite of all the above cautions, it is nearly impossible to avoid some mild infection if you exercise and shower daily. Constant walking in infected shower areas make the probability of catching this fungus very high. Left unattended, the infection can cause serious foot trouble. Using the towel of someone who has this fungus can result in athlete's foot to some painful, delicate areas other than the foot. Be cautious. The borrowed towel that dries you today may be needed to scratch you tomorrow.

WHAT CAN ATHLETES DO TO PROTECT THEMSELVES AGAINST ARTHRITIS LATER IN LIFE?

For football players, those in other contact sports, and anyone who has had a cartilage removed, it may be one of the unavoidable hazards of the game. Mild arthritic pain is common among former footballers over the age of 30.

Arthritis has numerous causes: rheumatic fever, infection, faulty metabolism, degenerative joint disease, circulatory and nervous disorders, glandular disturbances, allergy, trauma, to name a few. Symptoms include joint pain, swelling, tenderness, and loss of movement in the hands, wrists, fingers, knees, ankles, feet, or any other joint. A permanent cure is unknown. Arthritis patients are among the most victimized by quack cures (to the tune of $250 million annually). Medication to relieve pain and prevent further joint damage must be provided immediately by a physician. Special gadgets, apparatus, and quick cures do not work on anything but your pocketbook.

These suggestions, if followed, can help keep you from becoming an arthritis victim:

1. Maintain a high level of general health.
2. Exercise on a regular basis with a program designed to elevate heart-lung efficiency.
3. Protect the joints from injury, strain, and cold.
4. Avoid competing while injured, since repeated trauma is a causative factor.
5. Correct diseased tissues such as tonsils, teeth, eyes and infected sinuses immediately.
6. Avoid stress to weight-bearing joints (knee, ankle) later in life.
7. Dress warm when exercising in cold weather.

WHAT ABOUT BURSITIS?

Bursitis is a chronic or acute inflammation of a bursa (small sac of fluid between muscles, tendons, and bones). Common causes include trauma (single or repeated blows) and infection. Housemaid's knee, miner's elbow, and tennis elbow are laymen's terms for forms of bursitis. Symptoms include pain, swelling, tenderness, impaired motion, and muscle weakness.

Treatment involves rest and removal from the activity that may have caused the condition, immobilization of the extremity (sling or splint), medication to relieve pain, heat, gentle massage, and in severe cases, surgery.

Prevention for athletes involves proper care of injured parts and avoiding reinjury to a fully or partially recovered area. Playing while under local anesthesia to "hide the pain" can definitely lead to bursitis. It can also lead to permanent damage and the end of an athletic career.

WHAT IS TENDONITIS AND HOW CAN IT BE PREVENTED?

The location of tendonitis, an inflammation and swelling of the tendon, varies in different sports. In sports involving considerable running (cross-country, track, soccer, football, rugby, field hockey, team handball), the Achilles Tendon is affected; in sports involving repeated movement of the upper arms (swimming, baseball), it is the shoulder tendon; and in sports requiring repeated snapping or rotation of the elbow (tennis, handball) it is the elbow tendon (see Tennis Elbow).

Tendonitis is a serious, persistent inflammation involving pain that tends to disappear as one continues to exercise. Consequently, athletes are reluctant to take a week or two of rest or change their workout routines to eliminate the causative factors. After the workout, pain returns fully and the inflammation grows worse.

Both prevention and treatment focus on stretching the involved tendon. The problem is caused by tightness and hard exercise. Stretch daily and exercise lightly until the pain and inflammation disappear.

WHAT CAN BE DONE TO PREVENT BLISTERS?

Blisters no longer need to be a problem in athletics. With proper care, no one should lose playing time due to blisters. Without proper care, blisters can have a crippling effect that keep you out of action for weeks.

Blisters are caused by shoe friction. Reduce friction and a blister cannot occur. A porous innersole has been developed that is about 95 percent effective in preventing blisters in any sport including, tennis, basketball, handball, squash, and badminton. These innersoles are reasonably priced and on sale at any sporting goods store. Under controlled tests, athletes who were disabled with blisters were found to be able to return to action when the innersole was used. No one who has soft or blister-prone feet should do without this innersole.

Additional preventive measures are:

1. Socks should be clean at all times.
2. Shoes should fit comfortably and be laced tight.
3. Tincture of benzoin (toughskin) followed by dusting talcum should

be used in early workouts to reduce friction. Blisters of the feet and hands are most common before these body parts have had an opportunity to callous. Place 1½-inch tape over tender areas and around the entire foot. Cut off any tape that is not touching the foot (a gap will be present just below the ball of the foot) to prevent tape from wrinkling up and placing friction on the foot instead of on the tape.

4. Two pairs of socks should be used. Coat feet with Vaseline and use either a lightweight sock under the heavy socks or two pairs of medium-weight socks.
5. If a friction area or "hot" spot develops, stop activity immediately and apply petroleum jelly or a piece of tape tightly over the area.
6. Train gradually with the first four or five workouts, slowly building up to intensified cutting action.
7. Use the porous innersole described above.
8. Shield all known pressure areas with felt padding.

In 1924, Calvin Coolidge, Jr., son of the president, developed a blister on his big toe from a friendly tennis game. Two weeks later, he died of blood poisoning from this minor injury. Hundreds of unnecessary deaths occur each year from neglect of some kind. Blisters should now be removed from the list—they are too easy to prevent.

IS IT DANGEROUS TO CONTINUE PLAY WITH A BRUISE?

A bruise or *hematoma* occurs from a direct blow. It is very much like an incision wound or cut, except that bleeding is internal and can be mild or very extensive depending upon the trauma.

Tenderness, swelling, and discoloration occur at the site of the injury. Ice should be applied immediately to minimize swelling and bleeding. Days later, heat treatment and oral enzymes are indicated.

Some athletes bruise more easily than others. Constant sudden bruising after mild or moderate trauma is a symptom that should be investigated by a physician. Continuous reinjury of a bruised area *can* lead to a serious condition. Sensitive areas should be protected with sponges and other padding. If adequate protection is not possible, the athlete should *not* participate.

Weight training and the acquisition of additional muscle mass can make body parts a lot more difficult to bruise. The big game of life is the important one. Competition that continually reinjures a bruise can shorten the quarters. Also, the second half of the game of life may not last nearly as long.

WHAT CAN BE DONE TO PREVENT HEEL BRUISES?

Bruises to the heel result from a direct blow against a hard object such as a stone or extremely hard surface. It is a common injury for competitors in the high jump, broad jump, hurdles, and the pole vault and also occurs in team sports. An injury to the heel is a complex one and requires weeks of rehabilitation and inactivity.

Following are suggestions to help prevent such bruises:

1. Place a plastic heel cup in your shoes. These cups are inexpensive, adaptable to any heel, and most effective.
2. Be certain that shoes are snug at the heel, cupped, and fit properly.
3. Master proper running habits.
4. In contacting the surface for jumping events, learn to roll from the heel to the ball of the foot.
5. Avoid jogging or running on unknown terrain that may contain rocks and other dangerous objects.

If you have a history of difficulty, use the plastic cup. You would then have to be hit by a sledgehammer to do any damage.

WHAT CAN BE DONE TO PREVENT CAULIFLOWER EAR?

A deformed, painful ear, particularly the outer ear, is referred to as a "cauliflower ear" (hematoma auris). It is common in wrestling and rugby and is caused by continuous friction, hard blows to the ear, and wrenching in a headlock position. Injury to the ear heals slowly because of poor circulation. Thus, fluid resulting from injury is absorbed slowly and the ear may remain swollen, sensitive, and discolored for a considerable length of time.

There is no reason why anyone should develop cauliflower ear. Prevention involves use of protective ear guards, Vaseline to reduce friction, and application of ice as soon as a sore spot is indicated. These precautions must be taken both in practice and match competition. Remember: once a deformed ear develops, only the plastic surgeon can return the ear to normal appearance.

WHAT IS A CHARLEY HORSE AND HOW CAN IT BE PREVENTED IN CONTACT SPORTS?

A charley horse is merely a contusion of the thigh caused by a direct blow. The contusion occurs by direct, hard contact on a relaxed thigh muscle, compressing tissue against the surface of the largest bone in the body—the femur. How severe the injury is depends upon the force of the blow and the degree of thigh relaxation.

A charley horse is easily detected by examining the type of blow that was received, palpating the area, administering a muscle function test (to see if flexion of lower leg is impaired) and checking for swelling and discoloration.

Preventive efforts are centered around use of proper protective equipment in contact sports and a high level of conditioning. But even the most highly conditioned athlete will suffer injury should a hard blow occur to relaxed thigh muscles.

WHAT CAN BE DONE TO PREVENT AND TO TREAT THE COMMON COLD?

Since a common cold is an infection of the upper respiratory tract, you could cut off your head. Nothing else seems to help. There are some suggestions that may reduce the incidence of colds, which usually occur through exposure and chilling and have no known cause.

Contributing factors include low resistance, poor physical condition, improper nutrition and sleep, tension, bacteria entering the respiratory tract, and the tendency to remain indoors in fall, winter, and spring. A cold can also catch you as fast as you can catch it. A sneeze travels nearly 100 miles per hour, spraying thousands of germs in your direction. It may be helpful to:

1. Dry properly after a warm shower, particularly in hairy areas, before going out of doors.
2. Use a hat, scarf, and appropriately warm clothing out of doors and remove same when entering a building.
3. Avoid chills on the athletic field after sweating.
4. Use heavy warm-up clothing out of doors in cool weather.
5. Avoid crowds and contact with people in poorly ventilated areas.
6. Avoid contact with contaminated individuals through talking or kissing, even with a spouse or girlfriend or boyfriend.
7. Obtain proper sleep and diet, consuming fruit juice and possibly vitamin A and C supplements.

The effectiveness of cold treatment is debatable. With medication, it should go away in seven days; without medication, it will last a week. Contrary to popular opinion, vitamin C, vitamin E, cod liver oil, alcoholic beverages, and avoidance of chills do not appear to protect you from a cold. Also, antihistamines, decongestants, and cold tablets are of little value in removing symptoms and the course of the common cold, and penicillin is of no value. Save your money—over $5 million are spent annually for cold remedies. Aspirin, rest, and plenty of fluids remain sound advice. Home remedies are as effective as no treatment at all. Take preventive measures and pray a lot.

SHOULD ATHLETES CONTINUE TRAINING WHEN STRICKEN WITH A COLD?

Yes. Training, however, should be altered to a mild maintenance program. While you will not progress or improve your conditioning level, you can hold deterioration to a minimum. Although rest, adequate fluids, and aspirin provide the only sensible approach, complete rest for the athlete is not recommended in season.

One argument for complete rest and isolation is that teammates will not be contaminated. Colds are spread by a group of viruses through talking, sneezing, hand shaking, coughing, and handling of infectious materials, and the closeness of athletic teams makes spreading inevitable.

HOW COMMON ARE INJURIES TO THE EYES IN ATHLETICS?

Fortunately, eye injuries are rather rare in all sports because of (1) protection provided by fat, the bridge of the nose, and the overhanging bones, (2) the elasticity of the globe of the eye and its absorptive powers, (3) the small entrance to the eye, causing blows to be deflected by surrounding parts, and (4) the depth of the eye. It is obvious that nature has provided excellent protection to this apparently fragile area.

Injuries do occur, however, although contact with elbows, basketballs, footballs, team handballs, and volleyballs are unlikely to cause serious injury since these instruments are too large to enter the eye. Lacerations and contusions of the lids or eyeball occasionally occur and need immediate professional attention. If you wear glasses, unbreakable glass or contact lenses should be used, and proper precautions should be taken (see the next question).

IS IT DANGEROUS TO USE CONTACT LENSES IN ATHLETICS?

It *can* be dangerous to use contact lenses at any time. The original concept of contact lenses dates back to 1887, when a glass shell was placed over an eye without a lid. Today, lenses are smaller, lightweight, plastic, unbreakable, and available in color. The most popular type is the corneal lens that covers the cornea and the iris. Contact lenses are used by over 7 million people for cosmetic and practical reasons.

Let's first examine the favorable side of contact lenses:

1. Appearance is improved.
2. Efficiency in some occupations and activities is improved since contact lenses do not fog up, get wet in the rain, or reflect stage lights.
3. Some types of eye deficiencies such as myopia and corneal astigmatism are better corrected through use of contact lenses.

The unfavorable side is short of frightening. In fact, numerous eye injuries result from use of contact lenses. One survey of 50,000 users conducted in 1964 revealed that six eyes were removed due to infection, seven had permanently reduced vision to 20/200, one required a corneal transplant, and several hundred suffered less serious injuries that were corrected when contact lenses were discarded. Eye damage was generally a result of improper fitting, unsanitary practices, and prolonged use. Permanent eye damage *is* possible.

Participants in wrestling or boxing should not use contact lenses. Swimmers also should avoid use while competing or merely engaged in leisurely swimming, since lenses tend to wash out. There is no reason at this time to suggest discontinued use in other contact sports. If you are a user, follow these suggestions carefully:

1. Keep a spare pair handy on competitive days in case one is lost. Insure your contact lenses; they are very likely to be lost at one time or another in athletic competition.
2. Resort only to a skilled practitioner (ophthalmologist or optometrist) for fitting. Write to the Contact Lens Association of Ophthalmologists, 34 East 35th Street, New York, New York, 10016, or the American Academy of Optometry, 1508 Foshay Tower, Minneapolis, Minnesota 55402, for assistance in choosing.
3. Take heed if you are one of the approximately 15 percent who cannot be fitted due to infection, inflammation, allergy, discomfort, or other reason.
4. Maintain close supervision with the practitioner during the initial period of adjustment and discomfort. Pain during this acclimation period can reveal a poor fit or inability to use the lens.
5. Be extremely clean in handling lenses to avoid infection. Wash hands and lenses in a wetting agent and under tap water. Store properly.
6. Remove before sleeping. Failure to do so on even one occasion can cause permanent eye damage.

Contact lenses have been a tremendous aid to the athlete with poor vision. They appear to be much safer than regular glasses if proper care and caution are used. Carelessness can result in permanent damage. Regular glasses are available that are shatterproof, set in resilient frames, are shock absorbent, and almost indestructible. Even then, perhaps they are a second choice to a wise use of contact lenses.

WHAT CAN BE DONE TO PREVENT HAMSTRING PULLS?

It is possible to reduce the risk of a severe pull. First, let's take a look at what actually happens when a pull occurs. Hamstring muscle pulls range from a mild strain to actual tearing of muscle tissue. An involuntary attempt to stretch a contracting muscle results in torn tissue, ruptured blood vessels, severed nerve fibers, and severe pain. Prior to hamstring pulls, a competitor has often been observed to have one hip lower than the other; this position occurs when one makes a short radius turn on a track or athletic field. It is also apparent that form in sprinting plays some causative part. At the first sign of irritation, running should stop immediately. If leg movement ceased without another step at the first sign of irritation, no injury would occur. Unfortunately, this is not possible.

Other possible causes of hamstring pulls include lack of proper warm-up, lack of salt in the diet, tooth decay discharging harmful products into the bloodstream during the later stages of infection, poor flexibility, overtraining, and muscle balance.

Preventive measures include: (1) adequate warm-up or stretching prior to each training session and following every weight-training workout, (2) running on soft surfaces the first two or three weeks of training, (3) shorter indoor workouts in early basketball season with distance running and sprinting performed out of doors on grassy surfaces, (4) use of salt tablets if needed, (5) daily hamstring-stretching exercise, (6) mastery of proper sprinting form, (7) care in running around a wet area.

HOW COMMON ARE HEAD INJURIES IN FOOTBALL?

Head injuries in the form of mild, moderate, and severe concussions continue to occur in football at all levels of competition. Approximately four to six concussions per year for each football squad can be expected. The majority of head injuries occurs to the forehead, top of the head extending downward one or two inches, and the temporal area.

Numerous studies have been undertaken to examine causing factors. Most concussions are a result of a blow from an opponent's knee or helmet; occasionally, contact with the turf is the culprit. Running backs are twice as vulnerable as any other player, followed by interior linemen and linebackers. The safest position appears to be in the defensive secondary. Also, most head injuries occur during the second and third period of play or late in a practice session. This suggests a fatigue factor that limits the ability to avoid a direct head-on collision. The kickoff, punt return, and pass return plays result in the majority of head injuries.

HOW CAN HEAD INJURIES BE PREVENTED?

Complete prevention is difficult. There is some indication that fewer injuries occur each year. Prevention centers around the following: (1) continuous improvement of the headgear and hatband area, (2) possible padding of the outside of the headgear, (3) caution with athletes possessing a history of head injury, (4) alteration of rules on dangerous plays in football, (5) reevaluation of tackling techniques at all levels, (6) reevaluation of running techniques when trapped, (7) making the headgear an illegal offensive weapon.

WHAT CAN BE DONE TO PREVENT HERNIAS DURING STRENGTH TRAINING?

The danger of hernia from weight training, isometrics, and calisthenics is greatly exaggerated. Hernias are generally caused by congenital weakness in the abdominal muscles and develop over a long period of time. The truth is that your everyday chores are more likely to result in a hernia than engagement in strength training. In fact, research shows that weight lifters are much less prone to hernias than nonlifters; this activity may actually help prevent hernias.

A hernia is merely an outward protrusion of normal tissue. A muscle bulges through its protective sheath to become protruded and easily noticed. In addition to congenital defect, a hernia may occur from strain, improper lifting, a direct blow, or from tissue deterioration due to infection. Most hernias are noticeable upon coughing, as they protrude to an even more noticeable degree.

The following precautions will reduce the risk of hernia from engaging in strength training and athletics:

1. Avoid lifting extremely heavy weights early in a workout, early in a

workout program, or with a new exercise. Progressively build up to heavier weight in each case.

2. Do not place too much stress on the stomach with any type of exercise such as a very low squat.
3. Avoid breath holding while lifting heavy weights.
4. Utilize bent leg sit-ups in your program.
5. Remain in top condition. If you have been inactive for several years, use a two- to three-month training program prior to an explosive movement.

HOW CAN GYM ITCH OR "JOCK STRAP ITCH" BE PREVENTED?

Physicians indicate that gym itch is acquired by contact and is associated with bacteria, fungi, molds, and ringworm. However, the fact remains that an infection is not always present when there is an itch. The crotch provides the right type of warm, moist climate for skin irritation and may become red, inflamed, scaly, or itchy.

Prevention includes proper habits of hygiene (showering in warm water, and use of antiseptic soap, powder, and proper drying); adequate water intake; regular change of underwear, supporter, and shorts; disinfecting locker benches, mats, and other equipment; and avoidance of long hours of sitting in warm moist environments such as autos and classrooms. Avoid using other people's towels, shorts, and supporters. The gym itch is a mild problem compared to what could be communicated.

WHAT CAN BE DONE TO PREVENT KNEE INJURIES?

Preventive conditioning definitely is necessary for adequate knee protection. The anatomical structure of the knee simply does not provide adequate stability against lateral movement. Conditioning should be directed at the development of the musculature to provide greater structural support; however, it must be pointed out that this approach also has its limitations, because the design of the knee precludes greatly increased stability through supporting muscle strengthening. Both ligament and muscular strength determine knee stability, however, and can be favorably affected by strength training programs.

Exercise approaches may take the form of (1) isometric training or muscular contraction against an immovable object, (2) isotonic or weight-training movements through use of a leg flexor apparatus or iron boots, (3) movement against spring resistance, (4) two-man exercises utilizing the resistance of a partner, or (5) movement against only the body as resistance. All approaches must be systematically applied over a suitable period of time.

Preventive measures include:

1. Overstrengthening the ligaments and supporting musculature of the joint. While in a seated position, try to extend the lower leg eight times with 75 pounds attached to your foot.
2. Mastering proper movement, with emphasis on pigeon-toed walking and running.
3. Removing heel cleats for contact sports and substituting a regular heel to prevent sticking during cutting and turning maneuvers.
4. Eliminating full-squat exercises (duck walk, squat, jumps, full squat with or without weights) and all exercises requiring full flexion and compression of the joint. Squat exercises should require flexion to right angles only.
5. Avoiding play in contact sports when very fatigued.
6. Maintaining a high level of conditioning. This will delay fatigue and keep you at your quickest throughout the game.

It may also be helpful if you do not tape your ankles unless absolutely necessary. Remember, if contact occurs on the side of the knee, a body part other than the knee should share the shock. With heel cleats firmly into the turf and the ankle tightly wrapped, there is no chance of a sliding foot or rotating ankle being of assistance; thus, there is a great chance of cartilage or ligament damage to the knees.

DO FOOTBALL SHOES CONTRIBUTE TO KNEE INJURIES?

Yes. Research clearly indicates that the heel cleat of the standard football shoe (regardless of the composition) is associated with knee injury due to the locking of the heel in the turf, preventing the foot from releasing during contact or cutting. Thus, the knee becomes the cushion. Numerous studies show that both the incidence and severity of knee injuries are reduced by approximately 60 percent when conventional football shoes are replaced by shoes with a regular heel or a soccer style, locked-on bar heel. A short one-half inch cleat would also be an improvement over conventional cleats. The low-cut shoe, so common in today's football, results in the highest incidence of knee injuries.[2]

Keep in mind also that the knee is more vulnerable during the adolescent years, when ligaments are looser than in other stages of growth. Yet, heel cleats are common also for this age group. The next logical question is: "Why are heel cleats still used?" Removal does not interfere with performance. No one runs on his heels. They only serve to lock the heel when cutting and isolate the knee as the major point of strain when contact occurs. The only answer is that heel cleats have always been used. No one is quite sure why. We now know why they should be removed. Ten thousand knees that underwent the knife and shortened their owners' athletic career can still benefit by reducing the chance of recurring injury. Get smart—the real heel is the user.

IS A "POPPING" OR SNAPPING KNEE A SIGN OF SERIOUS TROUBLE?

Not necessarily. This sound comes from a tendon flipping over bony fulcrums and may be quite natural in some athletes who just never really noticed the sound before. Often, warm-up reduces the sensation and sound.

Bone or cartilage damage is not indicated unless other symptoms are present such as inflammation, swelling, fluid, and knee locking.

IS THERE ANY WAY A COACH OR TRAINER CAN DETECT THE TYPE AND SERIOUSNESS OF A KNEE INJURY?

Yes. However, it takes a skilled physician who is experienced in the treatment of common athletic injuries to make an accurate diagnosis. Even for a physician, an on-the-spot diagnosis is not always possible.

The skilled coach or trainer may use the tests listed below as a preliminary examination before referral is made to the team physician:

1. *McMurray's sign* is used to uncover injury to the cartilage. The patient lies on the back with the knee bent and foot drawn up to the buttocks. With one hand on the knee (index finger and thumb on opposite sides of the joint) and the other grasping the ankle, the trainer rotates the lower leg to the right and left. If a sharp pain or clicking sensation is detected, cartilage damage is indicated.
2. *The drawer sign* is used to uncover cruciate ligament damage. These ligaments cross and provide lateral support to the knee. The patient lies on the back with the injured leg flexed at right angles. The tibia (bone between knee and ankle) is then pulled forward, then pushed backward. Any abnormal movement or pain indicates injury to the cruciate ligaments.
3. *The abduction test* is used to uncover damage to the medial ligament which gives support to the knee. The patient lies on the back with the injured leg completely extended and flat on the table. The trainer kneels on the table and places his knees directly against the inside of the patient's knee to form a fulcrum point. Grasping just above the

knee with one hand and at the ankle with the other, the trainer pulls the ankle toward him with his knee firmly in place. A sharp pain indicates damage to the medial ligament.

During each examination, compare the injured knee to the normal knee. This is helpful in noting the amount of swelling, deformity, position of lower leg, and range of motion in the joint.

Results of these tests along with detailed information concerning exactly how the injury occurred should be supplied to the team physician. Professional team physicians will carefully review game films to detect the exact position of the athlete at injury. This information is very valuable in diagnosing the difficulty and beginning corrective treatment.

IS THE KNEE MORE LIKELY TO BE INJURED DURING THE GROWTH YEARS?

Yes. In fact, a hard blow to the knee can produce very serious injuries at certain ages.

Certain years (high school) find individuals more susceptible to injury than others (college). The following general traits are present at various age levels:

8 years. General looseness of collateral and anterior cruciate ligaments; high degree of bilateral knee hyperextension.

8–13 years. Tightening of collateral ligaments and reduction of bilateral hyperextension; great flexibility in cruciates remains. General knee stability increased.

13–14 years. Hyperextension of knees, ligament laxity, general looseness of knee.

14–16 years. Still greater looseness evident in the right medial, left medial, and left lateral ligaments; bilateral hyperextension increased; hyperextension increased; bilateral looseness of the anterior cruciates decreased.

16 to college years. General tightening of ligament tension and total joint structure.

College years up. General leveling off with ligament tension remaining fairly constant.

It is obvious that the knee is not fully developed for contact sports until about age 16. The exact age differs for each athlete depending on his physiological development. Before this time, contact sports can be dangerous. A hard blow from the side when the foot is planted would cause more serious injury in this age period.[3]

WHAT HAPPENS TO THE KNEE WHEN CARTILAGE TROUBLE DEVELOPS?

The knee is a hinge joint that moves only in one plane: flexion and extension. Located between the joint (separating the bones of the upper and lower leg) are pads or cartilage (much like gristle found in chicken) which must absorb the shock or weight of the entire body.

Extreme rotation stress on the knee or contact on either side often causes cartilage damage. In football, this occurs when a foot is strongly planted on the ground and an opponent makes contact with either side of the knee. The result is usually torn or damaged cartilage tissue. Rotating the body with the foot firmly planted will have a similar effect.

Symptoms of serious cartilage damage include: (1) immediate pain that is often accompanied by a "locked" knee—inability to extend the leg and (2) discoloration and/or swelling, and fluid formation. The cartilage may be torn loose, compressed, or actually severed in half. One or both of the pads may be damaged from the same injury. Contact on the outside of the knee with a planted foot, for example, could compress the cartilage on that side and tear the pad located on the inside of the knee from its attachment.

For proper diagnosis and treatment, the injured athlete must be examined by a physician. Only a doctor's diagnosis can determine the need for surgery or rest. One thing is certain: removal of a cartilage condemns you to arthritic knee in middle age—a condition that is far from pleasant. It also shortens your athletic career.

WHAT TRAINING PROGRAM CAN HELP ME RECOVER FROM CARTILAGE SURGERY?

The most important objective is to restore muscle strength and full range of motion. Don't be alarmed by the loss of strength and motion and the atrophy and weakness of the muscles following surgery. It happens to everyone. Your program should progress somewhat as follows:

First week: Muscle setting, leg lifts (straight knee) to begin on fifth day if possible. Begin partial weight bearing on crutches.

Second week: Discard crutches unless leg is in cast. Begin weight training only if incision area is pain free. Lift one-half of your maximum weight 8 times, holding for 10 seconds with the leg fully extended. Repeat using three-fourth's maximum weight. Repeat with maximum weight.

Third week: Use 5 pounds of weight on the first 8 repetitions, increase to 7, then 10.

Fourth week: Progress to 15 pounds using above method.

Fifth week: Progress to 25 pounds.

Sixth week: Progress to 35 pounds. Begin straight running with knee in a wrap. Fast walk up stadium stairs; start bicycling and swimming.

Seventh week: Progress to 45 pounds, bicycling, swimming, running up stadium stairs.

Eighth week: Progress to 55 pounds. Continue after eighth week until you reach 75 pounds. Continue bicycling and swimming.

Keep in mind that you should not begin the weight-training program until full range of motion has returned. Each case is different. Work closely with your physician. He will adapt the above program to your recovery rate.

WHAT IS A STRESS FRACTURE?

A stress fracture is a small crack in the bone's surface, generally the feet, legs and hands. Athletes may experience unexplained pain over one of the small bones of the foot. Stress fracture pain should hurt when you grasp the foot from below and above and squeeze the affected spot. An Xray generally will not reveal small cracks in the bone until after it heals and a callus (scar tissue) forms. The fracture will heel properly if you rest or change to another activity for a few weeks.

WHAT IS ORTHOTICS?

Among cross-country runners, distance runners, high mileage joggers (100–300 miles monthly), basketball players, and athletes in other sports involving a lot of running, knee, hip and back problems are common. In most cases, these injuries are a result of improper foot/ground contact due to excessive foot pronation (foot rolls inward), high arched feet, unequal leg lengths, flat feet, knock knees, bowlegs and muscle imbalance. Miles and miles of hard pounding on uneven road surfaces add to the problem.

A podiatrist, who may also be an orthotics specialist (not all podiatrists are), analyzes your problem and develops a shoe insert made from a cast of your foot. This cast is designed to correct faulty ground contact and to eliminate your injury problem. Lets examine some of the common problems that orthotics can help:

1. Excessive foot pronation and flat feet—In the correct mechanics of running (not sprinting) you land on the heel first. Weight then transfers to the outside part of the foot as the foot moves forward. At this point, the foot rolls inward to shift body weight to the inside bottom of the foot and distribute the shock throughout the foot and leg. Runners who tend to be flat-footed roll the foot inward too far. The most common injury from excessive pronation is pain behind the kneecap; the kneecap is rubbing against the femur bone (long bone of upper leg). Check your old shoes for excessive wear on the outside back of the shoe heel.

2. High arched feet—These individuals have the opposite problem and fail to pronate enough to distribute body weight properly. Stress fractures and pain on the outside of the knee is common in athletes with this structural problem.

3. Unequal leg lengths—Even slight differences of ⅛ to ¼ inch can lead to hip, back or leg pain. You can measure overall leg length while standing erect, ankles together, and having a helper measure the distance from the floor to the same spot marked with a magic marker on each side of the top of your pelvis. If the two bony protrusions of the ankle do not meet at the same point, your length difference is below the ankle. If, while sitting on a chair, feet on the floor, heels together, toes pointed, a carpenter's level placed on both knees is uneven, your problem is above the ankle.

4. Morton's Foot—Approximately one person in three has a short first metatarsal (big toe) and long second metatarsal (second toe). The second toe is longer than the big toe, must take more force of the initial foot strike (particularly in stopping and changing direction), and is more susceptible to stress fractures and irritation. Orthotics and padding to even the alignment of the first and second toes can prevent injury.

WHAT CAUSES SOMEONE TO BE KNOCKED OUT?

A knockout may occur from many different types of blows to the head, chin, solar plexus, or testes. The most common, a blow to the head, results in a concussion due to injury to an area of the brain stem. Trauma causes breakage of small blood vessels that supply the brain; the resulting hemorrhage that spills into various sections causes unconsciousness, loss of sight, paralysis, loss of reasoning, depending upon the affected area. A blood clot is always a possibility with head injuries.

With each injury, scar tissue forms and decreases blood supply to brain tissue—damage is irreversible.

Each knockout seems to occur a little easier than the previous one. On each occasion, more scar tissue forms. A series of knockouts can and often does prove fatal. Fortunately, the scalp, skull, and facial bones absorb considerable energy when a blow occurs. On the other hand, a hard, well-directed blow can and has caused death due to the brain's striking sharp surfaces in the cranial cavity, or from thrombosis or hemorrhage.

The head is an unwise choice of weapons in any sport. In fact, spearhead tackling in football can put both your opponent and you out of commission for a considerable length of time. Protect your head at all times in any sport—it's the only one you have and a transplant is highly unlikely even in this modern era of medicine.

IS AN INDIVIDUAL WHO HAS HAD HIS WIND KNOCKED OUT IN DANGER?

No. Although you will not convince a gasping victim, the temporary inability to breathe following a blow, usually unexpected, to a relaxed midsection will slowly subside until normal breathing is restored. Meanwhile the victim will gasp for breath, possibly suffer from dizziness, nausea, all-around weakness, and may even collapse. Technically, a hard blow to the solar plexus increases intra-abdominal pressure, causes pain, and interferes with the diaphragmatic cycle reflex due to nerve paralysis or muscle spasm. Obviously, breathing is temporarily affected from such a blow.

A physician or trainer should be called and emergency treatment begun immediately by instructing the victim to breathe slowly through his or her nose. Clothing should be loosened at the neck and waist and ice applied to the abdomen. The practice of lifting the victim up by the belt and dropping him or her to the ground is of no value and could be harmful should stomach injury be present.

It may be helpful to know that it is nearly impossible for death to occur from such an injury, which merely paralyzes the nerve control of the diaphragm. This may be little consolation to a gasping victim who is 100 percent convinced that death is only seconds away. One of the most severe cases observed occurred during a rugby game in which the victim's gasping was heard throughout the playing area, suggesting a rather severe injury. Approximately 20 seconds later, normal breathing returned and not a trace of pain was evident on the victim's extremely pale face.

WHAT CAUSES LOWER BACK PAIN?

Lower back pain in the form of sharp stabs or a "toothache" similar to that experienced by the late President John F. Kennedy is extremely common. It is estimated that more than 2.5 million backs are permanently impaired. The typical victim is a middle-aged individual who bends, sits, stands, or slouches too much and is inactive and overweight.

The first seven vertebrae or bones of the spinal cord control your head, neck, and upper back. The next twelve dorsal vertebrae provide attachments for the ribs. The five remaining lumbar vertebrae of the lower back *support the weight of the entire upper half of the body* and are most vulnerable to injury and strain. Most severe back pain originates here in the sacroiliac at the base of the spine.

The back muscles must be protected. Preventive measures include:

1. Correcting faulty posture.
2. Avoiding exercises that irritate the back: toe touches, leg lifts, rocking on the stomach, or other hyperextension movements.
3. Strengthening the abdominal muscles; the stomach muscles keep you erect by supporting the spine and are linked to most back ailments.
4. Avoiding the placement of the back in a mechanically unsound position—bending over with legs straight to lift an object from the floor or an infant from a crib.
5. Avoiding chairs with a low, soft seat.
6. Avoiding walking or running on an uneven, sloping surface such as a beach.
7. Checking the length of each leg. It is not uncommon to have one leg shorter than the other by ¼ to 1 inch; this has the effect of walking on a hill and causes lower back problems. Corrective shoes may be indicated (see Orthotics).
8. Avoiding a girdle since this keeps the stomach muscles from functioning.
9. Getting out of bed correctly by pushing up with one arm and sliding the legs over the sides.
10. Consuming adequate minerals and getting regular checkups. Women, after menopause, may suffer from microscopic fractures linked to hormonal imbalance.
11. Exercising regularly and maintaining normal weight.
12. Avoiding a slow jog that tends to jolt the lower back area. Pick up

the pace to a run (8–10 mph or 6:00–7:30 mile pace) and cover less distance.

Since all back ailments differ, visit an orthopedic physician for an accurate diagnosis. There is some difference of opinion concerning the protection of the back in athletics, ranging from very specific exercises to complete absence of any movement designed for the back. If you place both hands on each side of the back as you walk or run, you will note the involvement of these muscles. As one expert puts it, "The best exercise for the back is none at all." Obviously, this physician is very much aware of the fact that certain exercises aggravate back conditions. He is not advocating inactive living—merely the elimination of specific calisthenics.

The exact cause of lower back trouble is often difficult to diagnose. Preventive medicine is the best choice, for once a chronic condition develops, it can be incapacitating and affect both your work and marriage.

WHAT CAN BE DONE TO HELP PREVENT NECK INJURIES?

Prevention is centered around the improvement of flexibility in the neck region, strength training, and proper techniques of tackling or making contact.

Neck flexibility exercises should be used daily in conjunction with strength training. A normal range of flexibility must be maintained to allow free movement away from pressure when contact is made. Strength training, on the other hand, will assist in applying the necessary force when the neck is made rigid to resist contact.

Athletes must learn to "bull" their necks prior to contact. Both shoulders are elevated, the hand is raised slightly, and neck muscles are contracted. Keep in mind that the neck loses most of its power when the head is down and is most powerful with the head up in a bull neck position.

Proper equipment is another preventive measure. For greater protection of the face, football helmets now come equipped with various types of face masks. However, a face mask is the number one enemy of the neck, since it provides a lever that increases force to the neck region by as much as 90 percent. If the mask is lifted, the back of the helmet jams the cervical vertebra and can damage the spinal cord.

Keep your chin up. It helps your pride while it protects your neck!

WHAT CAN BE DONE TO PREVENT SHIN SPLINTS?

The shin splint syndrome, which generally affects the lower distal third of the shin, has become a catch-all phrase for any pain below the knee. Technically, a shin splint is merely an inflammation or slight strain of the anterior and/or posterior tendons of the large bone in the lower leg. Once symptoms of this condition are present, treatment is immediately indicated. The condition may be caused or aggravated by running on hard surfaces for long periods of time, lack of sufficient warm-up, fallen arches or other preexisting foot problems, and improper running habits.

Preventive measures include use of grass or other soft terrain in early training sessions, use of a shorter spike, use of a sponge heel or sneakers prior to vigorous sprinting or long-distance running later in the season, and exercises designed to strengthen the arch and supporting muscles.

WHAT CAN BE DONE TO PREVENT SHOULDER INJURIES?

The shoulder is a vulnerable area. Its intricate musculature and loose construction make it susceptible to numerous injuries in contact sports, since it has little resistance to traumatic force. Injuries generally occur from a direct blow to the top of the shoulder, from falling on an outstretched arm or from throwing motions (tennis, baseball).

Preventive measures evolve around extra care in properly fitting each individual with high-quality protective equipment in contact sports, and use of weight training to improve muscle strength and bulk of supporting muscles. The following weight training exercises are suggested:

Bench press	Shoulder shrug
Bent-arm pull-over	Two-handed snatch
Forward raise	Two-handed clean and jerk
Rowing	Straight-arm pull-over

DOES A MOUTHGUARD ACTUALLY PROTECT THE TEETH?

Yes. Unfortunately, it is somewhat like the seat belt—it works only when inserted in the mouth. Although many schools require a football player to use a mouthpiece, it is a requirement that is difficult to enforce. The fact remains that the number of chipped, damaged, and lost teeth, as well as lip and gum tears, is greatly reduced through use of a mouth-piece. There is also some evidence that a mouthguard will reduce the incidence of head (concussions) and neck injuries.

The best type, as indicated by an elaborate study of several dentists, is the custom-fitted guard that forms an identical model of the user's mouth. Such guards are generally placed in boiling water for 20 seconds, removed, and immediately and firmly placed on the upper teeth. They are odorless, tasteless, tight fitting, comfortable, and strong enough to prevent penetration by the teeth.

Basketball, rubgy, wrestling, ice hockey, and team handball are additional sports where teeth injuries are common. Only basketball completely ignores the use of this protective device. Tradition has retarded the use of a mouthpiece in an indoor activity. Strangely enough, it doesn't matter whether you are inside or outside when contact occurs—teeth can fall out on the floor equally well. The hours of work, pain, and the cost of tooth restoration convince an athlete, all too late, that a mouthpiece would have been a wise choice.

WHAT IS TENNIS ELBOW?

"Tennis elbow" has become a catch-all phrase for any pain affecting a player's arm. There are several conflicting viewpoints concerning its prevention, cause, and treatment. It appears that microtears of the tendon unit which eventually become inflamed may be the cause. Actually, microruptures of the tendinous unit as it inserts in the bone is suspected. "Lateral epicondylitis" involves pain located at a bony point on the outer side of the elbow and spreads to the forearm muscles. "Medial epicondylitis" involves pain located at a bony point on the inside of the elbow. The movement producing the pain is a forehand drive, backhand drive, or serving motion involving a straightening of the elbow as the forearm rotates away from the body.

WHAT CAUSES TENNIS ELBOW?

Factors contributing to tennis elbow are numerous. The type of elbow problem (lateral or medial) depends upon the level of play, which obviously reflects stroke mechanics and technique:

Intermediate Players—90% suffer from lateral (outside of elbow)
10% suffer from medial (inside of elbow)

World Class Male Players—25% suffer from lateral
75% suffer from medial
World Class Female Players—50% suffer from lateral
50% suffer from medial

"Poor stroke mechanics" is a common cause for the beginning player. The elbow should not be completely locked at ball contact; however, muscle structure should be firm. Late forehand ground strokes, late volleys, off-center hits, a flexed elbow at impact, and the American-twist serve contribute to the problem. A change from soft (slow) to hard (fast) courts often results in late hitting and poor stroke mechanics. It should be noted that top spin roduced by hitting below the ball and up and through will not cause tennis elbow. Also, medial problems are rare among players using the two-handed backhand.

DOES TENNIS EQUIPMENT HAVE ANYTHING TO DO WITH TENNIS ELBOW?

Yes. Three excellent articles appeared that provide valuable data for racket selection aimed toward prevention of tennis elbow. One was written from the manufacturer's view, *Tennis U.S.A.*, February 1976, one from the orthopedic view, *The Physician and Sports Medicine*, February 1977, and one from the view of the independent researcher, *Tennis U.S.A.*, February 1977. Surprisingly enough, all three are very much in agreement in their rating of rackets and choices for prevention of tennis elbow. Vibration transmitted by a racket during off-center hits either causes or aggravates the problem. Even when the ball is hit dead center on the sweep spot, some vibration occurs at the grip of the racket. The ideal racket is one that causes this vibration to die after a short period of time (referred to as damping). The chart shows the damping qualities of 12 rackets tested, range is between .022 and .035 with higher numbers indicating a higher rate of damping and better choice for the prevention of tennis elbow. Rackets are also ranked according to the best choice for prevention or cure to the poorest choice. The best racket in wood is the Bancroft-Borg while the better metal choices are the Wilson T-4000 and the Head Comp II. If none of these rackets fit your fancy, search out one that is not head heavy, has good racket balance and avoids both extremes of flexibility and stiffness. String it with 50–56 lb. gut and secure the largest racket handle you can tolerate cushioned with foam rubber. It is also wise to avoid heavy tennis balls (all purpose) or play when balls become damp or wet from slight rain.

DAMPING CHARACTERISTICS OF SELECTED RACKETS

Tennis Elbow Ranking	Racket	Measured Damping	Rating (Vibration)	% of Highest Rating
1	Bancroft-Borg	.035	Low	100
1	Wilson T-4000	.035	Low	100
2	Head Comp II	.034	Low	97
3	Yonex T-7500	.033	Low	94
4	PDP Fiberglass	.031	Rather low	89
5	Dunlap Fort	.030	Rather low	86
6	Slazenger	.029	Medium	83
6	Tony Trabert	.029	Medium	83
6	Prince	.029	Medium	83
7	Wilson-Kramer	.027	High tendency	77
8	Davis-Classic	.026	High tendency	74
9	Head-Pro	.022	High tendency	62

From *Tennis U.S.A.,* February 1977.

HOW SHOULD TENNIS ELBOW BE TREATED?

Therapy for tennis elbow is not very advanced. Home treatment is generally recommended with injection and surgery used only for the worst cases. Expect no miracle cures from your physician nor help from prescription medications, although several new anti-inflammatory drugs appear promising in early tests. Corticosteroid injections may provide some relief; however, only two to three are recommended. Constant injections and return to the irritating activity will eventually lead to surgery. What can you do? Almost anything imaginable has been tried, including heat, cold, acupuncture, splints, injections, oral medication, copper bracelets, hypnosis, faith healing, witch doctoring, and surgery. Three orthopedic surgeons offer three similar programs that appear quite sound (*The Physician and Sports Medicine*, February 1977):

Program #1 suggests the use of a proximal forearm band, a reduction in the frequency of play, a change from wood to metal racket, and increased strength and flexibility of the affected part through weight training.

Program #2 suggests the use of heat, massage, and removal of the inflammation; static stretching by extending the elbow, pronating the forearm, and volar flexing the hand with the other hand for two minutes; wrist curls using three to five pounds and 20–30 repetitions (lateral problems—palm down or reverse curl, medial problems—palm up or regular curls), and repeating the exercises 2–3 times daily as pain permits.

Program #3 suggests an increase in strength through weight training, use of a proximal forearm band, a reduction in the frequency of play, a change from a wood to a metal racket, and a change to a two-hand backhand.

Surgery and injections are a last resort. Use of aspirin or anti-inflammatory medication several hours before play, ice immediately after for 15 minutes, followed by heat that evening, rest, and back to the aspirin should get you through the summer, providing pain is not too great. If you have not developed tennis elbow, it may be wise to consider some precautionary measures: (1) avoid playing too long at any one time, (2) warm-up slowly and thoroughly before stroking hard, (3) switch to a light weight, large-handled, gut-strung racket with good damping quality, (4) correct faulty stroke mechanics, (5) consider using a two-handed backhand, (6) avoid playing in the rain, (7) avoid use of all-purpose balls which tend to be heavier, (8) do not use the American twist serve, and (9) avoid changing from one court surface to another (particularly slow to fast).

HOW CAN TOENAIL DISEASES BE PREVENTED?

Deformed, painful toenails can keep you out of action. The condition of the nail is very revealing, since it is sensitive to body changes and reflects general health. Enlarged, thickened, brittle, split, atrophied, or ingrown nails can be painful. Causes for each condition are numerous.

Nail trouble that can take you out of action is best avoided by:

1. Adequate nutrition.
2. Carefully fitting athletic shoes to avoid sliding or pressure against toenails.
3. Selecting good athletic socks that are of sufficient length.
4. Proper nail cutting; eliminating ragged edges and sprawls at the corners. Cutting a "V" in a toenail can add to the problem. Digging into the corner of nails also can cause difficulty.
5. Proper care of feet—drying, use of medication for invading fungus.

Surgery may be needed in some cases to relieve persistent nail trouble, particularly for those with a hereditary tendency to ingrown nails.

HOW CAN VARICOSE VEINS BE PREVENTED AND PROTECTED IN ATHLETICS?

Varicose veins are merely abnormally lengthened, dilated, sac-like superficial veins. Surrounding muscles provide support to deep veins;

however, superficial veins lie in subcutaneous fat and get little support. The upright position places excessive burden on the veins of the legs. Normally, valves prevent the blood from backing up; however, as a vein enlarges and loses its elasticity, valves are not very effective and allow blood to regurgitate and remain in the same area. As a result, tissue dies and pressure rises to dilate the walls of the veins; this causes swelling and waste accumulation. The end result is pain and decreased performance.

Fortunately, varicose veins are not common in the young athlete except when obesity is present. In the older professional athlete, they may be very much a problem and contribute toward early retirement.

Prevention and treatment for athletes with symptoms or with a family history of difficulty include:

1. Antigravity measures—bed rest, leg elevation.
2. Avoiding prolonged standing or sitting in one position.
3. Elimination of intra-abdominal pressure—obesity, tumor, tight girdle for women, tight fitting gear, etc.
4. External support—elastic bandages and stockings.
5. Surgery for severe cases.

WHAT CAUSES A MUSCLE CRAMP?

The exact cause is unknown. Cramp appears to be a result of a muscle's shortening too much (contraction of any muscle causes shortening). It could also occur from a rigorous muscle contraction that takes place when that muscle is already partially shortened. Low levels of salt, potassium, and magnesium also increase the possibility of a cramp.

The much-feared stomach cramp during swimming rarely occurs. One investigator failed to find one single case of stomach cramps ever experienced by 30,000 swimmers studied.

In most athletes, cramps can be prevented by:

1. Using static flexibility exercises (steady pressure at maximum range of movement) instead of bouncing hard.
2. Avoiding jerky movements until properly warmed up.
3. Using a 10–15 minute warm-up period.
4. Drinking plenty of water, before, during, and after practice; fatigue is also delayed with water intake during practice.
5. Using salt tablets (or combination salt/potassium) in hot, humid weather and when sweating is excessive.
6. Eating more fruits and vegetables.

Severe cramps in the back of the lower leg (calf area), back of the upper leg (hamstring muscle group), and front of the upper leg (quadricep muscle group) are common in sports.

HOW IS A MUSCLE CRAMP RELIEVED?

If a cramp does occur, it can be relieved by stretching the involved muscle. To relieve a cramp in the back of the lower leg, assume a seated position on the court with the leg fully extended. Instruct someone to apply steady pressure forward on the ball of the foot. If you are alone, place a towel around the toe of the tennis shoe and pull steadily for several minutes while the leg is fully extended. For a cramp in the front of the upper leg (quadricep group), assume a seated position and instruct someone to push down on top of the ankle to fully flex the knee (steady, firm pressure only for several minutes). To relieve a cramp in the back of the upper leg (hamstring group), pull your knee (extended) up toward your chest and hold for several minutes. Very firm massage is also helpful in some cases.

WHAT CAUSES A STITCH OR PAIN IN THE SIDE DURING EXERCISE? IS THIS A DANGER SIGN?

The exact cause is a mystery. Pain occurs on either side of the chest, in the center of the chest and stomach, or in the liver area. It generally happens during severe exercise such as cross-country running, soccer, rugby, ice hockey, or basketball.

Since the pain occurs while the body is adjusting to the demands of exercise, it is thought that it is caused by ischemia (insufficient supply of oxygen to a muscle) of the diaphragm or rib muscles. It is interesting to note that ischemia of any muscle will cause pain. Another theory places the trouble at the site of the liver. It is noted that pain often is relieved when an athlete bends over at the waist and presses hard in the area of the liver.

A stitch in the side is more common in the untrained athlete; it also occurs more frequently when one is exercising after a meal (circulatory adjustment at the beginning of exercise is slower in both instances). Do not stop at the first sign of pain. It will often disappear if you continue to exercise, because the respiratory system catches up and adequate oxygen is supplied to the muscles. However, if severe pain remains, stop exercise and rest for 15–30 minutes. Train hard and warm up thoroughly and you may never experience a stitch in the side.

HOW IS APPENDICITIS DISTINGUISHED FROM A COMMON STITCH IN THE SIDE?

For the layman, the difference is not easy to detect. A stitch in the side generally occurs during exercise, whereas appendix inflammation is more apt to be noticed while at rest. An inflamed appendix is usually acute in the teenage athlete, beginning with severe stomach pain, tenderness, and rigidity on the right side. Other possible symptoms are nausea, vomiting, fever, and rapid pulse. Drawing the right leg toward the stomach provides some comfort.

If you suspect an appendicitis attack, call a physician immediately, apply ice to the stomach, and administer no food, fluid, laxative, or heat. Don't panic at the first sign of these symptoms. Let the physician diagnose; it's difficult enough even for him.

Good appendices have been unnecessarily removed because of gas pains. Luckily, no one is certain what function they serve.

HOW CAN YOU SAVE A CHOKING VICTIM WITH THE HEIMLICH MANEUVER?

More than 2,500 persons choke to death each year on food and other objects. Typically, the victim is eating at home or in a restaurant, drinking several cocktails, talking, laughing, relaxing, when he or she suddenly inhales a piece of meat or vegetable into the larynx, thus partially or completely closing off the air passage.

The next 30 seconds are critical. Now, thanks to Dr. Henry Heimlich, an easily administered, effective method of expelling the object has been devised. To apply the Heimlich Maneuver, wrap both arms around the victim from behind, allowing his or her head and torso to slump forward. Clasp the back of the wrist of one of your hands with the other and squeeze upward (hard and quick) against the person's diaphragm, repeating several times. Proper hand placement is easy; place your hand just under the victim's lower rib. Chances are the object will pop out like a cork as the diaphragm compresses air into the lungs and in turn expels the object blocking the passage.

A few other points to remember:

1. If it is a baby choking, place the baby face down across your knee and push firmly against his or her buttocks, or use the index and middle finger to perform the Heimlich Maneuver.
2. If you choke while alone, fall with your stomach against the edge of a table to expel the object.
3. Distinguish between a heart attack and choking. Mouth-to-mouth

resuscitation, lifesaving for a heart attack victim, can drive an obstruction in tighter. Ask the victim a question. A choking victim will be conscious but unable to answer.

To prevent choking, cut your food in small particles. Believe it or not, particles of food as large as cigarette packs have been found lodged in a victim's throat. Also, avoid talking and laughing with food in your mouth. If serious choking occurs, zap the person with the Heimlich Maneuver. It is nearly 100 percent effective.

CAN MOST MINOR INJURIES BE TREATED AT HOME?

Yes. Provided someone has the skill to distinguish between a minor and a serious injury. Common sense goes a long way in most cases. Consult the chart below for suggested home treatment and determination of whether a physician is needed for the common injuries listed.

The first aid treatment of most strains, sprains, muscle pulls, suspected bone breaks, bruises, and aches and pains is similar and involves four simple actions:

1. Ice—to decrease blood flow to the injured part
2. Compression—to limit swelling
3. Elevation—to help drain excess fluid through gravity by raising the injured limb above the heart level
4. Rest—to prevent additional damage to injured tissue

Ice is applied immediately and can be combined with compression by wrapping a bandage around the ice pack.

COMMON INJURIES AND THEIR TREATMENT

Injury	Emergency Home Treatment	Need for a Physician
Abrasions (with skin or layers scraped off)	Clean thoroughly with soap and warm water or hydrogen peroxide. Use bandage if wound oozes blood. Remove loose skin flaps with nail scissors if they are dirty; allow to remain if clean.	If all dirt and foreign matter cannot be removed Signs of infection
Ankle and Knee Sprains	Stop activity, apply ice pack immediately. Continue ice three times daily for 48 hours before switching to heat. Use crutches 2–3 days if pain is severe when walking. Recovery	Swelling and severe pain continue for more than three days

COMMON INJURIES AND THEIR TREATMENT (continued)

Injury	Emergency Home Treatment	Need for a Physician
	should take this course: swelling and pain for 24–72 hours, decreasing symptoms for 6–10 days, full return to normal in 6–8 weeks.	Pain prevents any weight bearing Knee injury other than contusions Ligament or tendon damage
Broken Bone	Look for a suspicious break. Apply ice packs. Protect and rest the injured part for 72 hours. No additional damage is likely to occur if proper rest and protection is provided; or immobilize, call rescue squad and transport to emergency room.	Limb is cold, blue or numb Pelvis or thigh are involved Limb is crooked, unusable Considerable bleeding and bruising Shock symptoms are present Pain lasts more than 72 hours
Burns	Diagnose the depth of the burn: First Degree (superficial), Second Degree (deeper burns resulting in splitting or layers or blistering from scalding, sunburn, etc.) and Third Degree (destruction of all layers with damage into the deeper tissues). Apply cold compress for 5–10 minutes to reduce skin damage and pain; avoid rupturing blisters. Aspirin may be used for pain.	All third-degree burns Second degree burns involving an area greater than 25–35 sq. in. Pain continues for more than two days
Dental Injury	Chipped tooth: avoid hot and cold drinks. Swelling of face due to abscessed tooth: apply ice pack. Excessive bleeding of tooth socket after extraction: place gauze over socket and bite down maintaining pressure. Toothache: aspirin and ice packs may be used.	Chipped tooth Abscessed tooth Excessive bleeding of socket Toothache
Fainting and Dizziness	Lack of blood flow to the brain commonly occurs with increasing age and may result in a temporary loss of vision or lightheatedness. Avoid sudden changes in posture, reduce anxiety levels.	Loss of consciousness occurs Room appears to be spinning Dizziness occurs frequently
Frost Bite	Thaw rapidly in a warm water bath. Avoid rubbing frost bite with snow. Water should be comfortable to a normal, unfrozen hand (not over 104°). When a flush reaches the fingers, remove from the bath immediately. For an ear or nose, use cloths soaked in warm water.	Always see a doctor

COMMON INJURIES AND THEIR TREATMENT (continued)

Injury	Emergency Home Treatment	Need for a Physician
Head Injury	Apply ice bag to bruised area. Observe patient every two hours for the next 72 hours for: alertness (unresponsiveness, deep sleep), unequal pupil size (one-fourth of population have unequal size all the time), severe vomiting. Pressure inside skull may develop over a 72 hour period.	Bleeding from ears, eyes or mouth Black eyes Unconsciousness, unequal pupil size, lethargy, or severe vomiting
Infected Wounds (Blood Poisoning)	Bacterial infection in the bloodstream or septicemia. Keep area clean, change bandage twice daily. Soak and clean in warm water several times daily. Have patience—10–12 days may be needed for normal healing.	Presence of fever above 99.6° Thick pus, swelling since the second day
Insect Bites/ Stings	Apply cold compress, use aspirin or other pain relievers. Identify the insect—a black widow spider has a glossy black body about ½" in diameter, red "hour glass" on abdomen. Bite produces sharp pain at the site; cramps appear within an hour and may involve the extremities and trunk. Breathing becomes difficult; nausea, vomiting, twitching, tingling sensations of the hand may occur.	Evidence of wheezing, difficulty in breathing, fainting, or hives or skin rash Bite from a black widow spider Severe local reaction
Minor Cuts	Clean the wound vigorously with soap and water or hydrogen peroxide, removing all dirt and foreign matter. Use a butterfly Band-Aid or steri-strip to bring the edges of the wound tightly together without trapping the fat or rolling the skin under. Avoid antiseptics: they may destroy tissue and retard healing and are not as effective as soap and water.	Cuts on trunk or face, deep cuts that may involve tendons, ligament, blood vessels or nerves Blood pumping from a wound Tingling or limb weakness Signs of infection Cuts that cannot be pulled together without trapping the fat
Nose Bleed	Squeeze the nose between the thumb and forefinger just below the hard portion for 5–10 minutes while seated with the head back. Do not lie down. Apply cold compresses to the bridge of the nose and avoid blowing.	Occurs frequently and is associated with a cold History of high blood pressure
Object in Eye	Avoid rubbing, you might scratch the cornea. Close both eyes for several minutes to allow tears to wash out the foreign body. Grasp the lashes of the upper lid and draw	Foreign object is on the eye itself Remains after washing Object could have

COMMON INJURIES AND THEIR TREATMENT (continued)

Injury	Emergency Home Treatment	Need for a Physician
Object in Eye (continued)	out and down over the lower lid. If it feels like the foreign object is present but is not, cornea scrape probably occurred and will heal in 24–48 hours. Using a medicine dropper, flush eye with plain water. If speck is visible, touch lightly with moistened corner of handkerchief. If chemical was splashed in eye, dilute immediately by placing face under luke warm shower with heavy spray.	penetrated the globe of the eye Blood is visible in eye Vision is impaired Pain present after 48 hours
Poison Ivy and Oak	After initial exposure, 12–48 hours may pass before a rash appears. If plant oil is removed from the skin with vigorous washing (2 or 3 times) a rash may be prevented. Apply cool compresses of Burrow's Solution. Cleanse the skin thoroughly. A hot bath will release histamine and cause intense itching; however the cells of histamine will eventually be depleted and 6–8 hours of relief will follow.	Rash occurs without itching, redness or exposure to oak or ivy. Contact may be direct from pets, clothing, or smoke from burning Rhus plants
Puncture Wounds	Let wound bleed as much as possible. Clean thoroughly with soap and water or hydrogen peroxide diluted to 3%. Soak the wound at least twice daily in warm water for 3 or 4 days to keep it open to allow germs and foreign matter to drain.	Head, abdomen or chest puncture wounds; danger of internal damage Object still inside wound Wound is deep, cannot be cleaned thoroughly, tetanus shot is needed
Sunburn	Apply cool compresses using Aveeno or one half cup baking soda in a tub of water. Avoid Vaseline and other lubricants the first day.	Presence of abdominal cramps, dizziness or second degree burns

Exercise, Aging and Health

This chapter examines age and sports from two aspects: (1) the effects of sports upon the aging or degeneration process, and (2) the effects of age upon performance, learning, and injury resistance. There are many questions to answer concerning participation in various sports at both a very young and old age. At both extremes, there is considerable danger unless control is exercised. It must be said that we probably make two serious mistakes in this area. First, we begin to compete in some types of athletic activities too soon, imposing numerous physical and psychological dangers. Second, we quit too soon under the false assumption that we are "over the hill" and unable to remain active. Both errors are more common in the United States than in other countries. While we cannot guarantee that through exercise and sports you will live longer, we can say that you "will have more life while you live." To receive this benefit, exercise or participation in sports must be continuous throughout life.

This chapter provides accurate information that will guide you in receiving the utmost enjoyment and benefit from sports and exercise throughout life with minimal danger of bodily harm while getting the most out of your body.

WHEN DOES THE GROWTH SPURT TAKE PLACE?

Two growth spurts generally occur: the mid-growth spurt and the adolescent growth spurt. The mid-growth spurt occurs at about 5–7 years of age for boys and girls; the adolescent growth spurt begins around the eleventh to thirteenth year for girls and the thirteenth to fifteenth year for boys.

Females grow faster during their adolescent spurt with the pelvic width continuing to expand after growth has ceased. Males have approximately two more years than females to grow before the adolescent growth spurt which extends growing time and allows the legs to become longer.

There are exceptions in both sexes that fall outside these ranges.

IS IT HARMFUL FOR YOUNG CHILDREN UNDER 10 TO ENGAGE IN VIGOROUS EXERCISE?

There is no physiological evidence to indicate that vigorous training has any harmful effect on the body. This is not to imply that the potential for harm is not present. Under competent leadership, almost any sports activity is relatively safe for young athletes. Without such leadership, hazards are present in any sport or activity. Much also depends on the sport, the child's emotional makeup, parental expectations, the growth stage of each child, and the basic philosophy of the league.

Consider these factors before deciding on a specific sport or program:

1. Boxing is an inappropriate sport for this age group unless radically altered in approach.
2. The hazards of collision sports are associated with the leadership and the conditions under which a sport is administered more than with the sport itself. Collision sports can be conducted for youngsters with limited risk.
3. Marathon running for children of this age group is a questionable activity, imposing considerable joint stress during training and excessive energy requirements at a time when surplus calories are needed for growth and development.
4. A thorough physical examination is necessary prior to any type of participation.
5. Leagues or sports that group athletes by body size, sex, skill and maturation, not age, should be selected for your child.
6. Children should undergo a good physical conditioning program before starting the new activity.

There is no sport in existence that requires your child to begin organized, competitive play during this age range. All-star games, play-offs, high pressure from the public, paid admissions, and other commercialization are things a 6–10 year old does not need. There is no evidence that exposure to these aspects of adult athletics at an early age has any carry-over value whatsoever.

Protect your child from emotional and physical damage by avoiding high pressure, win-at-all-cost programs. A child's self concept is far more important than a victory. Look into your local YMCA age group programs if you want a sane, fun approach to sports. Work on basic motor skills such as running, jumping, throwing, catching that have carry-over to most sports. Children should be encouraged to compete against their own standards and feel good about themselves at any level of competition.

IS WEIGHT TRAINING HARMFUL TO YOUNG ELEMENTARY SCHOOL CHILDREN?

The ideal time for the start of *vigorous* weight training programs appears to be during late adolescence, after the growth spurt and widening of the shoulder girdle. A properly devised program at this time aids recovery from injuries, helps prevent injuries to the major joints (knee, shoulder, ankle, neck), provides needed recognition, and allows youngsters to carry out athletic activities more successfully.

It must be said that elementary school children, ages 6 to 12, are extremely weak in the upper body. A *modified* weight-training program beginning at approximately 8 or 9 may eliminate the need for intense programs in later years and actually allow more rapid development in physical education and athletic skills requiring above-average strength. Age group swimmers continue to utilize weight training several times weekly as a part of their regular training routine. The truth is that no other program is as effective in the development of strength. For the elementary school child, however, there are some pitfalls that must be recognized:

1. Heavy weights can overstress the knee joint at a time when ligament strength is weak.
2. Shoulder and elbow joints are experiencing rapid changes and should not be subjected to heavy weights.
3. Injuries due to faulty lifting form and careless use of equipment may occur.

A modified program for young children should be prepared on an individual basis by the physical educator. In general, it should involve total body development (rather than concentrating on one or two areas), light weight (no more than 60 percent of maximum for any one exercise), and a high number of repetitions (8–15). Elementary age is a time for the development of general coordination through creative, active games. With competent instruction, strength development can be a concomitant activity. Take time to find out what's happening in your elementary physical education program. Your child will thank you for it years later.

HOW EARLY IN LIFE SHOULD I START MY CHILD IN SPORTS?

Let your child answer this question. Don't be too pushy or your child may reject a particular sport entirely. Family influences *are* great, particularly in early years. Parental interest and participation in sports are *often* transferred to their children. Exceptions do and will occur and the transfer is not automatic or guaranteed. Chances of transfer can be improved, however, with the correct approach.

Chances of your child pursuing athletics depend upon his ability and your respect for his individuality. The secret is to persuade and not command, lead and not pressure, nurture and not force. An interest in physical activity can be developed through a child's own curiosity, directed and encouraged through *indirect* family influences. At very early ages (under 6), a two- to five-minute exposure to a parent's favorite sport is adequate. Moments of interest, within a child's attention span, are used wisely by parents with *no* pressure to continue when the child chooses to do something else.

The Law of Readiness also prevents you from starting your son or daughter too early in many activities. Until finer muscular movements are possible, some sports are virtually impossible.

IS LITTLE LEAGUE BASEBALL PITCHING HARMFUL?

Yes, according to Dr. Joel E. Adams, orthopedic surgeon and researcher in this area. Pitching at early ages apparently can cause arm muscles to pull on the growth centers of the bone which are not yet closed. Of 80 young pitchers tested, all were found to have some degree of separated and fragmented bone centers and accelerated arm growth. Permanent elbow and shoulder injury is a serious danger to Little League pitchers under present rules. A number of rule changes are suggested:

1. Curve ball pitching should be abolished.
2. Fathers should not build backyard mounds or encourage youngsters to throw hard for long periods of time.
3. Children under 12 should be permitted to pitch only two innings, children 12 to 17 only three.
4. Pitchers with arm pains should immediately move to another position.
5. Playing seasons should be shortened.
6. A 10- to 14-day rest period should be required between games for pitchers.
7. Physicians should examine the physiological growth state of pitchers more carefully to determine the stage of bone development.
8. Practice throws should be reduced or eliminated.

Little League baseball can hurt your child, in more ways and places than the elbow and shoulder.

IS THERE ANY ASSOCIATION BETWEEN EXERCISE AND AGING?

Yes. There is little doubt that speed of aging is related to your health habits—mainly exercise, eating, and resting patterns. A summary of some comments by researchers specializing in this area may help:

1. Regular physical exercise can reduce degeneration associated with aging to a minimum.
2. There is a relationship between aging and fattening. Exercise is a valuable means of maintaining normal body weight.
3. Long-term exercise and proper nutrition retard the aging process.
4. Changes due to aging are the opposite of those appearing from training.
5. Long-term exercise protects the cardiovascular system from disease by postponing the unfavorable changes occurring to the heart and blood vessels, reducing the probability and severity of coronary heart disease. It also improves survival chances should a heart attack occur.
6. Exercise helps various body organs to adapt to restrictions imposed by disease.
7. Exercise can also benefit those who suffer from arterial disease, emphysema, diabetes mellitus, and asthma.

It is obvious that long-term exercise and proper eating habits will prevent weight gain, help maintain a healthy appearance, improve ability to exert physical effort, slow the aging process, and provide a healthier life while living. Even if not one day is added to your life, the results are worthwhile.

Many athletes become sedentary when their competitive days are over. The smart athlete continues to exercise throughout life. You have already invested 5–10 years in active living. Several years of complete inactivity and poor eating habits can negate the dividends accumulated and eventually place you into the high-risk group as a candidate for a coronary.

HOW DOES LONG-TERM EXERCISE AFFECT THE BODY SYSTEMS OF THE AGING INDIVIDUAL?

The majority of evidence is extremely favorable as we examine older individuals who have engaged in regular, vigorous exercise throughout life. In general, we might expect the following to occur:

1. *Cardiovascular system.* The amount of blood pumped per minute declines with age; however this reduction need not occur in the exercising individual. In addition coronary arteries are somewhat larger than those of the population of inactive individuals. Stroke volume (amount of blood ejected per heartbeat) will decline much more slowly.
2. *Respiratory system.* The amount of oxygen that can be taken in from the atmosphere and utilized declines with age. This rate of decline is slowed in the active individual who is engaged in endurance exercise. The right kind of exercise will improve the efficiency of the respiratory system.
3. *Muscular system.* Strength loss of 10 to 20 percent occurs with advanced age; however, progressive resistance training can cut down on this loss; the strength of such individuals can actually exceed that of some younger people, particularly those who never engaged in strength training during their youth.
4. *Nervous system.* Psychomotor slowing occurs with age; however, there is some evidence that this process is delayed by vigorous activity that causes hypertrophy of nerve cells.

In general, all body systems, including the excretory, endocrine, and digestive systems, function more smoothly in active individuals. Limited scientific data are available to make the information above conclusive; however, evidence is continuing to suggest that exercise has a strong influence on maintaining the efficiency of the body systems in the aging individual.

HOW DOES AGING AFFECT INJURY AND HEALING?

Unfortunately, older individuals are more easily injured and slower to heal than younger individuals. Age results in numerous physical changes that bring this about:

1. The quality of distensibility disappears from connective tissue, limiting flexibility or range of motion and increasing the possibility of injury.
2. Localized areas of cartilage soften from injury, disease, or wear, particularly in weight-bearing areas of the legs, leaving one more injury prone.
3. Muscles, ligaments, and tendons lose their elasticity and are more susceptible to injury; a return to complete normalcy following injury is unlikely.
4. In the healing of broken bones, age is an important factor. Bones of growing children unite more quickly and heal faster. The more rapidly a bone is growing (the younger the patient), the more quickly it unites.

Explosive movements and contact sports should be avoided after age 50, and substituted with vigorous activity of another nature. Again, for those who have exercised continually throughout life, injury is less likely to occur. Pushing oneself too far beyond the maximum at later ages can lead to strain.

HOW MUCH IS PERFORMANCE AFFECTED BY AGE?

Researchers point out numerous rates of deteriorating and the rate certainly differs among individuals. The athlete who has been involved in a continual, vigorous exercise program throughout life will definitely decrease in performance at a much slower rate than the inactive individual. Regardless of the most herculean efforts, however, performance slowly diminishes with age.

One writer suggests that musculoskeletal efficiency diminishes about 1 percent annually (slightly more in women) after the age of 25–30. At age 50, then, you are approximately 75 percent as effective as you were at age 25. From the age of 20 to the age of 70 you will lose about 50 percent of your physical efficiency.

More specific findings concerning various body systems and aging are listed below:

1. Oxygen consumption during strenuous exercise declines slowly with age, with a 20 percent decline evident by age 40.
2. The maximum heart rate increase possible during exercise declines with age. A maximum rate of about 190–210 between the ages of 18 and 25 declines to approximately 160–170 at age 50.
3. The capacity for endurance-type exercise suffers a much slower rate of decline after age 30 if some type of training is continued.
4. Maximum anaerobic power (capability of sprinting full speed for extended distances) increases to about age 20, declining slowly thereafter.
5. Muscles, ligaments, and tissues lose their elasticity with age, making one more susceptible to injury.
6. Muscular strength decreases very slowly with age, although weight training at practically any age can improve strength. Even at age 60–65, only a 15 to 20 percent decrease is evident.
7. Coordination is not greatly affected by age.
8. Following exercise, recovery to normal oxygen intake, carbon dioxide elimination, and blood pressure is slower with age.
9. Reaction time is hindered by age.
10. Stroke volume (amount of blood ejected per heartbeat) decreases at about 1 percent per year after maturity.
11. The area of the coronary artery open to allow blood to pass through is 20 to 30 percent less in middle age.
12. The amount of fat-free weight decreases with age. To maintain a constant fat/muscle ratio throughout life, body weight must be reduced. The change is generally due to inactive living and atrophy of muscle tissue due to disuse. Continuous training could eliminate the need for weight loss.

It is nearly impossible to say how much of the preceding deterioration is due to aging and how much due to inactive living. It is known, however, that in some of these areas, little deterioration occurs for some active, older individuals. Your best protection against rapid or even normal physical decline is daily exercise, sensible eating, normal weight, and adequate sleeping habits. Daily exercise helps you in all other areas. Physiological age is much more important than chronological age. A heart transplant from a 35-year-old inactive, obese man may not be much of a bargain.

SHOULD THE INTENSITY OF EXERCISE REDUCE WITH AGE?

Not necessarily. There are a great many misconceptions concerning what should decrease or increase with age. In many cases, these myths evolved out of convenience and self-justification for the easy life. Examine the list below and use it as your guide:

Food intake: Should decrease with age. Metabolism slows and fewer calories are needed to maintain weight.

Blood pressure: 100 plus your age is poor advice. Ideal bood pressure will not increase with age, but remain within safe limits of less than 90 (diastolic or low reading) and less than 140 (systolic or higher of the two readings).

Exercise: Increase the volume as you get older, assuming that you have been involved in a program throughout life. Select a program that will develop and maintain heart-lung endurance and avoid contact sports and explosive exercise in later years.

Weight: Should decrease with age. Weight charts that allow you to be heavier as you grow older are misleading. If you weigh the same at age 50 that you weighed at 30, you are probably overweight due to greater percentage of body fat.

Sexual activity: Tends to decrease with age although there is some indication that prostate difficulty is less likely to develop in sexually active males.

"We are too soon old and too late smart." This Pennsylvania Dutch quote describes the normal course of events concerning exercise and activity. Get smart early and stay with exercise throughout your life. You may find that the "too soon old" applies to chronological age only.

DOES EXERCISE REALLY RELIEVE TENSION?

Yes. There is experimental evidence to support reduced tension from exercise. A strong logical argument also can be advanced: Since increased body temperature synchronizes cortical activity and reduces muscle activity, and exercise elevates temperature, the same results should occur.

Exercise has been shown to reduce residual neuro-muscular tension immediately following a workout or sports activity with lowered tension increasing slowly back to the initial level during the post-exercise period. In addition, long-term exercise has been shown to produce a significant reduction in the body's electrical activity, promote deeper sleep, and aid in the treatment of individuals with emotional disorders.

WHAT IS A HEART ATTACK?

Let's examine briefly what actually happens when a so-called heart attack occurs. The heart muscle is rarely at fault; rather, inadequate supply of blood to the heart, usually due to clogged coronary arteries and their branches, causes tissue death to certain areas of the heart that are left temporarily or permanently without blood and oxygen.

The heart receives nourishment from two main arteries. These coronary arteries branch off the aorta and carry oxygenated blood from the heart throughout the body. The right coronary artery covers the back side of the heart by branching into smaller and smaller arteries which penetrate the heart muscle. The left coronary artery is divided into two parts which nourish the front and left side of the heart. These coronary arteries are most susceptible to fatty deposit build-up, atherosclerosis, and clogging.

"Coronary thrombosis" may occur due to a clot in a coronary artery with artery closure caused by an accumulation of atheromas (plaque-like lesion in the inner lining of an artery). In most cases, only a branch of an artery supplying a portion of the heart muscle is affected. This may explain why many attacks are not fatal. Blockage in the larger sections of a coronary artery would diminish blood supply to a large area and generally result in death. Keep in mind that the heart muscle must be properly nourished second-by-second to function.

"Angina Pectoris" refers to a symptom of heart disease caused by diminished blood supply to a portion of the heart muscle. When any muscle fails to receive adequate blood supply (oxygen and nutrient material), pain results. This condition is referred to as ischemia. When the heart is involved, the victim experiences a tightness or pressure in the chest and pain that may radiate to the shoulders or arms.

WHAT CAUSES HEART ATTACKS?

Although capsule form has the effect of greatly oversimplifying a complicated problem, it is helpful to summarize four common theories:

1. *The Lipid Theory.* A high number of fatty particles (lipoproteins) in the bloodstream cause atherosclerosis or the accumulation of these

particles on arterial walls. Particles increasing the tendency for atherosclerosis are called lipoproteins which consist of fat (triglyceride), a blood protein (to make the fat soluble), and cholesterol (actually a steroid which has many traits of fat). A high fat diet, common to Americans, elevates blood lipid levels and enhances the atherosclerotic process.

2. *The Personality Behavior Theory.* Individuals are classified as either: Type A Behavior: in a hurry, pressed for time, clock watcher, competitive, aggressive, hates to lose, lack of patience, and an underlying hostility.
    Type B. Behavior: unaggressive, not concerned with job advancement or time pressures, a contented "cow" enjoying life as it is. Individuals exhibiting Type A Behavior patterns are supposedly more likely to suffer an early heart attack.

3. *The Risk Factor Theory.* A number of risk factors in combination make one more susceptible to heart disease: heredity, history of early coronary heart disease in the family, high blood pressure, obesity, inactivity or sedentary living, tobacco smoking, high blood lipid levels. Proneness to coronary heart disease seems to increase with every additional risk factor to which one is exposed.

4. *The Fibrin Deposit Theory.* It is suggested that sticky fibrin deposits on the inside of artery walls are the cause of atherosclerosis. Eventually, reduced flow of blood or a complete block due to clotting or narrowing of coronary artery branches results in a heart attack. The theory is somewhat compatible with the lipid theory.

Unfortunately, everyone can cite one example of longevity or tragedy to provide the rationale for a particular behavior or lifestyle. There will always be examples failing to fit the mold. Good genetic lines may allow some individuals to reach a ripe old age regardless of lifestyle. Conversely, poor lines may result in early death in spite of the most ideal lifestyle. This is not, however, percentage ball that should guide the masses.

Experts continue to voice causative theories while few are actively involved with prevention. There are few, if any, 40–50 year studies in progress that will prove, beyond a shadow of a doubt, the exact percent each theory or risk factor plays—coronary heart disease does not have a single cause and this type of research support will not be forthcoming. There is already enough evidence available to show that certain lifestyle changes can alter what is now considered the inevitable by the layman.

HOW DOES EXERCISE HELP TO PREVENT PREMATURE AND REOCCURING HEART ATTACKS?

It assists in many ways by causing certain physiological changes within the body. Before discussing these, however, we should point out that to reduce the risk of a reoccurring heart attack, lifestyle changes must be made in *all* major risk areas: increased physical activity, decreased blood pressure, lowered cholesterol level, elimination of smoking, and a reduction to normal weight. A change in only one or two areas cannot be expected to prevent further deterioration of vessels and protect from another attack. In fact, even these changes cannot undo the damage that was 25 years or more in the making.

Exercise, then, is a valuable factor in preventing a heart attack and reducing the risk of reoccurring attacks. In fact, the active man is three to four times less likely ever to have an attack and three to four times more likely to survive should one occur. The exercising cardiac patient who has already suffered an attack is also less likely to have another than is the inactive patient, and much more likely to survive should one occur. The chart below examines the changes brought about by exercise to the major risk factors cited previously.

Risk Factor	Effect of Regular Aerobic Exercise
Obesity/overweight	Reduction of body fat, return to ideal weight
High lipid levels	Reduction of atherogenic fatty particles in the blood, lowered cholesterol and tryglyceride levels, enlargement of coronary arteries and their branches
Hypertension	Aid in the control of high blood pressure and maintenance of normal pressure
Tension and stress	Increased tolerance for stress, release of tension and nervous or emotional energy
Lack of physical activity	No longer a risk factor for the active person
Diabetes	Assist in the control of diabetes
Genetic history	No change
Smoking	No change; cessation of smoking essential
Age	Slows degenerative process

Change is slow. For generations, patients who suffered from myocardial infarctions (damage to the heart muscle) were prescribed prolonged, strict bed rest. Today, the average patient is placed on an endurance exercise program that eventually would tax a highly conditioned athlete. This change has greatly improved survival rates of patients.

A great deal of research has been conducted concerning the cause of heart attacks. One hundred percent conclusive evidence is lacking; however, indirect evidence is overwhelming. Most studies reveal the same thing: patients who suffer heart attacks are less active, eat more fat and have higher cholesterol levels, smoke more, have higher blood pressure, and have more stressful occupations than the controls who have not suffered attacks. On top of this, many have a history of cardiovascular disease in the family. It may be a long time before absolute proof is available. In the meantime, it is a good idea to exercise regularly—you'll then have a better chance of being here when absolute proof is uncovered.

Research suggests that to greatly lessen the risk of heart disease, your exercise program should result in a weekly energy expenditure of 2,000 calories or more. Study the chart on page 180 and evaluate your program.

HASN'T THE FEMALE SEX HORMONE BEEN SUCCESSFUL IN PREVENTING RECURRENT HEART ATTACKS IN MALES?

Yes. There is some evidence to suggest estrogen is beneficial to men who have had heart difficulty. A change in lifestyle is probably the most important preventive measure, starting with the elimination of smoking, weight reduction, lowering of blood pressure and cholesterol levels, and regular exercise (walking-running, cycling, swimming) for those who are diagnosed as capable.

While use of the female sex hormone for males may help, it is not without its problems. When the breasts enlarge, voice increases in pitch, and testicles atrophy, the patient begins to question its value.

DOES THE MEDICAL PROFESSION AGREE THAT EXERCISE REDUCES CHOLESTEROL LEVELS, LESSENS DEPOSITS IN THE ARTERIES, AND GREATLY REDUCES THE RISK OF HEART DISEASE?

Definitely yes. In fact, the biggest news about the heart in 20 years was released September 1, 1970, by a 19-man team from Harvard's School of Public Health and the School of Medicine at Trinity College, Dublin. The condensed findings of this historical study appeared in national magazines and newspapers and provides the source for the information in this discussion.

The two-country medical group conducted a nine-year study of 575 pairs of brothers, aged 30 to 65, born in Ireland. One of each pair remained in Ireland while the other emigrated to the Boston area of the United States. Brothers were chosen who had similar physical and psychological heritage and whose first 20 years involved similar habits of eating, comfort, and affection. Each brother was carefully analyzed by the team of physicians.

FACTOR	FINDING
Lifestyle	
Caloric intake	Irish brothers consumed 400 to 500 more calories daily than the Boston brothers. Tea, whole grain cereal, and brown bread were also more prevalent in the diet of the brothers living in Ireland.
Cholesterol intake	Irish brothers ate a higher percentage of animal fat.
Activity patterns	Irish brothers were *far* more active in their occupations and leisure pursuits than the Boston brothers.
Analysis of Body	
Fatty tissue as measured by skin calipers	Irish brothers had less fatty tissue.
Body weight	Irish brothers were significantly lighter.
Cholesterol level	Irish brothers had a much lower blood serum cholesterol level.
Condition of the arteries and heart	Hearts of Irish brothers appeared similar to those of Americans who were 15 to 28 years younger. Ireland brothers were two to six times healthier than those in Boston.
Mortality rate from heart disease	Considerably less among Irish.

As we examine the factors that were analyzed in the two groups, it would have appeared that both groups were heading for an early coronary—both ate a high number of calories and a high amount of animal fats. The single difference was the exercise of the Ireland brothers and the fact that the fluoride (contined in tea) and magnesium (contained in brown bread and whole grain cereal) may help to prevent cholesterol buildup in the arteries. The American diet is almost completely absent in magnesium.

No evidence concerning the importance of exercise in delaying heart disease in men could be more positive. Although additional research of a similar nature is still needed, this unique, well-controlled study shows how imperative it is that you engage in an exercise program three to five times weekly that is designed to develop heart-lung endurance. Exercise may not be the cure-all in preventing heart disease; however, it is one of the most important factors.

DOES EXERCISE HELP REDUCE BOTH TRIGLYCERIDE AND CHOLESTEROL LEVELS?

Yes. A reduction in triglycerides can be expected with regular aerobic exercise (exercise requiring high energy expenditure such as running, cycling, soccer, rugby, and many other sports. Regular exercise (3–4 times weekly) lowers triglyceride levels and keeps them low. Cholesterol, however, is lowered immediately following exercise, but will elevate to normal levels unless you exercise again within 36–48 hours. Exercising almost every day is the best approach. Exercising individuals have been found to have a higher percentage of high density lipoproteins (HDL) and less low density lipoproteins (LDL) in their composition of total blood serum cholesterol. A lot of HDL has been associated with protection from early heart disease.

Proper management of blood lipids (fats) requires a low cholesterol diet and regular exercise. High blood lipids are either inherited or of the environmental form (diet and exercise habits).

CAN DIET HELP PREVENT HEART ATTACKS?

Yes. Heart attacks (coronary thrombosis, myocardial infarction, angina) are generally caused by atherosclerosis, often referred to as arteriosclerosis or hardening of the arteries. A stroke (apoplexy), or failure of one of the tiny vessels to supply a portion of the brain because of blockage or a clot, is generally caused by the same underlying condition. Prevention and control of atherosclerosis, then, also prevents heart attacks and stroke.

The condition of atherosclerosis is influenced by factors such as cholesterol level, high blood pressure, diet, diabetes, age, sex, heredity, obesity, stress, smoking, and exercise habits.

The relationship between diet and atherosclerosis is revealed by numerous research findings: (1) animals fed a high cholesterol diet develop deposits in arterial walls and develop atherosclerosis, (2) habits of various countries indicate a relationship between fat consumption, cholesterol level, and incidence of heart attacks, (3) diet control has been shown to reduce blood cholesterol levels and subsequently lessen the risk of heart attacks and strokes, and (4) the fat intake of Americans (40–50 percent of caloric intake) is higher than that of other countries, and so is the incidence of heart attacks. Reducing blood fat levels is a complex problem; however, it can be done by substituting polyunsaturated fats for saturated fats to a reasonable degree. Merely eliminating foods high in cholesterol without substituting polyunsaturated fats does *not* solve the problem since the body will produce cholesterol from other types of fat. The substitution of polyunsaturated fats is essential and should occur for individuals with two or more of the following characteristics in their background: (1) an overweight or obese condition, (2) history of atherosclerosis or heart attacks in the family prior to age 65, (3) high blood pressure, (4) heavy smoking, (5) diabetes, (6) sedentary living, (7) a previous heart attack.

Athletes who suddenly become inactive when playing days are ended also fall into the sedentary group and are vulnerable.

Proper diet and exercise control over a long period of years does delay atherosclerosis and help prevent heart attacks and strokes. Exercise and diet control should be a part of one's daily life. Unless it is treated as such, benefits are sporadic.

WHEN IS THE BEST TIME TO CHANGE DIET IF PREMATURE HEART ATTACKS ARE TO BE PREVENTED?

No change is necessary if you begin at birth: "Heart attack prevention begins in infancy." Signs of atherosclerosis and cholesterol buildup have been noted in young children under ten years of age. A sensible diet should be initiated in the younger years with the use of skim milk instead of whole milk, absence of fried foods, potato chips, Fritos, ice cream and dairy products, hamburgers and milk shakes, butter, and limited use of meats as a source of protein. Eating habits established in youth will carry over to the adult years.

Everyone can cite examples of individuals who abused themselves in diet, exercise, and sleep and still lived a long life, as well as examples of those who selected their foods very carefully, exercised daily, and still died young. Both extremes are possible. People handle fat intake differently, with some able to handle high-fat diets and other unable to do so. Keep in mind that handling high-fat diets without developing signs of hardening of the arteries and plaque buildup is not the usual pattern. In fact, these individuals are now being studied to determine how they differ from you and me who must avoid high-fat foods in order to avoid a premature heart attack (prior to age 60). One person in five suffers from a heart attack before age 60 (one in three after age 60), and possibly almost all of us would if we lived long enough. In October 1971 tragedy struck the National Football League and the athletic world when a 27-year-old player died on the field from a heart attack. Autopsy revealed rather advanced atherosclerosis in the coronary artery. This is unusual at such a young age; however, it is possible.

Start your children off right. Also, regardless of *your* age, change now to a low-fat, medium-calorie diet and exercise daily. Consult your physician for advice in both areas. While it seems rather comical to tell a 60-year-old man he may eat only three eggs per week, it will assist in delaying further vessel damage—though it will not reverse a process begun many years before. By the time the first overt signs of heart attack are evident, it is safe to assume that the process began 25–30 years ago. Give your children the benefit of recent scientific knowledge. Develop the habit of exercise and proper diet. They will have more life while they live and live a longer life.

CAN AN ECG (electrocardiogram) UNCOVER HEART DISEASE?

It can assist in detecting heart disease if a "work" or exercise ECG is used. In this type of test, the patient is subjected to a standard work load such as the Master Step Test, bicycle ergometer, or treadmill, and monitored as the heart rate is elevated to a predetermined level (approximately 170 beats per minute for the under-30 age group, 160 for those 30–39, 150 for those 40–49, 140 for those 50–59, and 130 for those 60–90). The theory is that abnormalities are more likely to be noticed when the heart is under exercise stress or during the two- to six-minute period of recovery than when it is under minimal use at rest. In spite of this, resting ECG's have, until recently, been more common.

Even the exercise ECG has its limitations. There are some conditions that are not revealed by this or any other test. In addition, some marathon runners and athletes in high endurance sports may have different ECG tracings than the so-called normal population. Physicians are now aware that such findings may also be normal for the athlete; changes that occurred through training and impose no health hazard.

Blood pressure (BP) during exercise should be measured along with an ECG. Unusually high pressure may be a sign of oncoming hypertension even though resting pressure is normal. It is interesting to note that the BP of a hypertense individual will decrease during exercise. Also, several ECG's over a period of time allow comparisons that may reveal changes indicative of heart disease.

There still is no one single test that will plot the progress and/or rate of acceleration of heart disease. You can be certain of one thing, however: it does not occur overnight, but develops from a rather early age, with progression depending upon lifestyle (eating, sleeping, exercise habits and emotional stress).

Remember, a so-called normal ECG is no guarantee of freedom from heart disease. Reduce your intake of animal fats, give up smoking, maintain normal weight and blood pressure, and begin a daily exercise program that develops heart-lung endurance. Begin early in life and continue into old age. The start of your first year of inactivity should begin in the casket.

IF EXERCISE IS NOT HARMFUL, WHY DO SO MANY MEN DIE SHOVELING SNOW EACH YEAR?

A number of middle-aged men do die each year while shoveling, or shortly after shoveling, the winter's first snow. It would be unjust, however, to conclude that exercise is harmful and dangerous and should be avoided. Let's take a look at what actually may have caused death.

The victim is probably middle-aged, overweight, and possessing some danger signs of heart disease such as high cholesterol level, diabetes, history of heart disease in the family, hypertension, or heavy smoking habits, and has probably been inactive for many years, including the 364 days before snow fell. In many cases, the victim is a cardiac patient. He then decides to engage in strenuous exercise that can place demands on the heart (when the snow is wet, shovel is full, and haste is great) equal to walking up seven flights of stairs in one minute. Obviously, the heart is not accustomed to such demands. Considerable blood is now needed to supply working muscles, leaving too little to pass through narrowed arteries (due to atherosclerosis) to feed the heart muscle itself. The result is a heart attack that could be fatal. It is unlikely that this would occur in an individual who has been active and whose heart is accustomed to such effort.

Exercise, then, is not the killer. It is a combination of eagerness to remove snow quickly, conditions of the snow, past exercise habits, and lack of common sense in trying to change from an inactive to an active role in one day.

It might be wiser for the wife to shovel the first and second snow. Women are much more cautious, will use rest period, and not try to remove the snow in giant portions and record-breaking time. Meanwhile, the husband should begin a conditioning program, in consultation with his physician, to get ready for the third snow. That one is his, and as a bonus, he will get a crack at snows of the future.

EACH YEAR A NUMBER OF CASES OF COLLAPSE OCCUR DURING STRENUOUS EXERCISE. WHAT CAUSES THIS?

Although such cases are rare, they do occur occasionally and exercise receives the blame. Numerous causes may have contributed. (1) use of drugs, such as amphetamines, that remove warning signs of fatigue and overstrain and allow one to continue exercise when he or she should rest, (2) heat stroke due to hot, humid weather, heavy perspiration, limited fluids, loss of salt, poor evaporation, (3) sudden vigorous exertion in a previously inactive individual, (4) presence of undiagnosed heart difficulty or other ailments, (5) aneurism or weakness in a vessel wall that suddenly gives out.

The body normally operates under adequate safety devices; signs of fatigue prevent excessive exertion. Sometimes this feeling of fatigue is accompanied by weakness, abdominal pain, headache, sweating, nausea and vomiting, or a combination of several of these symptoms. Although the condition generally disappears quickly, it may last several hours. Collapse may occur unless the patient is placed in a lying or sitting position. The explanation for this type of "sickness" is unknown. Some feel it is due to a drop in blood sugar level. In any case, these warning signs require a rest period rather than continued exercise. Know your limitations. If any unusual symptoms of sickness occur during exercise, stop and rest immediately.

IS EXERCISE DANGEROUS FOR OLDER INDIVIDUALS AND THOSE WHO HAVE BEEN INACTIVE?

It can be, and certain precautionary measures may be necessary. Obviously, an individual (anyone over 30) who has been relatively inactive in the past must undergo a physical examination and initiate an exercise program according to the starting intensity prescribed by the physician. Additional precautionary measures should be considered:

1. Heavy sweating results in loss of salt, potassium, magnesium, and water, necessitating greater salt intake and diet changes to avoid exhaustion or heat cramps on extremely hot, humid days.
2. A workout is too light if sweating does not occur and too heavy if

breathlessness persists ten minutes after exercise, the heart pounding continues ten minutes later, fatigue remains the following day, or sleep is interrupted.

3. Realistic starting levels should be selected and overwork avoided in early sessions.

4. If the body continues to move after a vigorous endurance repetition, it can slowly return to normal physiological functions without undue bodily stress or muscle cramp.

5. Slight muscular stiffness following early workouts is a normal occurrence; it should not be considered an injury or a reason for a deaccelerated program.

6. Proper rest is essential when one is engaged in a systematic exercise program.

7. During involvement in an exercise program, crash diets such as fasting or use of ergogenic aids should be avoided.

8. Smoking and drinking are both harmful and detrimental to top performance and attainment of peak conditioning levels.

9. Strenuous exercise immediately following an illness should be avoided.

10. Competition in contact sports with those who are much more highly conditioned, or who are of significant different size and weight, should be avoided.

11. Adequate warm-up prior to rigorous activity may prevent injury and improve performance for some individuals.

12. A pre-test such as the 1.5 mile run or 12-minute run to determine your initial conditioning level can be very dangerous for any sedentary individual over 30 years of age who decides to begin an exercise program. One-and-one-half miles is too far to run without a pre-conditioning program tailored just for you.

It is impossible to condition the body in one training session, although this is a common approach for older inactive males. This approach is a leading cause of injury, illness, death, and discontinuance of an exercise program.

DOES GOLF IMPROVE PHYSICAL FITNESS AND THE FUNCTION OF THE HEART?

No. Not all golfers are unfit, but those who are highly conditioned did not get that way by playing golf. Research and expert opinion provide considerable insight into the question of the effects of golf upon heart-lung efficiency, general fitness, or conditioning. The limited demands of golf upon the heart are dramatically emphasized by the work of

Ender,[1] who telemetrically monitored 67 golfers during play before concluding that *most* cardiac patients could play golf without undue risk. No significant changes were found in blood pressure, blood chemistry, or electrocardiogram findings after play. Obviously, there are very few physical restrictions that prevent involvement in golf.

Studies examining the effects of golf upon physical fitness are in general agreement. No appreciable gains are evident after even four to six months of golf three times weekly. Golf does not improve or maintain functioning levels of (1) the heart and circulatory system, (2) the respiratory system, or (3) the muscular system. It will not help prevent heart disease, improve general health and vigor, or raise conditioning levels. Golf is a very challenging recreational sport that can aid mental and emotional health. As played by some Sunday golfers, it is much more likely to cause a heart attack than prevent one.

Slow walking does help circulation and, for the very elderly in particular, this is valuable and may be the only form of exercise permissible. There is also a chance of slight enlargement of the wrists, arms, and shoulders, which is of no practical value to anyone, anywhere except on a golf course.

DOES GOLF HELP YOU LOSE WEIGHT?

As you can see in the chart on page 91 golf has a caloric cost of about 290 per hour for the average 150-pound person. While this expenditure is above that of carpentry, a 2.6-mph walk, shoemaking, driving a car, sweeping, dishwashing, ironing, typing, dressing, sewing, and sitting, it is much inferior to most other sports.

On the other hand, it must be said that three to four hours on the golf course and a caloric expenditure of 870–1,160 calories (over one-quarter pound of fat) is a significant amount for weight watchers. It is far superior to a TV-and-beer afternoon. Nevertheless, it is far inferior to an afternoon of activity in practically any other sport.

WHAT TYPE OF SOUND EXERCISE CHOICES ARE AVAILABLE?

You have two basic choices: the sports approach or a specific exercise program approach. Either method can effectively improve heart-lung efficiency, provide some protection from heart disease and contribute toward weight control and improved physiological functioning of the body.

If you select the sports approach, it is wise to get involved in an activity that is fun and has a high cardiovascular rating. Choose from those evaluated on the chart below and plan to exercise a minimum of four times weekly. Start slow the first 3 to 6 weeks, have fun, and work into more competitive, vigorous competition by choosing more advanced opponents.

BEST AND MAXIMUM AGES FOR COMPETITIVE SPORTS PARTICIPATION

Sport	Cardiovascular fitness value	Best age	Maximum age
Archery	Low	26-28	No limit
Badminton	Moderate	26-28	No limit
Baseball	Low	27-30	40-43
Basketball	High	26-28	40-45
Boxing	Moderate	23-27	34-37
Cycling	High	26-31	No limit
Fencing	Moderate	26-28	No limit
Football	High	23-30	37-40
Golf	Low	30-35	No limit
Gymnastics	Moderate	21-23	34-37
Handball/Squash	Moderate	23-27	No limit
Ice hockey	High	24-29	37-40
Jogging	High	24-29	No limit
Rugby	High	26-31	37-40
Running (cross-country)	High	26-31	No limit
Skiing (cross-country)	High	26-31	No limit
Soccer	High	26-28	37-40
Softball (fast pitch)	Low	26-28	40-45
Softball (slow pitch)	Low	26-28	45-60
Sprinting	Moderate	21-24	32-35
Swimming	High	21-23	34-37
Tennis	Moderate	23-27	No limit
Volleyball	Low	26-28	No limit
Water polo	High	23-27	34-37
Wrestling	High	23-27	34-37

The best and maximum ages are very much individual matters. In fact, there is really no limit or maximum age for participation in practically any sport on a recreational basis—for the individual who has been active throughout life. It is not advisable to start any of the above sports on a vigorous basis at the maximum age if you have been inactive. Your start and finish may closely coincide.

EVALUATION OF EXERCISE PROGRAMS

Characteristics of the Ideal Program	Calisthenics	Canadian 5BX	Circuit Training	Exergenie	Isometric	Weight Training	Running Programs	Sports[b]	Wall Pulleys	Kennedy Adult
Easily adaptable to individual's exercise tolerance	Y	Y	Y	Y	Y	Y	Y	P	P	Y
Applies the progressive resistance principle	Y	Y	Y	Y	Y	Y	Y	P	P	Y
Provides for self-evaluation	P	Y	Y	P	N	Y	Y	P	P	Y
Practical for use throughout life	N	P	P	P	N	P	Y	P	N	P
Scientifically developed	P	Y	Y	Y	Y	Y	Y	—	N	Y
Involves minimum time for users	N	Y	Y	Y	Y	N	Y	N	Y	Y
Involves little or no equipment	Y	Y	Y	N	Y	N	Y	N	N	Y
Performed easily at home	Y	Y	P	Y	P	N	Y	N	N	Y
Widely publicized	N	P	P	P	P	Y	Y	Y	N	P
Accepted and valued	N	P	Y	P	Y	Y	Y	P	N	P
Challenging	N	Y	Y	P	N	Y	Y	Y	N	Y
Limits psychological barriers	N	P	P	P	Y	N	P	P	N	P
Appealing	N	Y	Y	Y	P	Y	Y	Y	N	Y
Develops muscular endurance (anaerobic)	Y	Y	Y	Y	P	Y	Y	Y	Y	Y
Develops cardio-vascular endurance (aerobic)	Y	Y	Y	P	N	P	Y	Y	P	Y
Develops strength	Y	Y	Y	Y	Y	Y	Y	Y	P	Y
Develops explosive power	Y	Y	Y	N	P	Y	P	Y	P	Y
Develops flexibility[a]	Y	Y	Y	P	N	P	P	Y	Y	Y

[a]Flexibility can be improved only if subjects go through the complete range of movement in each exercise, applying static pressure at the extreme range of motion before returning to the starting position.
[b]The value of the sports approach depends upon the activity and the level of competition.

Y = yes, P = partially, N = no provision, U = unknown (referring to meeting ideal characteristics)

From George B. Dintiman and Loyd M. Barrow, *A Comprehensive Manual of Physical Education Activities for Men*. New York: Appleton-Century-Crofts, Inc. 1970. Used by permission.

If you choose to try a specific exercise program, select one that meets most of the characteristics of the ideal program and your specific training objectives from the chart below. For heart-lung development and preventive heart disease, no approach is more valuable than a jogging (8:00 minute mile pace or more) or running (7:59 mile pace or better).

The one best method for improving your physical fitness level has not been developed. It is accurate to say, however, that your choice should place primary emphasis on the development of the heart and lungs through cardiovascular or aerobic training. The primary objective of an aerobic program is to increase the amount of oxygen that can be processed by the body within a given period of time while exercising (maximum oxygen uptake).

HOW CAN I SAFELY START A JOGGING PROGRAM?

Consult your physician for a thorough physical examination and the possible need for a Stress Test (Exercise ECG), particularly if you are over 30 years of age and have been previously inactive. When you get the green light, start in category I on the following chart. Begin easy and slowly improve your conditioning level. Don't rush things. It takes time to improve oxygen consumption so attempts to "get in shape" in one week will not help, except to endanger your health.

If you are under 30 or have been previously active for one year or more, take the 1.5 mile test on a track or measured 1.5 miles on a road. Warm-up with light jogging for 10–20 minutes (walk/jog) before starting. Run the entire distance without stopping and record your time. Find your category on the chart and begin your program. If you have been an active individual, but have not been running previously, be careful. Pace yourself and emphasize finishing the 1.5 mile test rather than setting a track record. Running is one of the most strenuous activities known and over-exertion can be dangerous even to young people. If you have been inactive, skip the 1.5 mile test and begin with category I.

CAN YOU OFFER SUGGESTIONS TO ASSIST IN TRAINING REGULARLY?

Although thousands of people initiate daily exercise programs, the majority eventually disband their efforts long before actual weight loss

TEST	RATING	WEEKS	AEROBIC TRAINING PROGRAM	COMMENT
1.5 Mile Under 30 30–39 40–49 50+	**I. VERY POOR** *Male* 16:00+ 17:00+ 18:00+ 19:00+	INITIAL WORKOUT *Female* 17:00+ 18:00+ 19:00+ 20:00+	On a track, begin running at a comfortable pace until you sense the onset of fatigue (mild). STOP IMMEDIATELY and note distance covered. Walk at an average pace until fatigue symptoms subside. Note the distance walked. Return to running until fatigue symptoms reappear. STOP. Record the total distance covered during the two running phases and one walking phase. This is your first "target." Until you can run this entire distance nonstop, do not add any mileage to your workout.	This is a run/walk workout. Do not overdo it on the first day. After several weeks you should be able to run the target distance nonstop.
		3rd Week	Begin LSD (long-slow-distance) Training—Use a pace that permits a pleasant conversation and causes only mild distress. Continue running nonstop for as long as possible. Rather than walk, slow the pace and attempt to finish the workout pleasantly tired but not exhausted. Do not be concerned about time.	Continue LSD training, add 30 seconds to 1 minute to each workout until you can run nonstop for at least 20 minutes.
		6th Week	Test yourself in the 1.5 mile run on a track. If your category has changed, move on to the program for Rating II. If there was no change, continue LSD training until you can run 30 minutes nonstop.	
1.5 Mile Under 30 30–39 40–49 50+	**II. POOR** *Male* 16:00–14:00 17:00–15:00 18:00–16:00 19:00–17:00	*1st Week* *Female* 17:00–15:00 18:00–16:00 19:00–17:00 20:00–18:00	Use LSD training described above, covering a minimum of 1 mile each workout (nonstop) for several weeks before walk/running 1–2 additional miles at the end of each workout.	Increase the number of weekly workouts to four.
		3rd Week	Begin to time each mile, running at a 9:00* pace for as long a distance as possible. Attempt to achieve two miles in 18:00 or less.	Run a minimum of 6 miles weekly.
		6th Week	Test yourself in the 1.5 mile run, moving to Category III if you qualify. If there was no change, continue LSD train-ing until you can run one mile in 8:45 and two miles in	

III. FAIR

1.5 Mile	Male	Female
Under 30	14:00–12:00	15:00–13:00
30–39	15:00–13:00	16:00–14:00
40–49	16:00–14:00	17:00–15:00
50 +	17:00–14:00	16:00–13:00

1st Week: Continue LSD training at 9:00 pace. — Increase weekly mileage volume to 10–12.

3rd Week: Increase nonstop run to three miles.

6th Week: Retake the 1.5 mile test, moving to Category IV if you qualify. If you do not qualify, continue to increase weekly mileage volume by 2–3 miles.

IV. GOOD

1.5 Mile	Male	Female
Under 30	12:00–10:00	13:00–11:00
30–39	13:00–11:00	14:00–12:00
40–49	14:00–12:00	15:00–12:00
50 +	14:00–12:30	16:00–13:00

1st Week: Adapt the Fartlek Program to your conditioning level. — An alternate method for those in this category is to acquire a minimum of 35 aerobic points weekly (see Chapter VII).

3rd Week: Adjust Fartlek program, attempting to complete the sample workout described in this chapter.

6th Week: Retake the 1.5 mile test, moving to Category V if you qualify. If you do not, continue Fartlek training for two additional weeks.

V. EXCELLENT

1.5 Mile	Male	Female
Under 30	10:00	11:00
30–39	11:00	12:00
40–49	11:30	12:30
50 +	12:00	13:30

Continue with whatever program you have been using if this was your original test category. See Chapter VII and accumulate a minimum of 45 aerobic points weekly (include tennis play in point count). — Increase the number of aerobic points weekly if you want to improve rather than maintain present level.

Take the 1.5 mile test once monthly to judge the success of your maintenance program.

Each workout at all levels begins with a slow one-mile warm-up run/walk and ends with a ¾ to one mile slow warm-down jog.

*Female runners add 1 mile to all times.

or physiological value is attained. For the athlete, this may become a problem in the off-season period.

Even the most ideal exercise program demands three to four weeks of systematic involvement if observable results are to accrue. A strong effort must be made in both diet and exercise habits to avoid early termination before a program becomes an important part of the daily routine. Following are tips for maintaining regularity:

1. Establish an exercise goal in terms of desired outcomes and choose a program most conducive to the attainment of these objectives.
2. Set realistic starting levels well within your physical and psychological limits.
3. Fight off early desire to miss a training session.
4. Set aside a time daily for your program and prevent any type of conflict.
5. Incorporate some method of periodic self-evaluation.
6. Vary your program through alternate activities of a vigorous nature.
7. Follow each session with a warm, then cool shower.
8. Maintain both weight and exercise progress records to ensure a systematic approach and uncover any unusual weight changes.
9. Maintain a balanced diet, secure proper rest, and avoid use of drugs to curb appetite.
10. Do not expect instant results.
11. Consult your physician for a thorough physical examination and the type of program best suited for your age and conditioning level.
12. Alternate hard and easy days. While exercising, if you seem tired, slack off and make it an easy day.

Women in Athletics

Competitive athletics for women has finally received impetus from Olympic sports and from the fact that accurate, factual information is replacing the myths that have retarded their participation for hundreds of years. Even to this day, some parents and girls avoid both competitive and recreational athletics because of unfounded misconceptions. There are still those who oppose athletics for women in any form. This chapter takes a hard look at the sociological, psychological, and physiological effects of participation and responds to the most commonly voiced concerns in the area of women's athletics.

WHEN DID WOMEN FIRST BEGIN TO PARTICIPATE IN SPORTS?

Little reference is made to women in sports until the time of the Greeks, when women exercised under the supervision of female trainers. From the fall of Rome to the Renaissance, sports for women were almost obliterated. During the Renaissance, women again become active, although child rearing was considered their primary function. During the seventeenth century, women engaged in handball, club ball, and archery to set the pattern for participation in only moderately vigorous activities. With the Turnverein movement and the influence of Jahn, father of gymnastics, women became active gymnastic participants. It wasn't until the late 1800's that the United States began to give recognition to women's sports, thus paving the way to programs as they exist today.

Obviously, women did not progress in sports at a rate comparable to men. Tradition, custom, prejudice, and outright ignorance retarded the influence of sport for women. These factors operate today and continue to plague the woman athlete. Biological, sociological, psychological, and philosophic justification is given to keep women in milder forms of sport. There *are* some physiological restrictions requiring concern in some sports for women; however, for the most part, women are capable of full participation in a wide variety of activities.

Women athletes no longer are content to be pushed into a corner. Athletics meet a definite physical and psychological need. The champion women track, swimming, tennis, golf, basketball, softball, and field hockey athletes in action give strong evidence of their physical prowess.

TITLE IX: WHERE ARE WE NOW AND WHAT HAS IT CHANGED?

Title IX is that section of the Educational Amendments Act of 1972 which forbids discrimination on the basis of sex in educational programs or activities in schools receiving federal funds. On July 21, 1975, this regulation officially became law. Secondary schools were given until July 21, 1978, to bring their athletic programs into full compliance with this mandate.

This law requires that each sex have equal opportunity to participate in intramurals and interscholastic programs. The selection of sports, the levels of competition and the interests and abilities of both sexes must receive the same attention. Other areas of importance to be given equal treatment were: provision of equipment and supplies, scheduling of games and practice facilities, publicity, and insurance coverage available to athletes. The regulation, however, does not require equal expenditure or budgets for each athletic team.

According to Dr. Jude Pennington, authority on Title IX problems, female athletes across the nation are making substantial strides because of Title IX. More and more females are becoming active participants in sports. They are achieving a higher skill level. The level of competition has improved drastically. The future for female athletes grows increasingly more favorable.

The impact of Title IX has not been fully realized. Some problem areas remain. The majority of those people affected by the law agree that passage of Title IX was necessary if females were to share a rightful place in the athletic world.

WHAT TYPE OF WOMAN IS ATTRACTED TO ATHLETICS?

Personality profiles of female athletes are surprisingly similar from sport to sport. This is not true for the male athlete. In general, the female athlete and physical educator is happy-go-lucky, extroverted, sociable, and anxiety prone. World class tennis champions differ somewhat from these traits, tending to be more adventurous, troubled, depressed, anxious, introverted, emotionally sensitive, and less confident.

With age, female athletes become increasingly similar to each other in personality traits.

There is not much evidence to show whether girls with these personality traits are attracted to athletics or whether athletics develop these personality traits. Both factors appear responsible. One thing is certain: the female athlete is a likable individual who can adapt to practically any social setting. You can't go wrong if some of these traits rub off.

IS IT TRUE THAT PARTICIPATION IN ATHLETICS MAKES WOMEN LESS FEMININE?

No. This is another myth that continues to flourish in the minds of many mothers and daughters throughout the world. Girls also worry about exercise increasing their growth rate, muscle bulk, and weight, and about becoming masculine after leaving competition. There is no evidence to support any of these beliefs.

If a program of exercise is designed correctly, it will *improve* femininity. Gymnastics, swimming, hockey, basketball, and racket games in no way tend to develop superior strength even in men. Attend a gymnastics meet in any school to convince yourself of this fact. In practically all women competitors, a high level of femininity and grace is evident. It is also interesting to note that the 1969 Miss America winner majored in Physical Education and was a very athletically skilled woman.

Some female athletes are muscular. This is most often observed in track and field; however, muscular women are more likely to succeed in this sport and are thus attracted to it. It is doubtful that running and jumping events or the training routines required for this competition can alter feminine qualities.

Don't avoid the wonderful experience of athletic competition for women because of unfounded claims.

DOES PARTICIPATION IN ATHLETICS DECREASE DATING OPPORTUNITIES?

Definitely not. In fact, one questionnaire study went directly to the woman athlete for the answer. Nearly one-half of the women felt that dating opportunities were actually enhanced. Approximately 40 percent felt that it made no difference, while only 10 percent indicated that chances were reduced.

Ogden Nash's quote that "Men do not make passes at athletic lasses" is hogwash. A feminine girl with a pleasant personality is quite popular regardless of her sports interests.

WHY ARE RUSSIA'S WOMEN TRACK AND FIELD ATHLETES SUPERIOR TO U.S. WOMEN?

The answer is very simple. Russian women athletes are respected and undergo highly organized, long-term training programs with excellent instruction and training routines. The United States, on the other hand, does not emphasize women's athletics. We expect our women to defeat the Russians and even criticize them for losing, but we do not provide them with the same kind of opportunities to develop their athletic talent.

Track and field for women in high school and college is grossly lacking. Only a few schools have organized programs, give girls equal opportunity to use institutional facilities, or offer coaching to girls. Thus, potential super track athletes are often never identified. For those who are identified as having high potential, it is an uphill climb to secure invitations to top caliber meets to develop their talent. Track clubs for girls are springing up in some parts of the country. Thousands more are desperately needed to allow women athletes to continue training into their thirties. Russian women athletes are approximately six to seven years older than the American women who compete in Olympic competition. Obviously, it requires a number of years of training in various events to reach maximum potential. In 1952, less than 50 percent of the countries represented in the Olympics even bothered to send women competitors.

As one critic puts it, "The only competition we're giving our modern female is the kind she finds in the back seat of a car."

Obviously, something must be done at all levels (elementary, junior-senior high school, college-university, track clubs) if our women are to develop athletic talent to the fullest.

WHAT PRECAUTIONS SHOULD BE TAKEN BY THE POTENTIAL WOMAN ATHLETE?

Women should follow the excellent practice of the male athlete and subject themselves to a thorough physical examination followed by periodic checkups. Routine items include: blood pressure, pulse rate and response to exercise, blood count, urinalysis, and skeletal examination. Women also are advised to have a pelvic examination to uncover such abnormalities as general prolapse (falling down or slipping of the uterus), ovarian cysts, vaginal discharge, or pruritus (itching).

After you get the green light from your physician, few additional precautions are necessary. You may participate in practically any form of activity and training that is conducted in a sane, organized manner.

WITH PROPER TRAINING CAN WOMEN PERFORM AS WELL AS MEN IN ATHLETICS?

No. It is true that women have only recently begun to receive expert coaching in track and field and other sports. Although this new type of training will greatly improve performance, women will never be men's equal in athletics. Why? After puberty, there are numerous physiological differences between the sexes. Let's examine those that limit women's performance in athletics:

1. The ratio of strength to body weight is much greater in men; women possess a greater proportion of fatty tissue.
2. The chemical makeup of muscle tissue is different in women.
3. The ratio of heart weight to body weight is about 85 percent less for women.
4. The oxygen-carrying capacity of the blood is less for women.
5. The female is more susceptible to bruises.
6. The anaerobic capacity (ability to sprint at maximum speed for extended distances) and maximum oxygen consumption is less in women.
7. The tolerance to hot environment is less in women.

What does all this mean? Mainly, that a woman is much less responsive to training (progressing at about 50 percent the rate of men). It also means that physical limitations place considerable restrictions on performance in relation to that of men.

IN WHAT ATHLETIC AREAS ARE WOMEN SUPERIOR TO MEN?

In skill execution, women possess greater manual dexterity than men. Unless strength and endurance are involved, women have as great a skill-learning rate and capacity as men. Also, reaction time (time elapse from the sight or sound of a stimulus and the first muscular movement) is similar in both sexes. Women have greater buoyancy than men because of a greater portion of fatty tissue in the body. This is advantageous in swimming, requiring less effort to stay afloat, and may partially account for the tremendous success of young female swimmers. In the areas of grace and beauty of movement, so important to competitive gymnastics, women have a definite edge.

There is an age when girls are superior to boys in numerous areas, since girls mature somewhat earlier. However, by age 12–14, girls have neared their peak performance level in endurance and power-type activities. Boys, on the other hand, continue to progress beyond the level of girls until they reach their peak in late high school or college.

It becomes evident that women come closer to being able to compete with men in areas where strength and power are not overly important.

SHOULD WOMEN ATHLETES TRAIN WITH WEIGHTS?

Yes. There is no reason to be afraid of muscle. In fact, the lack of strength is the main limiting factor for women in many sports. Women possess a much heavier layer of fatty tissue than men. They also possess less muscle mass. To overcome these disadvantages, some form of strength training is needed. No program is more effective than weight training.

Weight training is not too dangerous for women. Nor will it produce an Amazon or detract from feminine appearance. It will (1) improve strength, endurance, and tone, (2) firm sagging areas, (3) reapportion various areas, (4) strengthen weak areas, (5) improve general conditioning, (6) improve appearance, (7) improve posture, and (8) improve athletic efficiency in most sports.

In sports where strength and explosive power are critical (basketball, field hockey, tennis, badminton, track and field, swimming, volleyball, for example) weight training is absolutely necessary for high-level performance. No male athlete, in spite of the fact that he is endowed with much more strength, would consider eliminating weights from his program.

Weight training for women is becoming increasingly popular in physical education and athletics. It has been used for years in the development of beauty pageant contestants and the figures of Hollywood actresses. As someone once put it, "No woman can be pretty as a picture if her frame is bent."

ARE WOMEN MORE SUSCEPTIBLE TO INJURIES IN ATHLETICS THAN MEN?

Yes. This is true although women do not normally participate in contact sports. Women possess a greater proportion of fatty tissue, have a lower ratio of strength to body weight, and are more delicate in almost all areas such as bones, muscles, tendons, and ligaments. Women are four times more likely than men to suffer injuries from mere overstrain.

Injuries are most common in sports that demand an explosive action. Sprinting, the long and high jump, shot put and discus, basketball, and field hockey are likely to result in numerous injuries from overstrain.

A woman's best protection from injury is adequate conditioning. At least the risk of serious injury in women's athletics is low. Minor strains are easier to treat, recovery time is more rapid, and prevention through specialized conditioning programs is possible. Such programs would attempt to improve the strength of the supporting muscles in critical areas: ankle, knee, shoulder, and neck.

SHOULD WOMEN CONTINUE TO EXERCISE OR COMPETE DURING THEIR MENSTRUAL PERIOD?

Yes. There is no evidence to show that this practice is harmful. Champion female athletes rarely alter their training program for the menstrual cycle. Use your own judgment based upon how you feel. Some women may be unable to continue in the normal exercise routine and others may be unaffected. Several researchers did find that performance was at its peak in the *post*-menstrual phase, at a lower level *during* menstruation, and at its lowest two to three days *prior* to menstruation. However, several other researchers disagree, having failed to find a decrease in performance during any phase. Evidence is obviously conflicting and inconclusive.

It is good practice to avoid swimming because of the presence of pathogenic bacteria in the vagina.

A regular menstruation is a sign of good health and any variation could indicate overtraining. Consult your coach or physician if irregularities occur and alter your program accordingly.

Do not stop exercise or training completely during menstruation. Loss of five or more days will definitely lower your performance and conditioning level. An iron supplement may also be helpful. If you are unable to continue in a normal routine, embark on a minimum level of exercise to maintain your present conditioning level. Your coach will help you to plan such a program.

DOES EXERCISE HELP RELIEVE PAINFUL MENSTRUATION?

Yes. Painful menstruation, referred to as *dysmenorrhea,* generally occurs in younger, unmarried girls whose cycles have not yet stabilized or become regular. Dysmenorrhea may be either *primary* (no organic cause) or *secondary* (caused by another ailment such as inflammation of a turned uterus). Only competent medical attention will cure the secondary type.

Primary dysmenorrhea is relieved and may even be prevented by following certain suggestions:

1. Exercise regularly to improve both your physical and emotional state. Active women are less apt to suffer from painful menstruation. In addition to regular activity associated with a sport, the exercises described below may help.

   Exercise 1: Stand an arm's length from a wall with one hand on your hips and the other against the wall. Push your abdomen forward as far as possible before rotating to the right, back, and to the left to complete a circular motion.

   Exercise 2: Lie on your back with the knees bent and drawn slightly upward toward your trunk. Place both hands over the stomach area. Now, tighten the abdomen, push up the pelvis, and relax to complete a 3-count exercise.

   Exercise 3: Place your head in crossed forearms on the floor while in a kneeling position. Contract the stomach muscles, hold for 3 seconds, and relax.

2. Restrict your fluid and salt intake one week prior to expected menstruation.
3. Get adequate rest and avoid nervous tension just prior to expected menstruation.
4. Avoid aspirin, since large amounts may increase the flow.
5. Hot coffee or tea or small quantities of whiskey or brandy may help.

IS IT PERMISSIBLE AND HELPFUL TO ALTER THE MENSTRUAL CYCLE TO IMPROVE PERFORMANCE?

Use of hormones can influence the menstrual cycle and would not be considered unethical conduct or "doping," since the hormone would not improve performance except by eliminating the possible psychological and physiological disadvantages of the premenstrual phase.

The value of adjusting the cycle to a competitive schedule may depend upon the individual. Performance is most likely to be reduced in the premenstrual phase (the two or three days before) due to hormonal changes. Altering this phase *could* prevent a decrease in performance.

WHAT METHOD OF MENSTRUAL PROTECTION IS THE MOST DESIRABLE FOR THE FEMALE ATHLETE?

Either external pads or internal tampons are adequate. Female athletes tend to prefer an intravaginal tampon since it is superior from a standpoint of aesthetics, comfort, and freedom of movement. The tampon is definitely superior for swimmers, offering optimum protection from pool contamination.

HOW DOES ATHLETIC ACTIVITY AFFECT CHILDBIRTH BEFORE AND AFTER DELIVERY?

During *pregnancy,* there is no need to discontinue participation in sports. It is a fact that exercise increases the work of the right section of the heart two times. During pregnancy, such demands, when coupled with work of fetal circulation, should not be harmful to most women. The kidneys and liver also function with very little reserve capacity due to the increased demands of pregnancy. Again, for a woman who has been accustomed to regular exercise, this imposes no health hazard. Exercise is an important aspect of the daily routine of pregnant women. Only contact sports (basketball, field hockey, lacrosse, etc.) and dangerous recreational activities should be avoided (mountain or cliff climbing, back packing). In addition, it is not the time to initiate a new exercise program, other than walking and light jogging, if one has been previously sedentary.

Delivery has been shown to be rather quick and easy with athletic women, relatively free from complications, and necessitates 50 percent fewer Caesarian sections. Good physical condition before pregnancy is a real asset to the expectant mother.

Childbirth does not hinder future athletic performance. In fact, of ten women athletes who had borne children during their careers, all felt that they were stronger and had more endurance after childbirth.

DOES THE USE OF BIRTH CONTROL PILLS IN THE FEMALE AFFECT ATHLETIC PERFORMANCE?

There is no evidence of decreased or increased performance. The pill is helpful in treating painful menstruation, as well as irregular and excessive flow. The side effects may interfere with training—nausea, weight gain, intermenstrual bleeding, mood changes, breast swelling and tenderness—but these symptoms usually disappear after a few months of use.

It does not appear that strength, speed, endurance, coordination, or explosive power are altered through use of this type of pill.

DOES THE USE OF THE MALE SEX HORMONE IMPROVE PERFORMANCE IN WOMEN?

Although there is almost no available literature on this subject, two things are evident: (1) male hormones are used by some female athletes, and (2) use of male hormones does improve performance in women.

It appears that the male sex hormone aids women in overcoming some of the physiological differences between the sexes—mainly, the ratio of strength to body weight (fat to muscle) and of heart weight to body weight.

There is one problem associated with use of the male hormone. Women begin to develop secondary sex characteristics as well as changes in voice, facial hair, and chest hair. For these and other reasons, its use is not recommended and is disallowed at all levels of competition. If you are considering their use, nothing will change your mind like a coarse, black beard.

HOW CAN WE BE SURE THAT OLYMPIC WOMEN ATHLETES ARE REALLY WOMEN?

There is one fast check that is 100 percent accurate, but the International Olympic Committee won't allow "panty checks."

Men do and have competed under the cloak of womanhood. Hormone-injected women can also change from a feminine appearance to that of a hairy male. The Olympic Committee has recognized the problem and has used a required "sex test" at the games since 1972.

1. Cells scraped from the gums of female athletes (saliva test) are analyzed under a 1,200-power microscope. An athlete with 20 to 60 percent of the cells revealing a distinctive extra dot is declared a lady; others are considered impostors. The test takes 20 minutes and can be followed by a more time-consuming hormone test should doubt exist.
2. The cells in the root of a single hair from any body part can also be examined to determine sex.

HOW COMMON ARE BREAST INJURIES IN ATHLETICS?

Very few injuries to the female breast occur in athletics. This may be due to the noncontact nature of most sports engaged in by women.

The female breast varies greatly in size during various stages of development. Large breasts are more susceptible to injury. When an injury occurs from a contusion, a hard nodule of fibrous tissue generally forms in the fatty tissue and may remain for years. This nodule is distinguished from cancer only by removal of a specimen, and such a test is advisable in order to avoid confusion in the future.

Fencing, paddle ball, squash, field hockey, team handball, basketball, and wrestling are a few sports demanding use of a protective brassiere. In fact, special protective cups are recommended for female participants in all sports.

CAN VIGOROUS RUNNING AND JUMPING EVENTS PERMANENTLY HARM THE DEVELOPMENT OF THE FEMALE REPRODUCTIVE ORGANS?

This is a difficult question to answer with a yes or no. Additional research is desperately needed. The uterus was one area that experts believed could be harmed by such exercise. It is protected by a water cushion and literally floats alone in a pool of pelvic viscera similar to the human brain. The truth is, however, that this water cushion protection is almost infallible. A violent blow to the body or violent jarring does not cause a similar jolt to the uterus.

Vigorous exercise is essential to proper growth and development. There is, at present, no evidence to suggest that a healthy female of any age can be harmed from vigorous exercise.

Contact sports for women should be avoided until more conclusive evidence is available. Other sports are a healthful, important part of life and should be enjoyed by all females who care to reap the benefits.

Specific Training Programs

A wide variety of training programs are being used in athletics to improve general conditioning levels, skill, and performance. Some of these programs have little application to specific sports, while others are very effective. All programs need special control in devising training routines that simulate the athletic movements and demands of the sport. This chapter covers all areas for agility training, endurance training (muscular and heart-lung), explosive power training, flexibility training, and strength training through a variety of specific programs. Sample programs of college and professional teams in various sports are presented. Attention is given to all aspects of training for practically any sport or purpose, along with proper steps in tailoring a program to your individual needs, goals, and abilities.

WHAT IS MEANT BY A "CRITICAL THRESHOLD" IN ATHLETIC CONDITIONING?

Many individuals feel that moderately vigorous activities are effective in improving their conditioning level. They are greatly mistaken. Walking, golf, bowling, slow jogging, and mild workouts of any type do little to develop heart and lung efficiency (cardiovascular/respiratory endurance).

Heart efficiency has been found to increase by attaining a "critical threshold" in raising the number of heart beats per minute, through exercise. A critical threshold is a heart rate approximately 60 percent of the distance between the resting and the maximum heart rates. For an individual with a resting heart rate of 60 and a maximum of 190, the critical threshold is 138 beats per minute if good results are to be obtained.

Training must therefore take the form of very strenuous walking, bicycle riding, distance running, bench stepping, rope skipping, or vigorous exercises if the heart, blood vessels, and lungs are to respond. Intensified exercises with limited and gradually decreasing periods of rest between repetitions are capable of developing these systems.

There is strong argument for distance running and repetitive sprinting becoming a part of the training routine in any sport. Don't be fooled by the fallacy that improvement occurs without hard work. It does not.

WHAT IS MEANT BY SPECIFICITY OF TRAINING?

This phrase merely implies that training is unique to an activity or sport. In other words, football or soccer players who have just completed their seasons will find that they are not capable of meeting the physical demands of wrestling or basketball. A transitional period will be needed before maximum efficiency is reached in the new sport. This principle can be observed in well-trained athletes attempting to make the transition from one sport to another.

The scientific basis for this principle is that training occurs, in part, within the muscles themselves, and training is specific in terms of lactic acid production during heavy muscular work. Thus, *complete* training transfer, regardless of the closeness of the activities, is not possible.

Even sprinting speed is specific to the body area or muscle groups used. You may possess high leg velocity and slow arm velocity or be fast in one muscle and slow in another. Speed is about 86 percent specific to the limb.

It is obvious that a high level of conditioning acquired in one sport does not necessarily carry over to another. Exercise programs must stimulate movements of the activity for which training is designed. You cannot improve speed by doing push-ups, nor will sit-ups help you jump higher. If you use any type of exercise program in the off-season (weight training, isometrics, calisthenics, and so on), be certain that you combine this with drills and movements used in your sport.

WHAT IS THE OVERLOAD PRINCIPLE?

For the development of strength and endurance, each person has an "optimal load," or a minimum exercise load needed to produce results. Suppose, for example, this optimal load for improving strength in the bicep muscles (front of upper arm) is five repetitions of the curl using 60 pounds on the barbell. Using less than 60 pounds is termed an "underload" and would not increase strength. Using 70, 80, or 90 pounds represents an "overload" and results in the greatest strength gain.

Your optimal load for strength training and local muscular endurance work is approximately 60 percent of your maximum. Actually, the closer you work to your maximum load, the greater the strength gains.

DO ATHLETES PROGRESS AT THE SAME RATE FROM TRAINING?

No. Responses to training are unique to the individual. Thus, one program will produce varying degrees of development for two or more subjects. Determining factors include body type, conditioning level, activity experience, physical-psychological interrelationship, and a host of additional factors that affect learning in general. Correct form or style of performing various skills will also differ from one athlete to another. Although basic principles underlie performance in most cases, unnecessary *patterning* or copying the form of champions is not always advisable.

Women's progress is about 50 percent that of men from the same training routines.

WHAT IS THE CONCEPT OF WORK HYPERTROPHY?

You will not progress automatically and may not improve your conditioning level at all unless you are careful. For the best protection, consult with your coach and jointly plan a program for the off-season aimed at your weaknesses.

Improvement in any area (speed, strength, flexibility, explosive power, agility, endurance, reaction time), regardless of the exercise program used, depends upon what is called the *concept of work hypertrophy*. Don't let the terminology scare you. It merely means that you must do more work tomorrow—*per unit of time*—than you did today. Running four 440-yard dashes with a four-minute rest interval today and repeating this workout tomorrow with ten-minute rest intervals is not more work. Let's examine this concept further. When you begin training, you are at a certain conditioning level. Your first workout destroys muscle tissue and actually lowers this level at the workout's end. However, at this point, nature goes to work and regenerates tissue, rebuilding the body to a point higher than that before the initial workout began. It is similar to nature's reaction to a man's hands after shoveling the first winter snow. Calluses form within a short time to toughen the hands in preparation for more vigorous shoveling. On the second workout day, you are equipped to perform more exercise than before and, to continue to apply this concept, you *must* perform more work each day so that nature again rebuilds the body beyond the level of the previous workout.

Does it sound complicated? It isn't. There are only a few principles to remember in order to apply the work hypertrophy concept:

1. Exercise must be intense enough to destroy tissue—nature's rebuilding process is somewhat in proportion to this intensity.
2. The second, third, fourth, etc. workout must take place without too much recovery time between workouts (24–48 hours). Allowing more time than this will result in a lower conditioning level.
3. Enough recovery time must be allowed for rebuilding to take place. If you exercise before full recovery occurs, you defeat your purpose. Some coaches and athletes make this mistake with double training sessions. Unless one session is conditioning oriented and the other devoted to skill development with minimum exercise, the conditioning value is limited and may actually slow down physical improvement in a sport.
4. Each workout should be progressively more strenuous than the previous.

Think through this concept. Apply it to your training program by recording daily workout sessions. Compare one workout to another. Set work goals and systematically train to reach them. Your physical punishment will be rewarded.

WHAT OTHER PRINCIPLES OF CONDITIONING SHOULD BE KNOWN TO THE ATHLETE?

Principle of Overcompensation. Vigorous exercise destroys muscle constituents. As lost materials and muscle fuel are replaced, nature overcompensates in preparation for more strenuous efforts; the result being increased strength or capacity to perform work. The degree of overcompensation is in direct proportion to the severity of the exercise. This principle also forms the basis upon which a callus on the foot or hand develops following early season play that removes superficial skin layers. The principle of overcompensation is the physiological explanation for the concept of work hypertrophy.

Principle of Progressive Resistance Exercise. Muscles must be exercised against a gradually increasing resistance. Increased loads (overload) beyond the demands regularly made on the body determine the ultimate effectiveness of an exercise program. This principle is applied by increasing the resistance to be overcome, the number of repetitions, the speed of movement, the duration of a training session, decreasing the rest interval and through a combination of the preceding. The nearer a muscle is worked to maximum capacity, the greater the strength gain. A training program must therefore provide gradual progression in terms of increased load. Progressing too fast in any sport (increasing running mileage more than 10 percent monthly, for example) can lead to injury and decreased performance.

Principle of Intensity, Duration, and Frequency (alternate hard and light workouts). There are no short cuts to improving conditioning. Fifteen minute programs, vibrators, mechanical devices, and others vary from very slightly effective to worthless. Your first concern is to alternate hard and easy workout days. The body needs time to recover (see principle of work hypertrophy) and conditioning will not steadily improve with consecutive hard workouts. For most sports, you should train 5–7 times weekly for 1½ to 3 hours, alternating hard and light days.

Principle of Warm-up. See pages 17–19.

Principle of Warm-down. See page 19–20.

DO CONDITIONING LEVELS CONTINUE TO IMPROVE THROUGHOUT AN ATHLETIC SEASON?

No. Although you should slowly improve, this is not the case. In fact, by "Super Bowl Sunday" it is estimated that players are functioning at about 65 to 70 percent of their early season efficiency. Numerous factors account for this: (1) injuries and loss of practice and playing time, (2) a change to less rigorous practice routines that emphasize strategy and the expected action of opponents, (3) rigorous travel schedules, and (4) lack of a systematic maintenance program for strength, general endurance, and sprinting speed.

For athletes in most team sports, maintenance programs are essential. One weight-training session weekly using near maximum lifts will help to maintain the strength acquired in the preseason. Speed and endurance will also decrease unless time is set aside two or three times weekly for the purpose of maintaining levels in these areas. The body is tremendously adaptable. Whether its powers diminish or increase depends upon you. Only by progressively increasing the demands on the body will improvement occur or powers remain at the same level. There just is no magic potion or easy method other than hard work.

ISN'T THERE ALWAYS THE POSSIBILITY OF OVERTRAINING?

Yes. Athletes sometimes complain that they are no longer improving in spite of the fact that training has been continuous. Once you are certain that this plateau or deterioration is not due to some physical factor (injury, disease, diet, lack of rest, unsuitable living), you should then consider overtraining as a possibility.

The term "chronic fatigue" may also be used to describe this condition. Chronic fatigue or staleness is definitely a source of difficulty for the athlete; however, it is generally not a result of strenuous training and does not always require a lightening of exercise loads. According to one expert, the symptoms of staleness are: (1) constant complaints of undue tiredness, (2) difficulty in sleeping, (3) bad temper and irritability, (4) loss of appetite, (5) loss of enthusiasm and drive, (6) lack of concentration, (7) listlessness, (8) constant complaints of trivial aches and pains, usually in joints and muscles, (9) inability to make target times where previous times were satisfactory, and (10) small but sustained weight loss.[1] Research has shown that chronic fatigue is generally caused by emotional and situational factors rather than physiological factors.[2] Maladjustment, lack of sleep, and worry are common causes and should be the focus of treatment when planning alterations in training to correct this emotional-situational state. Attempts to alleviate staleness or chronic fatigue may involve: (1) temporary suspension of training, (2) coach-player discussion of underlying causes, (3) an attempt to eliminate underlying emotional causes, (4) change in training routine through use of a wide variety of drills and activities in each workout, (5) proper use of motivational devices of various types, and (6) medical examination. Also, be certain never to train hard on two consecutive days; alternate hard and light days in your sport to ensure full recovery from one workout to the next.

IS IT NECESSARY TO TAPER OFF AT THE END OF THE WEEK, ALLOWING A DAY OF REST BEFORE A CONTEST?

Yes, this is desirable for two reasons: (1) maximum filling of the body's nutrition stores occurs which will provide the fuel and energy for competition, and (2) complete recovery and repair of the body is needed; a 24–48-hour period of rest will allow this to take place only if tissue destruction through activity is called to a halt.

For a Saturday contest, Wednesday should be the final heavy workout day, followed by a light workout Thursday and possible rest on Friday. For the "super bowl" of your sport, it is advisable to begin to taper off two weeks in advance.

SHOULD I TRAIN HARD EVERY DAY EXCEPT THE DAY BEFORE COMPETITION?

No. Although it does depend on the sport, the following rules for runners can be applied to other training programs:

1. Do your stretching exercises at the beginning of every workout.
2. Alternate hard and easy days; never train super-hard on consecutive days.
3. Train hard no more than three times weekly.
4. Schedule one extra hard, all-out workout once weekly; include a maximum effort session (discussed later in this chapter) in the all-out workout.
5. Know your body and allow it to direct you; if pain continues or worsens or you get heavy-legged, stop, regardless of whether it is a light or heavy day.

WHAT IS THE BEST METHOD OF IMPROVING ACCURACY OR SKILL IN ANY SPORT?

Obviously, the single best method of improving pitching accuracy, basketball shooting accuracy, quarterback passing, soccer kicking activity, and so forth is continuous practice "with the intent to improve." Research strongly shows that repeated practice or training (repeated work with instruction) improves performance in any motor task.

Self-analysis, concentration on weakness areas, analysis by coaches, and long hours of work after practice will eventually lead to higher performance levels. Normally, practice sessions are not long enough, nor are they organized for a high degree of skill development. There is too much other material associated with the sport to be learned, such as complicated defensive and offensive systems, strategy, and the behavior of opponents.

Keep in mind that this is a learned phenomenon. Precision passing in football and excellent shooting in basketball, for example, are not automatic to anyone. These and other skills evolve from repetitive practice. Start with one extra hour per day devoted to improvement of a particular skill. Be systematic and analyze your difficulties before correcting or altering form. Follow this procedure for a minimum of three to four *months*—the results will shock you. Instant improvement has still not been put in a can; however, long-term programs are successful. Ask some of the pros in your sport who have made it; they too have been through this procedure.

HOW IMPORTANT IS AGILITY IN SPORTS?

Maneuverability, or rapid change of direction with minimum loss of acceleration, is an important action in major sports competition. A positive relationship exists between the ability to move quickly and athletic success. Agility involves upsetting equilibrium in the direction of movement by placing one foot ahead of the center of gravity and leaning away from the original direction of motion. A forceful push-off with the plant foot initiates movement in the new direction while maintaining acceleration.

Agility can be improved through a number of approaches, including weight-training programs, trampoline training, isometric training, and agility drills that simulate desired changes of direction in a particular sport. Practically all football coaches use agility drills and are continuously seeking new, more effective approaches. Obviously, you must be capable of controlling your own body before you can be expected to control an opponent.

HOW CAN I IMPROVE MY JUMPING ABILITY?

The question is, how can explosive power or the ability to exert a fast, maximum force against resistance in a minimum time (amount of work per unit of time) best be improved. The term *quickness* often used in basketball, football, baseball, soccer, and track is often confused with *explosive power*. The speed at which the body is propelled in any direction or the rapid movement of a hand or foot should be referred to as explosive power. Jumping vertically into the air to rebound a missed shot, the running broad jump, or a rapid start from a stationary position are all explosive movements. Thus, an individual who moves 120 pounds a distance of 10 feet in five seconds has exerted three times the power of an individual who requires fifteen seconds to move the weight this distance.

Attempts to improve explosive power have centered around training programs designed to develop strength and speed, since these factors are largely responsible for the body's initiating a rapid, vigorous movement from a stationary position. Vertical jumping ability has been shown to increase significantly following use of ankle spats on each foot, maximum height trampoline jumping, and weight training. Vertical jumping ability has also been shown to increase 3–6 inches following brief weight-training programs. Greater gains are possible with continued devotion to a sound program. Even a 3–6-inch gain for every member of a basketball team could be a deciding factor in many games.

IS THERE ANYTHING A RUNNER CAN DO TO IMPROVE CUTTING AND FAKING SKILL?

Yes. This is another neglected area that receives very little attention in athletics.

First, let's examine the purpose of a fake. In order of importance, a fake serves to:

1. Neutralize the defender by slowing his movement, breaking his concentration, altering his center of gravity, delaying his total commitment, and placing doubt in his mind.
2. Change the direction of movement of the defender away from your intended move.
3. Draw the defender closer to you so that a cut is effective (cutting must occur 2–3 yards from the defender, therefore, a fake "straight-ahead" break will draw him within proper distance).

Keep in mind that you fake, first to neutralize, second to go by untouched. Any fake will help neutralize, and any fake is better than no fake at all.

You must practice all types of head, shoulder, and leg fakes daily to develop the proper skill. These basic cuts must also be mastered:

1. *Single cut.* Angle away from the defender to force his commitment before planting the outside foot and cutting in the opposite direction.
2. *Double cut.* Run at the opponent before planting the left foot and breaking right, only to plant that foot also and return left to go by the defender. The first cut will neutralize, the second will draw, and the third will be one he'll only be able to watch.

Once these two basic cuts are mastered in various situations at maximum speed, you can advance to more complicated faking.

WHAT GENERAL CONDITIONING STANDARDS SHOULD BE MAINTAINED IN THE OFF-SEASON?

Since the off-season period should be used to improve skill or physical weakness areas, a general standard is often not maintained. This is obviously a mistake. Regardless of the sport for which you are preparing, the following standards require a high degree of cardiovascular/respiratory endurance which is common to most activities:

Four-Minute Mile: Any of the programs below or any combination may be used.

1. 4 × 440 yards: 60 seconds
                    4-minute rest interval between each
2. 2 × 440 yards: 60 seconds
                    4-minute rest interval
   4 × 220 yards: 30 seconds
                    2-minute rest interval
3. 8 × 220 yards: 30 seconds
                    2-minute rest interval
4. 2 × 880 yards: 120 seconds
                    8-minute rest interval

Twelve-Minute Mile Test: Run around a one-fourth mile track for 12 minutes, noting distance covered at the end of this period.

1¾ miles:	Target for athletes of all weights and heights
1½–1¾ miles:	Good; however, low for athletes
1½–1¾ miles:	Poor for any sport
1–1¼ miles	Very poor

Six-Minute Mile: Complete one mile within six minutes.

Report to the first practice session of your sport capable of meeting the above standards and you'll be noticed.

ARE CALISTHENICS OF ANY VALUE TO THE ATHLETE?

As performed by many, they are a useless form of conditioning that only serves to bore athletes and bring about a dislike for exercise. Calisthenics, like any exercise program, require careful planning to ensure progression and maximum value. Let's discuss only the *proper* use of one of the oldest forms of conditioning in existence.

Exercises such as sit-ups, toe touchers, trunk rotation, jumping jacks, push-ups, and a wide variety of others must be performed with a high number of repetitions since the resistance (body weight) is relatively low. Since resistance also remains constant, the number of repetitions must be gradually increased, the rest interval between exercises decreased, the speed or rate of execution increased, and the duration of the workout increased. Use of weighted vests (ankle, back) or an exercise partner can alter the resistance variable and thus further develop strength.

Exercises must be carefully chosen to activate the major muscle groups and must involve endurance-type work to stimulate and develop the heart and lungs. A properly conceived program can yield significant changes in strength, endurance, flexibility, agility, and reaction time. The obvious *disadvantages* are boredom and lack of diversity. Additional principles affecting the administration of calisthenic programs include the following:

1. Exercises should be performed to the full range of motion with exact form of execution enforced.
2. Little or no rest should be provided between exercises. Exercises should alternately activate muscle groups to permit continuous performance.
3. All body areas should be taxed for general development.
4. General stretching exercises may be needed prior to vigorous calisthenics.
5. One maximum-effort exercise should be incorporated daily.
6. The program should be designed to tax the major muscle groups for which training is designed.
7. Progression is attained by selecting a realistic starting level such as performing all 2-count exercises for 8 repetitions and all 4-count exercises for four repetitions. The number of repetitions is gradually increased with a target of 36 repetitions for 2-count exercises and 18 repetitions for 4-count exercises. The maximum-effort drills are personalized and allow individuals to perform at their level of conditioning. Additional personalized items should be added as the level of conditioning increases.

Unless these principles are followed, calisthenics will not aid in raising your general conditioning level. Nor will it develop strength, explosive power, or flexibility. On the other hand, a carefully designed program of rapid, explosive, continuous movements will take up little time (12–15 minutes) and will yield great physical benefits. No program is of any value without your cooperation and hard work.

IS ENDURANCE TRAINING NEEDED IN MOST SPORTS?

Yes. In fact, a relatively high degree of cardiovascular/respiratory and local muscular endurance is necessary for the majority of team and invidual sports.

Local muscular endurance is best attained through prolonged duration under less resistance. The work load or resistance is not as important as a short rest interval (time between each repetition and set or bout). High work loads are possible if broken up into repetitions of shorter duration with a timed rest interval (slowly being lowered) between each repetition.

Cardiovascular and cardiorespiratory endurance training may take the form of strenuous walking, bicycle riding, distance running, bench stepping, rope skipping, running in place, or similar means if the heart, blood vessels, and lungs are to respond. Intensified exercise with limited and gradually decreasing periods of rest between repetitions of a strenuous exercise are capable of producing heavy breathing and increased heart demands with repeated work.

Approximately once weekly, a coach should time each athlete at two-thirds his racing distance. When this pace is applied to the full racing distance, simple mathematics and comparison of times can reveal conditioning levels or drop-off.

WHAT TYPE OF FLEXIBILITY EXERCISES SHOULD BE USED IN ATHLETIC TRAINING?

Flexibility training (stretching exercises) is a common aspect of the general conditioning program in major sports. In the improvement of performance it serves to:

1. Increase stride length.
2. Permit free arm movement in sprinting, through improved shoulder flexibility.
3. Limit internal muscle resistance.
4. Assist in the prevention of muscle injuries when fast limb action is involved.
5. Limit energy expenditure.
6. Prevent muscle shortening when used following heavy-resistance exercise.
7. Improve the harmony between the antagonistic or relaxing muscles and the agonistic or contracting muscles in the movement specific to sprinting, or the movements in your sport.

Flexibility training in athletics should concentrate on *ankle flexion* and *extension, hip flexion* and *extension, shoulder flexibility,* and hamstring (back of upper leg) and calf muscle (back of lower leg) stretching and involve static procedures with no bouncing and little movement.

Flexibility exercises should be performed early in the workout, prior to more vigorous activity, and should always follow a weight-training or other heavy-resistance workout.

In each static exercise, as much force as possible is applied in a position of maximum flexion or extension, to attempt to go beyond the maximum range of movement. In early training sessions each exercise should be held in a position of maximum flexion or extension for 30 seconds, working up to one minute by the fourth workout and two minutes and fifteen seconds by the twenty-fifth session or start of formal competition. Each exercise is repeated three times, with the rest interval (15 seconds) gradually decreased at each workout.

WHAT IS ISOMETRIC TRAINING?

Unlike weight training (isotonic contraction), in which the levers go through a complete range of motion with muscle shortening, isometric training utilizes a static pressure against a fixed, immovable object without muscle shortening. Isometrics can be performed against any stationary object with a chain or rope, heavy barbell, resistance from a partner (two-man isometrics), a doorway, a rapid contraction of any voluntary muscle in the body, or resistance from an opposing body part. Near-maximum effort is performed for a predetermined number of seconds. The length or period of contraction (6–10 seconds), number of sets (1–3), amount of force applied (two-thirds to maximum strength of a muscle group), and angle and type of exercise are the alterable variables that must be manipulated to ensure progression and strength gains. Normal breathing should be used during muscular effort.

Numerous college and professional athletes utilize isometrics in their training routine. Frank Budd, former world record holder in the 100-yard dash, used a series of exercises to improve sprinting speed. Bob Petit testifies that isometrics had improved his jumping and game performance and added years to his career. The rapid strength gains and the ability to simulate basic athletic movements appear to be the key features of this type of training. It has been estimated that one year's use can produce 100 percent strength gains for a normal individual. Since additional muscle bulk and viscosity do not accompany training, strength acquired is of the type desirable for improved sprinting speed.

Also, following muscle and joint injuries, isometrics is a sound rehabilitative approach when the injured area is not strong enough for weight training. On the other hand, it must be said that weight training is more effective for athletes in most team sports. It is strength through the complete range of motion that is important, not at one or two specific angles.

SHOULD EVERY ATHLETE ENGAGE IN ISOMETRIC TRAINING?

Review this summary of advantages and disadvantages of isometric training before making your own decision:

1. Strength increases, equal to those produced through weight training, are achieved in isometrics, although the workouts consume less than one-third the time. One workout weekly is sufficient to maintain strength gains.
2. Cardiovascular/respiratory endurance is unaffected by isometric training.
3. A 2 to 3 percent strength gain weekly can be expected. Studies have shown increases as high as 5 percent for ten weeks, or a 50 percent gain, with only one six-second contraction at two-thirds the maximum muscle strength.
4. Exercises must be performed at varied angles throughout the range of motion since static strength acquired at one angle may not carry over to other angles. Specific, rather than general, strength may be developed with limited carry-over to athletic performance.
5. Isometrics has been shown to improve vertical jumping ability, 30-yard dash times, and agility.
6. Motivation tends to be lower in isometric training than in weight training.
7. Boredom occurs rapidly since evidence of progress is not present.
8. Controlling the amount of force that is applied by each individual is near impossible in group situations.
9. Strength gains occur more quickly in the early stages of training and for the untrained athlete. Gains occur slowly for the highly trained athlete.

In view of the limitations of isometrics, it is evident that this form of training should *not* replace weight training if improved sprinting speed and power are desired outcomes. It is dynamic strength (through the complete range of motion) that is the important factor in athletics. Isometric training is not extremely helpful in improving dynamic strength.

WHAT IS MAXIMUM EFFORT TRAINING?

Maximum effort training involves the use of high-intensity exercises that take each individual to complete exhaustion. They serve the purpose of producing psychological toughness, increasing the pain threshold, and improving physiological development beyond that occurring from regular training. Only the best mentally and physically conditioned athletes will be capable of incorporating this type of training into their schedules.

This type of training also is one of the few good methods of equalizing exercise effort among athletes of varying abilities and conditioning levels. It offers training geared to the individual, with everyone working against his or her own previous distance or time record, each coping with his or her own stress and psychological barriers, until, finally, only complete physical exhaustion causes cessation of exercise.

A maximum effort session should be a part of every practice, occurring at the close of the workout, and should tax every individual to maximum capacity. It is also helpful to keep records and test periodically to determine individual progress. Once you condition your mind to quit only when physically no longer able to continue, you have made great strides toward becoming a champion athlete in any sport.

BASIC PROGRAM (DAILY):

1. *All-out sprint*: Perform an all-out sprint at maximum speed until no longer able to continue. Record the distance.
2. *Distance hop:*   Perform a one-legged hop at maximum speed until no longer able to continue. Record the distance and time. Repeat using the opposite leg.
3. *Squat jumps:* Perform a maximum number of squat jumps, falling to a right angle only and avoiding the full-squat position, in a period of 90 seconds. Slowly increase the time limit as progress occurs.

The above basic exercises can be supplemented by Concentrations I and II below to add variety and intensity to the program and condition the muscles affecting sprinting.

CONCENTRATION I:

1. *Running in place:* Lifting the knees to waist level, sprint in place until no longer able to continue. Record the time. Avoid pacing or barely lifting feet from the ground.
2. *Treadmill pacing:* Set the treadmill at 12 mph and run until no longer capable of continuing.

3. *300-yard run:* Record the time in a 300-yard sprint.
4. *Two-legged hop:* Record the distance covered in 45 seconds. Slowly increase the time limit.

CONCENTRATION II:

1. *440-yard dash plus:* Surprise runners at the finish of a 440-yard dash with the command to continue sprinting as far as possible. Each sprinter should be followed by a teammate to prevent collapse and injury.
2. *Treadmill sprint:* The trainer sets the treadmill at each individual's 100-yard dash pace. Repeat and accelerate the treadmill just slightly above maximum mph without the runner's knowledge. Continue with moderate speed acceleration of treadmill on each occasion. Increase sprinting time requirement from three seconds slowly to ten seconds.
3. *Isometric charge:* With the legs moving continuously and shoulder and hands placed against an immovable object (sled, wall, post), continue to drive forward until no longer able to continue.

Think positively during exercise exertion. The thought process must be carefully controlled during high-intensity work, focusing on the value of exertion rather than yielding to psychological fatigue factors such as muscular discomfort, breathlessness, and pain. Learn to run through pain and continue far beyond early signs of fatigue.

Maximum effort tends to train both the mind and the body. Unless the mind is clearly the "boss," you will never be capable of enduring enough punishment to use this type of program effectively.

DESCRIBE A TRAINING PROGRAM TO IMPROVE REACTION TIME.

Reaction time (RT) can be improved through weight training, isometrics, calisthenics, and specific drills such as sprint starts that apply the principle of specificity and simulate actual game and skill movements of the activity. Total body and lower torso RT are the key areas of concentration for sprinters. Both have been improved through calisthenics (sit-ups, push-ups, side straddle hops), weight training, and sprint starts. For improvement in these two areas, note the following basic suggestions, which incorporate major research findings:

1. Concentrate on total body and lower torso RT through weight training, isometrics, calisthenics, and specific drills that simulate the movement or skill for which this quality is being developed.

2. Utilize drills that simulate the choices that will be present in game experiences. The reactor should be forced to concentrate on alternative moves at all times with an awareness of body position and weight distribution; these remain neutral, favoring a particular side only if a gamble is justified—for example, if guarding a strong right dominant dribbler, a short sideline pass in football, or if defensive assistance is available from teammates.

3. From a stationary position, a preparatory posture conducive to maximum RT can be held no less than one second and no more than four.

4. Drills must alllow practice in both simple (one response) and choice (more than one possible response) RT.

REACTION DRILLS

Imitation-reaction. All players are in clear view of the leader and mimic the leader's actions in an explosive manner. Most movements originate from a set action such as running in place or right-angle squat.

Sample reactions include:

1. *Front and back drop.* From a running position, subjects drop to either a push-up position or to the hips and back before quickly returning to a stationary running position.

2. *Quarter eagle.* Running in place, subjects rotate one-quarter turn and quickly return to the starting position with the feet and legs in continuous movement.

3. *Vertical jump.* A high leap into the air with arms reaching for the sky is executed before returning to stationary running.

4. *Front and backward roll.* Executed with momentum which is used to return immediately to a running position.

5. *Hand/foot reaction.* Subjects mimic the leader as he or she performs series of rapid movements with the extremities.

6. *Pivot reaction.* Subjects mimic pivots in various directions, executed from the stationary running position.

7. *Plant foot/cut reactions.* Subjects mimic plant/cut movements and return to a stationary running position. For variation, subjects run through a series of dummies placed 10 yards apart, following one another at 6 yards and executing or simulating the fake and cut of the individual ahead. All basic cuts are performed.

8. *Agility running.* Subjects perform a series of 15-yard sprints forward, backwards, sideways to the left, and sideways to the right.

ADDITIONAL EXERCISES FOR SPRINTERS

1. *Sprint starts.* Explosive starts, reacting to a gun or other loud noise,

should be taken daily with runners continuing to stride for 25 to 40 yards.

2. *Mountain climber*. With the body in a front-leaning rest or push-up position, the legs flex forward in a climbing motion in alternate fashion. Each leg should come to a complete halt before again moving forward. With a leader at the front of the group, the same leg remains forward until the command "go," at which time the forward leg returns and the backward leg explodes forward.

3. *Forward dive*. From a standing position, runners dive forward as far as possible upon hearing the command "go."

4. *Sprint-and-cut*. Five players, acting as obstacles, are stationed 15 yards apart, either standing or seated in chairs. Subjects begin to run so that they achieve full running stride when they are 15 yards from the first obstacle. When runners reach a distance of 2 to 5 yards from each obstacle, seated players quickly point to either side, indicating the direction where the cut is to be made.

HOW EFFECTIVE IS WEIGHT TRAINING?

A variety of effective programs are in use today. The literature is replete with research in the area of weight training and its effects upon certain performance measures. A basic tendency of researchers in the past has been to consider weight training as a replacement for, rather than a supplement to, actual sprint training and training specific to the particular activity. Experiments incorporating this error have retarded some of the true value of such a program in athletics. No program of any nature can replace formal training in an activity and in the specificity of the movements involved.

The following represents a brief summary of findings to date:

1. Weight-training programs, regardless of the method employed, produce significant increases in strength and endurance. However, the use of between three to nine repetitions for one set appears to be the optimum number for strength improvement. Training with less than two or more than ten repetitions adds little to strength development.

2. For improving performance in running speed, the use of three sets of six to nine repetitions, three sets of three to five repetitions, or increasing the weight 5–10 pounds after each set, performing a maximum number of repetitions on the last set, appear to be most appropriate, since excessive bulk or muscle mass is not produced in spite of great strength increases.

3. Weight training has no detrimental effect upon the speed of muscular contraction of the arm. Some studies have uncovered significant increases following a weight-training program.

4. If speed is the desired outcome, it appears that weight-training programs should utilize rapid, explosive contractions or movement of the dumbbells, boots, or barbell through the complete range of motion.

5. Weight training, used as a supplement to sprint training, increases sprinting speed (30–100 yards) significantly more than sprint training alone.

6. Weight training has no deleterious effect upon body flexibility and, if increased flexibility is the desired outcome, can actually improve the range of motion in the major body joints.

7. Weight training has been shown to significantly increase the physical capacity of subjects following brief training periods.

8. The use of weight-training programs as an adjunct to off-season competition in the post- and preseason, and as a supplement to in-season training, will assist in the attainment of higher conditioning levels and significantly contribute to improved performance.

9. Weight-training programs, when altered slightly to apply the principle of *intensity* more adequately and also to include power exercises, will significantly improve cardiovascular/respiratory efficiency.

10. Weight training has been shown to significantly increase explosive power as measured by the vertical and standing jumps.

11. Weight training has been shown to be of tremendous value in the revitalization of injured and weakened muscles, as well as in the prevention of injuries common to specific activities, through increased strength in the supporting muscles of the ankles, knees, and shoulders.

12. Vigorous weight training, once weekly, is sufficient to retain much of the strength acquired through a systematic weight-training program. The length of retention following periods of inactivity will be in direct proportion to the time spent acquiring said strength.

It is evident that practically all programs produce significant strength gains; however, variables must be manipulated to secure maximum gains in accordance with training objectives.

WHAT IS THE GROVES' SUPEROVERLOAD METHOD?

Developed by Dr. Barney Groves of Virginia Commonwealth University, this unique method of weight training has potential for superior strength/power gains for athletes in all sports. Here is a step-by-step account of how the method works:

1. For each exercise in your program, establish your 1RM (amount of weight you can lift only one time).

2. Add 25 percent to this amount of weight (an athlete with a 1RM of 200 lbs. in the bench press, for example, increases that weight to 250 lbs.).

3. Begin each repetition in the "Up" position, using a partner to assist you in lifting the weight up for the first repetition.

    a. Bench press - the exercise begins with the arms extended overhead, elbows locked.

    b. Leg press (on weight machine) - extend your legs and lock both knees.

    c. Other exercises - begin in the up position rather than having to lift the weight from the floor or rack. The method cannot be applied to all weight training exercises.

4. The first repetition is only a slight bend of the joint—attempt to move the weight downward only 2–3 inches. Then return the weight to the starting position.

5. Continue taking the weight downward further each time until (on the 7th repetition) you are unable to return the weight to the up (starting) position.

6. Complete three sets (of seven repetitions) every other day. At the end of each week, redetermine your 1RM and repeat these steps using this new weight.

Superoverload has a number of advantages for athletes. Its biggest asset is the ability to handle heavier weight resulting in greater strength gains. In addition, the muscle being exercised is forced to work against heavier weight at its strongest angle. With traditional methods, weight is limited to the amount capable of being handled at the weakest angle.

WHAT ARE THE FACTORS THAT MAKE UP A GOOD WEIGHT-TRAINING PROGRAM?

Weight training should be a systematic program whereby muscles are gradually provided with increased resistance in weight and intensity, or work per unit of time, to tax and improve the functioning of the systems of the body. A sound program adapted to your purposes requires adjustment of numerous training variables such as repetitions, sets, rest interval, weight (RM), speed of contraction, and exercises. Prior to the initiation of any type of weight-training program, the basic objectives of training should be established. Based on desired outcomes, the alteration of the variables discussed below should be determined.

Repetitions. The number of times an exercise is performed without any intervening rest period should gradually increase from the lower to the upper limit within each three to five training days. A high number of repetitions tends to produce greater endurance changes, whereas a low number (with heavier weight) tends to favor strength/power development. For the development of both strength and endurance, the lower and upper limits of 6–9 are recommended. For speed development and use of heavy weight and explosive power-type exercises, repetitions tend to be low (1–5).

Sets. The number of times the group of repetitions is performed each training day is referred to as *sets* or *bouts*. Sets may be completed 1–5 times for each exercise, with each set followed by a brief interval of rest. One set of each exercise should be performed once before repeated sets are employed. One to three sets are recommended when an athlete is concentrating on speed improvement.

Interval. This variable applies the principle of *work per unit of time*, essential in the development of all body systems, and gives weight training tremendous versatility and potential for cardiovascular/respiratory development. This variable should be decreased slowly, allowing minimum rest between sets and exercises to increase the intensity of the program. This gradual decrease is an important factor in achieving peak conditioning in weight training, as in interval training for sprinters. The interval (I) and weight (RM) should not be decreased simultaneously. After the subject is able to perform three sets of ten repetitions, the interval is reduced to 45 seconds before weight is added and the subject returns to the lower limit of repetitions.

Weight (RM–Repetitions Maximum). The weight that permits an individual to perform a specific number of repetitions is termed the RM. The 10RM, then, is the amount of weight permitting a subject to perform an exercise a maximum of ten repetitions. The use of lighter weights will permit more rapid contraction and a higher number of repetitions for endurance improvement. Heavy weights, slower contraction, and fewer repetitions will tend to develop strength more than endurance, although both are developed concurrently but not in the same proportion. When the goal for a particular exercise is attained, in terms of maximum number of repetitions chosen, additional weight is added and the subject again returns to the lower repetition limit. A starting weight for power exercises being used to improve sprinting should permit an individual to perform one set of three repetitions (when utilizing 1–5 as the lower and upper limits). The starting weight obviously varies with the choice of lower and upper repetition limits.

Speed of contraction. The time required to complete one repetition or movement is also an important variable affecting muscular development. Slower contractions produce greater fatigue than rapid movements which fully utilize the initiated starting momentum to flex and return to the normal position. Choice of slow, moderate, or rapid contraction again depends upon the training objectives of strength, local muscular endurance, cardiovascular/respiratory endurance, and increased muscle contractual speed. If speed is the desired outcome, rapid, explosive contractions should be used.

Breathing. The importance of proper breathing in bodily development and lifting performance is a point of controversy. Basically, it is recommended that inhalation occur while the muscles are contracting and exhalation as relaxation occurs. The only apparent value of loud and timed breathing attempts may be its possible assistance in fixating the chest walls, in turn aiding shoulder girdle and arm movement. Forced breathing undoubtedly contributes nothing to cardiorespiratory development and may acutally impair a highly refined and efficient mechanism. Holding the breath while pressing heavy weights also tends to compress the chest, produce great intrathoracic pressure, increase blood pressure, and deter the return flow of the venous blood to the heart, producing a dizzy or faint feeling. A deep inspiration followed by forced expiration, often against a closed glottis, is also unendurable. Normal breathing alleviates the possible occurrence of this *Valsalva phenomenon* (see pp. 7–8) and is preferred over the two common patterns used by weight trainers: (1) forced inspiration and expiration before completing the repetition before breathing again, or (2) forced inspiration before completing the repetition, and forcing expiration following the lift. It is recommended that breathing adaptations during exercise stress to be left to nature.

Exercises. Weight-training movements are chosen on the basis of their contribution to the muscles involved in the sports action for which training is aimed. Whenever possible, exercises should simulate movements of the activity for which training is designed. For example, the squat walk, hip flexor, modified hip flexor, sprint-arm exercise and other simulated sprinting exercises are more adantageous. For total bodily development, a variety of exercises are needed to tax all body systems and activate each body region. Heavy explosive movements such as the clean and jerk, two-handed military press, and two-handed snatch are needed to improve cardiovascular/respiratory development and strength.

The exercises discussed in this chapter represent a cross-section of the variety of movements possible with the use of the barbell, dumbbells, and iron boots. In relation to body position and lifting hints, the following principles apply to practically all movements and will not be mentioned for each specific exercise.

1. For the basic stance, place the feet slightly wider than shoulder width apart, with the toes parallel side by side. Primary considerations are balance (maintaining the weight directly above the medial plane of the body) and agility. The stronger leg is sometimes placed back in a heel-toe alignment (left heel is even with the right toe), depending upon individual preference.

2. Toes should be placed just under the bar in the starting phase of exercises where the barbell is resting on the floor.

3. Maintain an erect back (unless this is the muscle group being exercised) with the head up and eyes looking straight ahead.

4. Grasp the bar at approximately shoulder width with the weight equally distributed on each hand. Utilize the alternate grip when heavy weights must be supported by the arms, as in the dead and straddle lifts.

5. Avoid leaning backward to assist the completion of a repetition designed to strengthen the arm muscles.

6. Do not alter the stabilizing body parts after the exercise is initiated.

7. Stress mechanical disadvantages of levers in arm exercises.

8. Carry each repetition to the extreme range of movement.

9. Master and follow correct form on all exercises.

10. Utilize a brief overall bodily warm-up session prior to lifting heavy weights.

11. In early training sessions, choose realistic starting weights that provide little strain, adjusting rapidly within three or four workouts.

12. *Maximum lift* days should be built into the program. Also take girth measurements periodically for self-evaluation. Administer a physical capacity test before and after a specified training period.

13. Overcome training plateaus, or points at which progress in terms of increased lifting is not occurring or not measurable, by altering the exercises and variables.

14. Grips: Pronated—palms face downward; Supinated—palms face upward; Alternate: one each direction.

WEIGHT LIFTING AND WEIGHT TRAINING

EXERCISE	EQUIPMENT	BASIC MOVEMENT	HELPFUL HINTS	MUSCLE GROUPS ACTIVATED
1. Bench press	Barbell, bench rack	Pronated grip, lying on the back on a bench or floor, with both knees raised, the bar is slowly lowered to the chest and pressed back to the starting position.	Keep both feet flat on the floor; avoid lifting the buttocks; extend the arms fully.	Shoulder extensors
2. Bent-arm pullover	Barbell, bench rack	Pronated grip; from the same position as above the bar is placed at the chest and lowered behind the end of a bench (arms flexed) as far as possible before a return arch brings the bar back to the starting position.	Flex the arms during the entire movement; pass the bar close to the face on the return phase.	Shoulder flexors Arm and shoulder extensors
3. Two-arm curl	Barbell	Supinated grip; with the bar resting at the thighs and the arms fully extended, the bar is raised to chest level and returned.	Keep all parts of the body erect and motionless throughout.	Upper arm flexors, wrist flexors, long finger flexors
4. Reverse curl	Barbell	Pronated grip; the same movement as above with only the grip altered.	Use less weight than in the two-arm curl.	Upper arm flexors, hand extensors, finger extensors
5. Wrist curl	Barbell, bench or chair	Pronated grip; with the bar held by the final joint of the fingers and the wrists in a position of maximum flexion, both palms are brought toward the body as far as possible and returned to the starting position.	Grasp the bar as far toward the end of the fingertips as possible; curl the fingertips to prevent the bar from rolling off; rest forearm on the thighs; keep feet flat on the floor, and back and neck erect.	Flexor carpi group
6. Reverse wrist curl	Barbell, bench or chair	Pronated grip; from the position described in Exercise 5, the hands are reversed with the knuckles pointed toward the floor. The knuckles are raised toward body and returned.	Support the bar with thumb and end of fingers; avoid elbow joint movement or leaning back.	Extensor carpi group

WEIGHT LIFTING AND WEIGHT TRAINING (continued)

EXERCISE	EQUIPMENT	BASIC MOVEMENT	HELPFUL HINTS	MUSCLE GROUPS ACTIVATED
7. *Forward raise*	Barbell	Pronated grip; from a standing position, with the bar resting at the thighs, the arms move upward to the height of the shoulders and return in the same arch.	Keep the entire body erect at all times, vary the exercise by continuing the movement to the overhead position.	Flexors, anterior and middle deltoid
8. *Forearm rotator*	Dumbbells, weight on one end only	Supinated grip; from a sitting position with forearm resting on a table, wrist and hand extended over, and the weighted end of the dumbbell away from the body, the wrist is rotated from a supinated to a pronated position and returned.	Do not raise the forearm from bench or table; maintain an erect upper torso.	Pronator-supinator group
9. *Lateral raise*	Dumbbells	Pronated grip; both arms extended from the thighs outward to head level and lowered to the starting position.	Maintain an erect upper-lower torso; avoid flexing arms; vary with the leaning raise (same movement with trunk flexed at right angles) or supine position (lying on back on floor or bench).	Abductors, shoulder horizontal flexors
10. *Military press*	Barbell	Pronated grip; the bar is slowly pushed overhead from chest level until both arms are fully extended.	Maintain an erect neck and back, and extended, locked knees; avoid jerky movements or lean.	Abductors, flexors, and arm extensors
11. *Upright rowing*	Barbell	Pronated grip; with the bar resting at the thighs and the arms and legs extended, the bar is raised to the chin and returned to the thigh rest position.	Use a narrow grip with the hands 6 to 8 inches apart; keep the elbows higher than hands; maintain an erect stationary position.	Abductors, arm flexors

WEIGHT LIFTING AND WEIGHT TRAINING (continued)

EXERCISE	EQUIPMENT	BASIC MOVEMENT	HELPFUL HINTS	MUSCLE GROUPS ACTIVATED
12. *Shoulder shrug*	Barbell	Pronated grip; with the bar resting at the thigh and the body erect, both shoulders are elevated until they nearly contact the face before relaxing and permitting the bar to return to the starting position.	Keep the extremities fully extended; heavy weight will ensure more rapid strength gains.	Shoulder girdle elevators
13. *Sprint arm exercise*	Dumbbells	Pronated grip; with one foot slightly ahead, knees flexed, body forward, work arms to simulate the sprinting action.	Dumbbells should move between the shoulder and hip.	Anterior and posterior thoracic muscles and upper arm muscles
14. *Straight-arm pull-over*	Barbell	Pronated grip; lying on a bench, with the head at the very edge, the barbell resting on the floor, and both arms extended, the bar is raised overhead and returned to the floor.	Maintain fully extended arms; do not elevate the lower back or remove the feet from the floor.	Pectoralis muscles, triceps, latissimus dorsi, serratus anterior
15. *Two-handed clean and jerk*	Power rack	Pronated grip; bar is brought in one continuous motion up to the chest through use of the squat or split; bar must be raised overhead with elbows and knees locked for 2 seconds.	The bar may not contact the chest; perform movement as rapidly as possible.	Abductors, flexors, arm extensors, quadriceps, gastronemius, foot plantar flexors, lower leg and back extensors
16. *Two-handed snatch*	Power rack	Pronated grip; bar is raised in one continuous motion from the floor to an extended position overhead and held for 2 seconds.	Place hands slightly wider than shoulder width, keep body directly under the weight at all times.	Abductors, flexors, arm extensors, lower leg and back extensors, quadriceps, hamstrings, gluteus maximus
17. *Triceps press*	Barbell	Pronated grip; the bar is placed in the shoulder rest position and then pressed slowly overhead until both arms are fully extended.	Place the hands 9 to 12 inches apart; follow hints for the military press; tilt the head forward to prevent bar contact as the movement is initiated.	Arm extensors

WEIGHT LIFTING AND WEIGHT TRAINING (continued)

EXERCISE	EQUIPMENT	BASIC MOVEMENT	HELPFUL HINTS	MUSCLE GROUPS ACTIVATED
18. Wrist abductor	Dumbbells, weight on one end only	Pronated grip; the bar is held parallel to the floor, with the weighted end pointing away from the body; the arm is extended and to the side. The weighted end is slowly lowered until it points toward the floor before it is returned to the starting position.	Place a dumbbell in each hand and alternate movements; keep the body erect at all times.	Wrist abductor
19. Wrist adductor	Dumbbells, weight on one end only	Grip and position same as Exercise 18. With the weighted end now behind the body, the weight is lowered until it points directly at the floor.	Same as for Exercise 15.	Abductors
20. Bench knee extension	Bench and lower bar	Sitting position, hook ankles in bar and bend backwards before returning to sitting position.	Alter angle of body to increase tension.	Supporting muscles of the knee
21. Balance shoot	Iron boots	Sitting position, raise legs simultaneously before drawing to chest, straighten and repeat.	Keep legs off floor until a set is completed.	Quadriceps, iliopsoas, rectus abdominus obliques
22. Abdominal side bender	Barbell	Pronated grip; with the bar in the shoulder rest position, the upper torso is alternately tilted to the right and left and brought back to the starting position.	Tilt as far as possible to each side; secure bar collars; perform movement with dumbbell in each hand.	Lateral flexors
23. Sit-ups (bent leg)	Barbell or disc	Pronated grip; from a supine position on the back, with the bar or weight held firmly behind the neck with both hands, the upper torso is raised until both elbows contact the knees.	Bring heels up tight with the buttocks; flex the neck forward to initiate the movement; hook feet under a bar.	Hip flexors, psoas major

WEIGHT LIFTING AND WEIGHT TRAINING (continued)

EXERCISE	EQUIPMENT	BASIC MOVEMENT	HELPFUL HINTS	MUSCLE GROUPS ACTIVATED
24. *Sit-ups (straight leg)*	Barbell or disc	Pronated grip; from the position described in Exercise 23 the upper torso is raised until both elbows contact the knees.	Same as for Exercise 23; vary by alternately touching opposite elbow to opposite knee.	Rectus abdominus
25. *Dead lift (straight leg)*	Barbell	Alternate grip; with the bar at the thigh rest position, the hips are flexed to lower the bar without flexing the legs.	Maintain arms and legs fully extended; use light weights.	Back and hip extensors
26. *Dead lift (overhead straight-leg)*	Barbell	Pronated grip; from a standing position, the upper torso lowers to grasp the bar, with the arms fully extended, before raising the weight in a semicircle to a position overhead.	Extend legs and arms; avoid jerky movements; use light weight.	Back and leg extensors, arm flexors
27. *Dead lift (flexed knees)*	Barbell	Alternate grip; with the bar resting on the floor, a crouch position is assumed, the knees are flexed, the arms and back extended; the bar is raised to the thigh rest position and lowered.	Maintain extended arms and erect back; lift weight by extending the knees and hips and moving to a standing position; keep the shoulders back to protect the back muscles.	Thigh, lower leg, and back extensors; quadriceps; hamstring, gluteus maximus
28. *Trunk flexor*	Barbell	Pronated grip; from standing position, with the bar in the shoulder rest position, the upper body is bent forward to a right angle, parallel to the floor, and then returned to the upright position.	Keep the head up; avoid bending the knees; alter the movement with hyper-extension of the trunk and/or twisting to the right or left as the body is returned to the starting position.	Back extensors

WEIGHT LIFTING AND WEIGHT TRAINING (continued)

EXERCISE	EQUIPMENT	BASIC MOVEMENT	HELPFUL HINTS	MUSCLE GROUPS ACTIVATED
29. *Lower torso heel raise*	Barbell, 2- to 3-inch board	Pronated grip; with the bar in the shoulder rest position, the toes together elevated on a 2 to 3-inch board, the body is raised upward to the maximum height of the toes.	Alter toe position from straight ahead, to pointed in and out; keep the body erect.	Foot plantar flexors
30. *Hip flexor*	Iron boots	From a standing position, the knees are alternately pulled toward the abdominal area and returned.	Perform this movement with explosiveness; combine with alternate knee extensor.	Hip flexors
31. *Knee curl*	Iron boots	Lying on back, raise both legs upward, then draw them rapidly to chest before extending legs and returning to starting position.	Rapid movement is stressed.	Quadriceps, iliopsoas
32. *Knee extensor*	Iron boots, bench or table	From a sitting position, with the lower legs extended over a table, the foot is raised by extending the knees alternately.	Maintain an erect back; stabilize the body by grasping the sides of the table.	Quadriceps group
33. *Knee flexor*	Iron boots	From a standing position, the knees are alternately flexed to move the boot as close to the buttocks as possible.	Can also be performed lying flat on the stomach; keep the body erect.	Hamstrings
34. *Leg abductor*	Iron boots	Lying on the floor on one side of the body, raise the top leg upward as far as possible and return to the starting position.	Stabilize the body by resting the head on a bent arm, maintaining floor contact with the other hand.	Abductors

WEIGHT LIFTING AND WEIGHT TRAINING (continued)

EXERCISE	EQUIPMENT	BASIC MOVEMENT	HELPFUL HINTS	MUSCLE GROUPS ACTIVATED
35. Medial ligament abductor	Wall pulley	With a strap around ankle and the knee flexed, the leg is pulled inward and forward.	Use when softening of a cartilage is present.	Supporting muscles of the knee
36. Modified leg lift	Iron boots	From a sitting position with the back erect and hands grasping a chair, the legs are lifted from the floor.	Keep back erect at all times.	Quadriceps
37. Modified hip flexor	Vaulting horse, iron boots	Lying prone along the horse with one pommel removed and height adjusted to allow feet to rest comfortably on the floor, the upper leg is flexed and brought toward the abdominal area.	Perform repetitions with one leg, then the other, begin with only the boot.	Hip flexors
38. One-legged squat	Dumbbells	Pronated grip; from a standing position with a dumbbell in both hands, squat rapidly to right angles and return to upright position.	Toe in slightly with the base foot, begin without use of dumbbells, avoid using back muscles to straighten, remain on the toes.	Thigh and lower leg extensors
39. Quadriceps exercise	Iron boot	Lying on back with one leg in iron boot elevated at 90 degrees against a wall, a leg is raised with knee locked directly overhead at right angles and returned.	Keep your back flat on the floor.	Quadriceps
40. Rhythm lift	Barbell, padded shoulder rest support	Pronated grip; with the bar in the shoulder rest position, back erect, knees slightly flexed, bounce on balls of feet trying to reach maximum height on each bounce. One bounce per second for 60 seconds.	Keep feet at shoulder width; bounce only on balls of feet, do not return to surface on heels or with knees locked.	Foot plantar flexors, gastronemius

WEIGHT LIFTING AND WEIGHT TRAINING (continued)

EXERCISE	EQUIPMENT	BASIC MOVEMENT	HELPFUL HINTS	MUSCLE GROUPS ACTIVATED
41. *Three-quarter squat*	Barbell, squat rack, bench, 2- to 3-inch board	Pronated grip; with the bar in the shoulder rest position, lower the body to a sitting position by flexing the legs until the buttocks contact the chair or bench placed underneath the body.	Avoid bending the back; keep the head up; point the toes outward slightly with heels elevated on a 2- to 3-inch board.	Thigh and lower leg extensors
42. *Squat jump*	Dumbbells	Pronated grip; with the feet in a heel-toe alignment and the body in a squat position (dumbbell in each hand), a forceful jump, or extension, is performed that completely extends and raises both legs from the floor. Foot position is reversed in midair before the body is returned to the starting position.	Maintain an erect position throughout; strive for maximum height on each jump; work from the balls of the feet.	Lower leg, thigh, and back extensors
43. *Squat walk*	Barbell, padded shoulder rest support	Pronated grip; with the bar in the shoulder rest position, short steps (1 to 2 feet) are taken while squatting down; squat toward the rear heel after each step until the thigh of the front leg is parallel to the floor.	After each step and squat, raise the body to a normal walking position; number of steps fulfill the repetition variable.	Thigh and lower leg extensors
44. *Straddle lift*	Barbell	Alternate grip: straddle the bar (one leg on each side), bending the knees with back straight, grasp the bar and lift until returning to a standing position.	Grasp the bar with one arm toward both ends; keep head, back, and shoulders erect.	Thigh, lower leg, and back extensors
45. *Supine leg lift*	Iron boots	Lying on the back, the legs are alternately raised, with the knees straight, to a vertical position.	Keep the lower back in constant contact with the floor; grasp a weighted barbell overhead to stabilize the upper torso.	Quadriceps

WHAT WEIGHT-TRAINING EXERCISES SHOULD BE USED IN ATHLETICS?

There are many exercises that can be adapted to the movement of the sport for which training is taking place. The chart(pps.220-27)lists 45 exercises by body areas and indicates the primary muscle groups activated. To select the correct exercises, have your coach identify the major muscle groups involved in your sport before preparing your program to develop the muscles.

WHAT EXERCISES SHOULD BE INCLUDED IN A PROGRAM DESIGNED FOR GENERAL BODILY DEVELOPMENT?

A sample program of this type is shown below. The basic program is followed for a period of four to eight weeks before you change to Alternate Program I, then Alternate II. All three programs involve similar muscle groups and will help prevent boredom while also attacking muscles from varied angles.

IN WHAT ORDER DO YOU USE SUPPLEMENTARY TRAINING PROGRAMS IN A WORKOUT?

Let's examine each key program and establish a logical order.

"Flexibility training or stretching exercises" have very little conditioning value. Their main contribution is to increase range of motion, help prevent injuries, and warm the body to prepare it for the more vigorous activity to follow. Such important warm-up exercises should be completed *first* in your workout.

"Calisthenics" are designed to improve general conditioning, develop strength and muscular endurance, and improve cardiovascular endurance. They are conditioning oriented and should *not* be in the beginning of your workout. Thirty minutes of hard calisthenics will only turn a fresh athlete into a fatigued athlete. Such fatigue will interfere with skill and timing and make you more susceptible to injury. Conditioning calisthenics should either be the *last or next-to-last* part of the workout. Maximum effort training replaces calisthenics on alternate days.

BASIC AND ALTERNATE EXERCISE PROGRAMS FOR GENERAL BODILY DEVELOPMENT

EXERCISES	Repetitions	Sets	Starting Weight	Speed of Contraction	Interval Min. Sec.
Basic Program					
Two-arm curl	6-10	1-3	8 RM	Moderate	2 to 30
Military press	6-10	1-3	8 RM	Moderate	2 to 30
Sit-ups (bent leg)	25-50	1-3	30 RM	Rapid	2 to 30
Rowing (upright)	6-10	1-3	8 RM	Moderate	2 to 30
Bench press	6-10	1-3	8 RM	Rapid	2 to 30
Squat	6-10	1-3	8 RM	Rapid	2 to 30
Heel raise	15-25	1-3	20 RM	Rapid	2 to 30
Dead lift	6-10	1-3	8 RM	Moderate	2 to 30
Pull-over (straight)	6-10	1-3	8 RM	Moderate	2 to 30
Alternate I					
Reverse curl	6-10	1-3	8 RM	Moderate	2 to 30
Triceps press	6-10	1-3	8 RM	Moderate	2 to 30
Sit-ups (flexed)	25-50	1-3	30 RM	Rapid	2 to 30
Shoulder shrug	6-10	1-3	8 RM	Moderate	2 to 30
Squat jump	15-25	1-3	20 RM	Rapid	2 to 30
Knee flexor	6-10	1-3	8 RM	Rapid	2 to 30
Knee extensor	6-10	1-3	8 RM	Rapid	2 to 30
Pull-over (flexed)	6-10	1-3	8RM	Moderate	2 to 30
Alternate II					
Wrist curl	6-10	1-3	8RM	Moderate	2 to 30
Dead lift (overhead)	6-10	1-3	8RM	Moderate	2 to 30
Side bender	6-10	1-3	8RM	Moderate	2 to 30
Lateral raise	6-10	1-3	8RM	Moderate	2 to 30
Straddle lift	6-10	1-3	8RM	Rapid	2 to 30
Supine leg lift	6-10	1-3	8RM	Rapid	2 to 30
Hip flexor	6-10	1-3	8RM	Rapid	2 to 30
Leg abductor	6-10	1-3	8RM	Rapid	2 to 30
Forward raise	6-10	1-3	8RM	Moderate	2 to 30

From George B. Dintiman, and Loyd M. Barrow, *A Comprehensive Manual of Physical Education Activities for Men.* New York: Appleton-Century-Crofts, Inc., 1970. Used by permission.

"Wind sprints" as commonly used in football, baseball, basketball, soccer, rugby, and some other sports are generally 15- to 75-yard runs at maximum speed for as many times and with as little rest between each as the coach desires. The amount of work performed from one day to another varies with the coach's mood. When used in this fashion, they are anaerobic conditioning sprints (see Chapter 11) and should be *near the end* of the workout.

"Sprint training" is specifically designed to improve your speed in short distances. In order to apply all the concepts presented in Chapter 11, sprint training must be scheduled *second* in the workout, immediately following your stretching exercises.

"Scrimmage" in team sports, competitive play in dual sports, and the actual workout in individual sports such as running should be *third* and follow sprint training. Keep in mind that the body is still unfatigued, less apt to be injured, and more likely to execute skills at high speed under desired game conditions.

"Drills" for the purpose of skill development, if applicable and needed on a particular day, are *fourth*; while you are still relatively free from fatigue and can execute under game conditions.

"Strength/power training" with weights is the most fatiguing of any program. It literally leaves you weak and vulnerable to injury. It is therefore placed as the very last item in your workout.

Sound complicated? It isn't.

The final order is listed below. Strength training and sprint training are used every other day, while others are needed daily.

Order	Program	Purpose
1.	Flexibility or stretching exercises	Improved range of motion, warm-up, injury prevention, decreased resistance through the range of motion.
2.	Sprint Training	Improved speed of movement
3.	Scrimmage	Simulate game conditions
4.	Drills	Skill development, conditioning
5.	Wind Sprints	Improved cardio-respiratory efficiency. Eliminate from program unless variables are controlled.
6.	Calisthenics and maximum effort training	Individualized conditioning, improved cardio-respiratory efficiency and local muscular endurance and power.

Order	Program	Purpose
7.	Strength/explosive power training	Improved muscular strength and power, increased bulk if needed, rehabilitation of injured muscles.

IS THERE ENOUGH TIME TO INCLUDE ALL OF THESE SUPPLEMENTARY PROGRAMS IN ONE WORKOUT?

Yes. The chart below shows you how to do it. Do not change the order.

Time	Item	Comment
5–7 min.	Flexibility exercises	Mild stretching routine, also serves as warm-up period.
5–18 min.	Sprint training/sprint-assisted training	Total time for flexibility and sprint training (20–25 minutes) is similar to time normally allowed for calisthenics
75 min.	Normal session in football, soccer, baseball, basketball, rugby, etc.	This time period also is vital to adequate conditioning and should provide the major thrust toward this outcome in any sport with the principle of specificity of training providing no deterrent force
15 min.	Conditioning calisthenics and maximum effort session or Strength training	Calisthenics are vigorous, progressive, with no rest between exercises and the number of repetitions slowly increased from day to day. One or two maximum effort exercises conclude each calisthenic session
		At least twice weekly, strength training substitutes the calisthenic training program

TOTAL PRACTICE TIME: 1 Hr. 50 min.
to
1 Hr. 55 min.

No competitor in team and individual sports achieves championship caliber without certain supplementary training programs. These programs do not, however, carry instant results. They must be carefully conceived, controlled, and systematically placed into a practice session. Determine the training effect desired in your sport, alter the variables accordingly, and place into the practice schedule for maximum effect.

WHAT IS HYPOXIC TRAINING?

Cardiovascular endurance training for competition in the mile, two mile, and marathon events traditionally has consisted of running miles and miles per week. Some runners complete in excess of 100 miles weekly through a system of LSD (Long-Slow-Distance) training. In LSD training, a slower pace is used to permit comfortable running, a moderately heavy breathing rate, and conversation. Certainly, this varies from individual to individual; however, surprising results have occurred even with training at a seven-eight minute mile pace. As a possible alternative to training approaches requiring such volume, time, and joint wear, hypoxic training, introduced by the Czechs, is being tested. Its purpose is to force the body to adapt to oxygen debt by holding the breath during training. By breathing less frequently, less oxygen is available at the cellular level.

A typical approach to hypoxic training might be: inhale for six steps, hold the breath for six steps, exhale for six steps, and so on. The practice of breath-holding when not exercising appears to be of little value. A summary of research on the value of hypoxic training follows:

1. Hypoxic training, as a supplement to training using normal breathing, can benefit the athlete in extracting more oxygen per unit of volume ventilated.
2. Under hypoxic conditions, oxygen debt and blood lactate are higher than those attained under the same training program with normal breathing.
3. Hypoxic training resulted in an improved maximum oxygen intake per minute of 16.6% compared to 5.5% for a control group using normal breathing. No detectable increase was found in the number of erythrocytes (red blood cells) or in the amount of hemoglobin.
4. Approximately one-fourth of the workout should be done hypoxically at controlled sub-maximal speeds.
5. A 25 percent saving in training time was reported by two Czech sports scientists.
6. Hypoxic training is potentially dangerous and can result in unconsciousness. Headaches also are common. If they persist for more than one-half hour, the amount of hypoxic training used should be decreased.

Hypoxic training is not a highly recommended approach to conditioning for the runner. Stay away from it until it is developed more fully and declared safe.

DOES ROPE JUMPING IMPROVE CARDIOVASCULAR AEROBIC ENDURANCE?

Yes. By counting the number of jumps per minute, regulating the rest period between different jumps and using some difficult high energy jumps, a program can be designed that will improve both agility and aerobic endurance. During the first week or two it may be helpful to warm up by jogging in place 50 to 100 easy steps. The program, in the chart that follows, includes three warm-up jumps (to be completed slowly) and five basic jumps (to be completed at the rate of 70 to 75 jumps per minute). Locate your level on the sample ten-week program and begin at that point, progressing each week as indicated. The Boxer's Shuffle and single-foot jumps are performed at the 70 to 75 per minute rate while the double jump is restarted when missed and continued for the specified number of repetitions.

Warm-up Jumps:

Two-foot jump with an intermediate jump (double beat), after the rope passes under the feet, a small hop is taken before jumping again to clear the rope.

Two-foot jump (single beat), no intermediate jump is taken.

Single-foot hop (single beat), the left foot used for a specified number of jumps, followed by the right foot.

Basic Program:

Boxer's Shuffle (single beat), use alternate right and left foot jumping as the rope passes under.

Running forward (single beat), jump while running forward; repeat running backward to starting position.

Cross-overs (double beat), jump with the rope turning forward, cross the rope by fully crossing the arms as the rope clears your head. Repeat with rope turning backwards.

SAMPLE TEN-WEEK ROPE-JUMPING PROGRAM

Week	Exercises	Sets[a]	No. Jumps	Rest Between Jumps
First Week	Warm-up jumps	1	15	Continuous
	Basic five jumps	1	15	2 minutes
	Practice session	1		15 minutes to learn jumps
Second week	Warm-up jumps	1	20	Continuous
	Basic five jumps	1	20	2 minutes
	Practice session	1		15 minutes to learn jumps
Third week	Warm-up jumps	1	25	Continuous
	Basic five jumps	1	25	90 seconds
Fourth week	Warm-up jumps	1	25	Continuous
	Basic five jumps	2	15	90 seconds
Fifth week	Warm-up jumps	1	25	Continuous
	Basic five jumps	2	20	90 seconds
Sixth week	Warm-up jumps	1	25	Continuous
	Basic five jumps	2	25	60 seconds
Seventh week	Warm-up jumps	1	25	Continuous
	Basic five jumps	2	35	60 seconds
Eighth week	Warm-up jumps	1	25	Continuous
	Basic five jumps	3	40	60 seconds
Ninth week	Warm-up jumps	1	25	Continuous
	Basic five jumps	3	45	30 seconds
Tenth week	Warm-up jumps	1	25	Continuous
	Basic five jumps	3	50	15 seconds

[a]Number of times the specified jumps are completed; a one-minute rest period is permitted between sets when multiple sets begin in the fifth week.

Single-foot hops (single beat), same as warm-up jump; progress from slow to fast or pepper jumping.

Double jumps (double beat), the rope must pass under the feet twice while in the air. Perform one double jump, one single jump, one double jump, alternating until completing the specified number.

On the first workout day, locate your level on the sample program and begin at that point, progressing each week as indicated. The Boxer's Shuffle and single-foot jumps are performed as fast as possible; the double jump is restarted when missed and continued for the specified number of repetitions.

11

Sprinting Speed Improvement: How to Run Faster

Every athlete can benefit from additional speed. In sports at all levels, there is no single greater concern than *how to run faster*. There is also no question more frequently left unanswered. Why are athletes so preoccupied with speed of movement? Without adequate speed, stardom in most sports is next to impossible, for it is *the* single greatest asset one can possess in football, basketball, soccer, baseball, rugby, field hockey, and track. Unfortunately, it is also one of the most difficult to develop.

There is no quick formula to automatically produce a faster running athlete. In fact, so much diversity is present among coaches and athletes that one wonders whether most aren't deer hunting with BB guns. Considerable inconsistency exists in the training of modern-day sprinters. An air of secrecy surrounds the training methods used by coaches of several foreign countries. The sudden dethroning of American sprint supremacy in the 1972 and 1976 Olympic games has some experts worried about our present training methods. There is reason for concern. Many of our efforts have been less than scientific, more aerobic than anaerobic, more haphazard than analytical, more mass oriented than personalized, and more superficial than comprehensive. Yet, it is difficult to argue with success since it is a fact that the U.S. has produced the world's best sprinters for many years. Obviously, many individuals have been involved in some excellent training regimes.

All factors considered, it must be stated that speed improvement is a much more complicated problem and involves greater sophistication than has been exercised in the past. This chapter draws from more than 300 research studies and also summarizes two entire texts by Dr. Dintiman: *How to Run Faster: A Do-It-Yourself Book for Athletes in All Sports,*[1] and *Sprinting Speed: Its Improvement for Major Sports Competition*[2] to present a comprehensive individualized attack plan for the athlete in any sport who is dedicated to becoming a faster runner in short distances.

CAN SPRINTING SPEED BE IMPROVED?

Yes. In 1890 the world's fastest human was John Owen, who ran the 100-yard dash in 9.8. The 9.4 100-yard dash performances by George Simpson (1929), Dan Joubert (1931), and Jesse Owens (1933, while a high school student at East Tech in Cleveland) were truly great feats in that athletic era. Even more outstanding is the 10.2 100-meter world record set by Jesse Owens in 1936 which, more than three decades later, is only three-tenths of a second off the current world record. Owens' 220-yard dash world record of 20.3 in 1935 is also still an outstanding performance in the 1970's. Today, athletes have run 8.9, with some sprinters improving nearly one full second over a three- to four-year period. An 8.5 100-yard dash is not unrealistic for the 1980's. Research findings also clearly demonstrate that speed can be improved.

WHAT ARE THE KEY FACTORS TO WORK ON FOR AN ATHLETE?

A valuable aid in identifying what factors are important for you is a thorough analysis of a 100-meter dash. For team sport athletes who accelerate to maximum speed occasionally from a stationary position and, more frequently from a moderate speed jog, it identifies the attack points that will have the most influence on improving speed for your sport.

Acceleration, maintaining maximum velocity, and deceleration vary among individuals. Superior runners will reach maximum speed sooner, hold maximum speed for a longer distance, and slow down less than the average or less conditioned sprinters. It is also safe to assume that variations exist among champion sprinters.

The chart below indicates the factors involved in a 100-meter dash and their approximate point of entry for champion sprinters. Reaction to the stimulus is important in providing a quick muscular movement forward while in contact with the blocks. Explosive power or forceful push-off both combine with reaction time (RT) for what may be the key phase of the race—the first 2–3 meters. Acceleration to maximum speed occurs at different rates and is generally attained at or slightly before the 60-meter mark. Stride length and rate now become the limiting factors for the next 15–20 meters and determine maximum speed (mph). Anaerobic capacity controls the degree of slowing in the final portion of the race.

It's important to note that maximum velocity involves only a small portion of the race (15–20m), a slowing effect a similar portion (10–15m), and acceleration the main portion (45–60m). Inferior RT, an inadequate start, and poor driving power can cause a runner to lose the race in the first 2–3 meters. Poor acceleration most certainly will affect the outcome of the race. An inefficient stride and leg rate will affect maximum speed. And, finally, poor conditioning or low anaerobic capacity will result in one's being overtaken late in the race.

DISTANCE OF ENTRY FOR FACTORS AFFECTING 100-METER DASH

FACTOR	0 10 20 30 40 50 60 70 80 90 100	Major Role
Reaction to gun	▓ 0.10 sec	Response to gun
Explosive power (departure from blocks)	▓ 0.5 sec	Block clearance
Accelerating power	▓▓▓▓▓▓▓▓▓▓▓▓	Reaching max. speed
Stride length/rate	▓▓▓▓	Maximum speed
Anaerobic capacity	▓▓▓▓▓▓▓	Holding maximum, minimizing slowing

WHAT ARE THE MAJOR ATTACK POINTS?

The preceding discussion helps to identify the major attack points to be used in speed improvement. At first glance, you might conclude erroneously that you can only take a longer or faster step. Obviously, these two aspects affect a small portion of the racing distance for the 100-meter sprinter. For the team sport athlete, these aspects are much more critical. The major attack points are:

1. RT and improved starting ability
2. Acceleration to maximum speed
3. Stride length and stride rate
4. Anaerobic capacity

MAXIMUM IMPROVEMENT OF SPRINTING SPEED THROUGH SPECIALIZED TRAINING PROGRAMS

Training programs

- Explosive Power/Strength Training
- Flexibility Training
- Form and Stride Training
- Reaction Time Training
- Sprint Training/Sprint-Assisted Training

Specific Objectives

- Increased strength and power in the muscles involved in the sprinting action
- Mechanically sound sprinting technique, including coasting
- Improved range of motion in the hips, shoulders and ankles
- Increased power of leg drive or push-off with each step, higher knee lift
- Forced striding using longer stop
- Decreased internal muscle resistance allowing efficient muscle movement, limited energy expenditure and harmony of antagonistic and agonistic muscles
- Increased strength and power in muscles involved in the sprinting action
- Forced action and increased leg movement speed
- Mechanically sound sprinting technique
- Mechanically sound starting technique
- Rapid acceleration to maximum speed
- Rapid response to the stimulus (gun or action of the opponent)
- Forceful thrust or push-off from blocks, forceful forward thrust of arms-upper body
- Extended period of maximum effort
- Holding maximum speed for longer distance
- Minimum slowing in final stages of race

Major attack points

- Lengthened Stride
- Increased Rate and Efficiency of Leg Movement
- Improved Starting Ability
- Improved Anaerobic Capacity

Ultimate goal

- Maximum Improvement of Sprinting Speed

At this point in your planning, the major areas have been identified. It has also been established that each of these areas can be improved. Study chart carefully. It contains the basic data for your total approach to the improvement of speed.

HOW CAN I GET STARTED?

Stop and analyze your sport and speciality from the information below. Identify the attack points most critical to your activity.

Sport	Attack Areas
Baseball, football, rugby, soccer, track, field hockey	Starting, acceleration, anaerobic capacity, stride rate, stride length
Basketball, racket games, handball	Starting, acceleration, anaerobic capacity

Continue to plan your attack by following these steps:

1. Test yourself in the 50-yd. dash, 100-yd. dash, and the 300- or 440-yd. run, using two testing days. Record your times on your personal record sheet.
2. Compare your 50-yd. time to your 100-yd. time and your 100-yd. time to your 300- or 440-yd. time. This will identify your anaerobic capacity. Use this information to determine the degree of emphasis needed in this area.
3. Test yourself for stride length. Apply the formula to evaluate your performance.
4. Trim off all excess poundage. Body fat is a detriment to speed of movement.
5. Use your test scores to determine improvement in speed every four-week period.
6. Begin now to study the remainder of the chapter to master the techniques of improving the major attack areas identified.

HOW DO I TEST MYSELF IN THESE AREAS?

Follow the instructions for each test described below:

TESTS FOR EVALUATION OF PROGRESS

MAXIMUM SPEED (mph)

Equipment: Stop watches (1–3), Finish tape (yarn)
Reliability: Test-retest reliability of 0.92.
Procedure: A 15-yard running start is allowed to eliminate reaction time and starting ability. Subjects reach full running stride prior to arrival at

the "starting tape" where timers start their watches. As the finish tape is touched (50 yards down the track), a white flag (folded on top of the tape) falls, keying the timers to stop their watches. The best of two trials is recorded in your personal record sheet. A 15-minute formal warm-up period is used before the test and a 10-minute rest period between the first and second trials.

40, 50, 100-YARD DASH

Equipment: Stop watches (1–3), Finish tape (yarn)
Reliability: 0.89–0.91
Procedure: Subjects assume a stationary start (3-point football or track stance) and respond to the commands: Runners to your mark, Get Set, Go. Timers are placed at the finish line. A 40-yard dash is used by professional football teams. Unfortunately, some officials stand 40 yards away and drop their arm; others have runners start when they want to. The difference in these methods can be as much as 5/10 of a second.

ANAEROBIC CAPACITY

Equipment: Stop watches (1–3), Finish tape (yarn)
Procedure: Method one–determine your 50-yd. and 100-yd. time (running start). Double your 50-yd. time. This figure should be more than 0.2 of a second less than the 100-yd. time. *Method two*—determine your 100 or 300-yd. time from a stationary start. Triple your 100 time. This time should be no more than 3–5 seconds less than your 300-yd. time. A sprinter who can complete 300 yards in less than 31 seconds is ready for national competition in the 100 and 200 meter races; 33–34 seconds for lesser caliber competition. *Method three*—a good sprinter or team sport athlete should be capable of performing a respectable 440-yd. dash at a pace approximately five times his best 100-yd. dash effort.

100-yard time	*440-yard target*
9.0	45.0
9.5	47.5
10.0	50.0
10.5	52.5
11.0	55.0
11.5	57.5
12.0	60.0

STRIDE LENGTH

Equipment: Tape measure, smooth track or surface
Formual: The best stride guideline for men and women is approximately 1.17 × height ±4″. Attempt to increase stride until you fall within this range.

Example: *Lynne Rose, 5′9″. Her optimum stride 69″ × 1.17 = 80–81″ ± or 77–85″*

Procedure: Place two markers 25 yards apart on a cinder track. Step off 50 yards from the first marker making this the starting line. Begin running from this mark, accelerating to maximum speed just prior to reaching the 25-yard area where you have smoothed out the surface. Note prints on the track. Measure two separate strides from tip to the rear toe (front of mark) to tip of the front toe.

Record your test results on the form below. After your initial testing, train for 4 to 6 weeks before re-testing in each area.

PERSONAL RECORD SHEET

Name _____   Height _____ Weight _____

Starting Date _____

Major Attack Points:

_____ Starting Ability   _____ Acceleration
_____ Stride Rate   _____ Anaerobic capacity
_____ Stride Length

Test Item	Conditions	Initial test	Post-test	Imprv.
40-Yd.				
50-Yd.				
100-Yd.				
300-Yd.				
440-Yd.				

Anaerobic Capacity: *Method One:*
                               Method Two:
                               Method Three:

WHAT TYPE OF TRAINING WILL IMPROVE STRIDE LENGTH?

Increasing stride length, without a reduction in the rate of leg movement, is probably the most practical and efficient means of improving sprinting speed. Lloyd Bud Winter, famed coach of San Jose State College, states: "The secret of sprinting is to have a long stride that carries you low to the ground."[3] Stride length is determined by applying the formula 1.7 × height, plus or minus 4 inches. Although strides vary greatly among sprinters (as long as 9 feet, 6 inches) stride lengthening is definitely indicated if you are not within the above range. Even individuals who fall within this range should engage in training to attain a maximum stride that is most efficient for their style, body type, and physical attributes.

Stride length is dependent upon several factors: (1) the flexibility of the hip and ankle joints, (2) leg and ankle strength, (3) unalterable anthropometric measurements such as length of levers, and (4) sprinting form. Basically, it is increased through increasing the *power of the leg drive* or the intensity of the push-off and cannot be improved by placing the forward foot ahead of the body's center of gravity. Correct stride training necessitates use of several specific programs: weight training, flexibility training, form training, and special sprinting-assisted methods.

Weight Training. Increased stride demands additional strength in the ankles, feet, legs, and shoulders to improve the propulsive force and thrust of the leg against the ground. The Basic Weight-Training Program for Sprinters (pp. 244–245) will serve to increase stride length.

Flexibility Training. Exercises designed to improve range of motion in the shoulders, hip, and ankle should receive major attention. These exercises should always follow any type of weight-lifting or heavy-resistance program to avoid muscle shortening.

Form Training. A long, low stride is possible only with correct form. For optimum stride, a sprinter must possess high knee action and good foreleg reach, run high on the toes, bound forward instead of up, maintain good forward lean (30 degrees), run tall and relaxed with the back straight, elminate back kickup, maintain a loose jaw and hands, and use a low front arm reach. These aspects of correct sprinting require form training and are by no means natural movements.

Following are some of the drills suggested by Winter[3] and Doherty[4], for improved stride length:

1. *Stride running.* Begin with a walk, slowly progressing to maximum speed in several repetitions. From a standing position, spring to the toe of one leg, reach out with the foreleg while high on the toes, and snap down to the ground. Bound forward with the toes when the leg contacts the surface, maintain forward lean, and keep the hips forward and the back straight while utilizing proper arm action. Touch each 5-yard marker with the left or right foot while sprinting the length of a football field.

2. *Knee lift.* Run in place, lifting knees high; then move down the track at approximately 2 mph before walking the turn and repeating the exercise for two or three laps.

3. *Foreleg reach.* Use an exaggerated foreleg reach while sprinting.

4. *Running on the toes.* From a standing position, rise on the toes as high as possible. Run in place high on the toes for one or two seconds, lean forward from the heels and sprint straight ahead.

5. *Low hurdling.* Place low hurdles at a distance that forces over-striding.

6. *Stride measurements.* Smooth out one lane for 30 yards before sprinting this distance from the blocks, noting stride length. Move blocks one lane to left and repeat, attempting to use fewer steps. Measure stride length periodically to determine movement.

7. *Arm reach.* From an even low stride while running with a partner, begin to exaggerate arm reach without attempting to accelerate, keeping arms low and reaching forward. Arms should reach forward from a position no higher than the navel. Note acceleration compared to partner who did not exaggerate arm reach.

8. *Bound forward.* Bound forward as far as possible on each step, keeping the head in a straight line. Combine by alternating with bounding with locked knees, only flipping the ankles. Walk a short distance and repeat.

9. *Relaxation striding.* Practice sprinting with an exaggerated loose jaw and hands. Compare the times for a 30-yard run, with a running start, first when stressing relaxation at nine-tenths speed and then when neglecting concentration on relaxation striding.

During the recovery phase or between repetitions, walk on the toes and avoid allowing the heel to contact the surface.

Sprinting-Assisted Methods. There are two additional means of improving stride that have been used both in Europe and the United States: downhill running and towing. Both methods attempt to reduce internal and external (wind) resistance and thus permit a longer stride that should be carried over to normal sprinting. Downhill running requires careful control of the degree of slope if stride is to be lengthened. Towing, or pulling a runner by a rope attached to an automobile or cycle, also seeks to force a lengthened stride, increases hip-ankle flexibility, and carry over to flat surface running under normal conditions.

BASIC WEIGHT-TRAINING PROGRAM FOR SPRINTERS

EXERCISES	Repetitions	Sets	Starting Weight	Speed of Contraction	Interval[a] Min. sec.	
Basic Program:						
Two-handed press	3-5	3	3RM	Rapid	2 to	30
Squat (¾, ½)	3-5	3	3RM	Rapid	2 to	30
Rhythm lift	Maximum	2	Squat. wt.	Rapid	2 to	30
Two-handed clean and jerk	3-5	3	3RM	Rapid	2 to	30
Upright rowing	6-9	2	6RM	Rapid	2 to	30
Sprint-arm exercise	6-9	3	5 lbs.	Rapid	2 to	30
Two-handed snatch	2-5	3	3RM	Rapid	2 to	30
Knee flexor	2-5	3	3RM	Rapid	2 to	30
Modified hip flexor	3-8	3	6RM	Rapid	2 to	30
Hamstring stretching[b]	15-25	2	Body only	Slow, static	0 to	30

EXERCISES	Repi-tions	Sets	Starting Weight	Speed of Contraction	Interval[a] Min. sec.
Alternate I: Lower Torso Concentration					
Bench press	3-5	3	3RM	Rapid	2 to 30
Squat walk	6-9 steps	3	6RM	Rapid	2 to 30
Heel raise	6-9	3	6RM	Rapid	2 to 30
Straddle lift	3-5	3	3RM	Rapid	2 to 30
Hip flexor	3-5	3	3RM	Rapid	2 to 30
Supine leg lift	3-5	3	3RM	Rapid	2 to 30
Leg abductor	3-5	3	3RM	Rapid	2 to 30
Balance shoot	6-9	3	6RM	Rapid	2 to 30
Hamstring stretching	15-25	2	Body only	Slow, static	0 to 30
Alternate II: Lower Torso Concentration					
Pull-over (straight)	6-9	3	6RM	Rapid	2 to 30
Squat jump	6-9	3	6RM	Rapid	2 to 30
Modified leg lift	3-5	3	3RM	Rapid	2 to 30
One-legged squat	3-5	3	3RM	Rapid	2 to 30
Knee extensor	3-5	3	3RM	Rapid	2 to 30
Knee curl	3-5	3	3RM	Rapid	2 to 30
Quadriceps exercise	3-5	3	3RM	Rapid	2 to 30
Modified leg lift	3-5	3	3RM	Rapid	2 to 30
Hamstring stretching	15-25	2	Body only	Slow, static	0 to 30

[a]Subjects slowly decrease the rest interval between repetitions and sets from two minutes to 30 seconds over a period of workouts.
[b]Several hamstring stretching exercises, using static procedures, should follow each workout.

From: George B. Dintiman, *How To Run Faster: A Do-It-Yourself Book for Athletes in All Sports.* Champion Athlete Publishing Co., Box 2936, Richmond, Va., 23235. 1979.

WHAT IS THE BEST METHOD OF IMPROVING STARTING ABILITY?

Training in this area evolves around the four basic components that determine starting speed:

1. Reaction time (RT). Can be significantly improved in the sprint start.
2. Speed of arm-leg movement. Can be significantly improved through sprint training, sprint-assisted training, explosive power training, and strength training.
3. Propulsive force of the legs against the blocks. Can be significantly improved through explosive power and strength training.
4. Starting form or technique. Can be improved through periodic practice using the various techniques discussed in this chapter.

High-speed starting practice should occur when you are not fatigued in order to simulate competitive conditions and reduce the danger of injury. Adequate warm-up always precedes starting practice with the pistol and should consist of five to eight starts.

WHAT TYPES OF TRAINING WILL IMPROVE EXPLOSIVE POWER?

Power is a product of strength and speed. It is vital to sprinting and athletic success. It is also a component that can be improved, although procedures are somewhat involved and necessitate attention in four areas:

1. Application of force (strength development).
2. Development of speed of movement.
3. Techniques involved in providing the right force-velocity relationship.
4. Coordination of movement.

Areas 1 and 2 require programs to improve overall strength and the strength of the muscles involved in the sprinting action. The other two areas are technique or form oriented. The bulk of this section deals with the development of explosive power through strength-oriented programs that simulate sprinting actions whenever possible and utilize heavy-resistance, rapid, explosive contractions. It is essential to select exercises that are closely related to the movement of sprinting.

Research indicates that strength training programs, when properly altered, result in both increased strength and explosive power. However, weight training and other programs must depart from the typical approach if improved explosiveness in terms of faster starting ability, quicker and harder charges, improved jumping ability, and rapid acceleration from a jog are to be realized. Weight training, hopping and jumping routines, and weighted ankle spats are all effective methods of improving this important quality.

Weight training for improved explosive power demands that each exercise be performed as an explosive, competitive lift, stressing rapid movement and correct form from the time the first muscle contraction occurs to completion of the exercise. The following exercises (see pages 244–245 for description) are suggested:

COMPETITIVE LIFTS	POWER RACK ROUTINE	OTHER
Two-hand military press	Dead lift	Bench stepping with
Two-handed clean and jerk	Military press, low and high	barbell and weight across the shoulders
Two-handed snatch	Squats—¼, ½, ¾	(20-inch bench).
	Heel raise	Strive for 6–8 repetitions with 2–2½ times your body weight.

Explosive power training with weights requires few repetitions (2–5), heavy weights (1–3RM), multiple sets (1–3) with a diminishing rest interval between sets and exercises, and a 10–12-second hold in the final position on the last repetition of each set. To prevent injury and ensure maximum benfits, follow these suggestions:

1. Work in partners, with one performer lifting and the other spotting or protecting.
2. Warm-up properly prior to lifting.
3. In initial workouts, use realistic starting weight (under your maximum) until the upper limit is established.
4. Utilize maximum lift days and alter exercises periodically.
5. Avoid extremely heavy weights when recovering from an injury or illness or if bothered by chronic back or knee difficulty.
6. Increase arm exercises 5–10 pounds and leg exercises 10–20 when upper limits are attained.

Hopping and jumping exercises are popular in the training of sprinters and have been used successfully by Russian athletes. This procedure is valuable in the development of leg strength, leg endurance, explosive power, and the strength of the supporting muscles of the knee and ankle so vulnerable to injury in contact sports. Hopping and jumping possesses the added advantage of simulating the sprinting action or involving similar muscle groups; thus, the principle of specificity of training ensures greater carry-over to the sprinting action. Following are some hopping and jumping activities:

1. One-leg hops at moderate speed for a maximum distance.
2. Two-legged hops at moderate speed for a maximum distance.
3. Repeat activities 1 and 2 at maximum speed for maximum distance.
4. Slowly increase the distance that can be covered at moderate-to-fast rate until a distance of one-fourth mile can be covered on the same foot.
5. Sprint 25 yards before going into a 25-yard maximum speed hop on one leg. Continue for two to four laps alternating hopping legs.
6. Stand parallel to a 20-inch bench, then with both feet hop to the other side and return, continuously jumping side-to-side for a maximum number of jumps. Slowly increase the number of jumps at maximum speed that can be performed within a specific time limit.

Weighted ankle spats are still a relatively unproven means of developing explosive power, although their use has been shown to improve vertical jumping ability. The following practice routines using 1–5-pound ankle spats are suggested:

1. Bench jumping–side-to-side 2-foot jumping of a 20-inch bench.
2. Explosive starting from a sprinter's position.
3. Maximum effort sprinting for distances of 10 to 25 yards.
4. Explosive high kicks with each leg.
5. Squat jumps.
6. Burpee exercise performed at maximum speed.

Calisthenics, performed as rapidly as possible, are also used to develop explosive power. Specific exercises should include total body movement through a wide range of motion and should stress quick, sharp movements. The following exercises are easily adapted: (1) squat thrusts or burpee (2) side straddle hop (3) speed push-ups (4) tail gunner (toe touch and half squat) (5) eight-count push-up (squat thrust with 2 push-ups), mountain climber, and sit-ups.

WHAT GUIDELINES SHOULD BE FOLLOWED IN STRENGTH TRAINING?

Strength-training programs should observe the following principles if maximum benefits in terms of increased sprinting speed and performance are to be attained.

1. Since muscle shortening (hamstrings in particular) does occur after heavy-resistance work, a series of stretching exercises should always follow each workout.
2. Strength training should be used in conjunction with actual sprint trianing, both in-season and off-season, rather than as a replacement for sprint training. When the two programs are used simultaneously, sprinting speed is significantly improved.
3. Concentration is placed upon the muscles (upper and lower torso) involved in the running action. Exercises are then chosen that activate and strengthen these muscle groups.
4. General principles of conditioning must be followed with the *hypertrophy cycle* (pp. 199–200) producing enough rest between workouts to allow maximum exhalation or regeneration that elevates conditioning beyond the pre-exercise level. A Monday-Wednesday-Friday-Sunday or every-other-day schedule is recommended for heavy-resistance exercise. Alternate-day programs are used only for sprint training, flexibility exercises, form training, stride training, and other special supplementary programs.

5. If speed is the desired outcome, exercises must be performed explosively.

6. Heavy-resistance exercise, such as weight training, should follow the sprint training session or formal practice in track and field, football, basketball, soccer, and baseball. Unless this procedure is followed, athletes are left more susceptible to injury (knee, ankle, shoulder), should contact occur, because of destruction of muscle constituents, decreased capacity to continue exercise, and general fatigue. The fact that most injuries occur late in an athletic contest supports this statement.

Strength-training programs may take the form of weight training (isotonics), isometrics, weighted boots and vests, two-man exercise programs, or calisthenics. Apply the Groves' Superoverload Method, discussed in Chapter 10, to the bench press and leg press exercises.

WHAT IS ANAEROBIC TRAINING?

A halfback is tackled from behind by a slower player. A sprinter is passed in the final 10 yards of the race. A baseball player "runs out of steam" and is tagged out at home. A soccer or basketball player is beat to the ball by a slower player. All are examples of poor anaerobic capacity that caused a player to either "slow down" or fail to accelerate and hold maximum speed due to fatigue. In most sports, a player is called on to make repetitive short bursts of speed. Ideally, his fourth or fifth burst is run as fast as his first. This is often not the case due to poor anaerobic endurance. The athlete with high anaerobic capacity has several advantages: (1) repetitive short sprints can be made with minimum rest all at the same high speed, (2) maximum speed is reached more quickly, and (3) maximum speed is held for a longer distance before slowing occurs.

High anaerobic capacity provides each athlete with a "fresh start" on each short sprint in his sport. It may also make you the player who is doing the catching. It is a vital training phase for athletes in track and field and all team sports. It is the phase that can give you the "edge."

Anaerobic metabolism comes into action at the onset of any type of exercise as an immediate source of quick energy until circulatory and respiratory adjustments occur. Sprinting always takes place in the absence of oxygen; a condition under which the skeletal muscles can function for only a short time. The intensity and short duration of sprinting is such that respiratory and circulatory systems have no time to adapt as the oxygen requirements and oxygen uptake possible during the racing distance as the chart indicates. Obviously, the ability to breathe in and use atmospheric oxygen is of very little importance to sprinting short distances.

OXYGEN REQUIREMENTS, UPTAKE AND DEBT

Racing Distance	O_2 requirement (liters)	O_2 uptake (liters)	O_2 debt (liters)
100 m	8–10	None	8–10 (100%)
200 m	20	1–2 (5–10%)	18–19 (90–95%)
400 m	22.1	4–4.5 (18%)	18 (82%)

Understanding the muscle as a machine for converting chemical into mechanical energy is a complicated phase of physiology. With sufficient oxygen available (aerobic exercise such as a 5-mile run), fatigue lactates in the muscles are absent. When oxygen supplies are insufficient (anaerobic exercise such as short sprints), pyruvic acid forms from glucose and is reduced to lactic acid. This process (anaerobic glycolysis) only occurs in the absence of oxygen to produce energy-rich phosphate bonds to allow muscle contraction to continue. These quick energy stores are nearly depleted in 8 seconds of maximum effort sprinting. At this point (much sooner for the unconditioned athlete) slowing occurs due to lactic acid build-up. Improved lactic acid tolerance and improved quick energy stores result from anaerobic training. The amount of quick energy available depends upon factors such as training, age (highest at age 20–25 decreasing slowly thereafter) and nutrition.

HOW CAN I TRAIN ANAEROBICALLY?

The following guidelines govern anaerobic conditioning programs:

1. Sprinting (up to 200 meters) is 90–95 percent anaerobic and training should reflect this percentage. Aerobic training should occupy only a small portion of a sprinter's regime. The availability of additional oxygen is of no value. It is impossible for the respiratory system to use atmospheric oxygen once the gun is fired. Therefore, improved oxygen uptake can in no way improve sprinting speed.
2. Aerobic training also has no effect upon lactic acid tolerance, stride length or stride rate.
3. An individual should avoid training anaerobically and aerobically at the same time. Two one-half hour sessions of aerobic training weekly are sufficient for sprinters.
4. Maximum work for short durations (10 to 60 seconds) should be used.

5. Rest periods of a few minutes should follow each maximum effort.
6. The principle of specificity should be followed. Maximum work for sprinters must involve all-out sprints.
7. A one minute maximum effort, followed by 4 to 5 minutes of rest before repeating the effort, produces high lactic acid concentrations in the blood and improves anaerobic endurance. Repetitive 400 meter runs in less than 60 seconds, followed by a 4 to 5 minute rest period, are an effective technique for sprinters.
8. The decisive factor in lactic acid concentration is the length of the work period. At maximum speed, distances closer to 400 meters will produce the highest lactic acid levels. Recovery time and the relationship between the rest interval and work are secondary.

A variety of sprint training methods are effective in improving anaerobic capacity: Pick-up sprint training, hollow sprints, interval sprint training, and Fartlek training. A discussion of these common programs follows.

WHAT IS PICK-UP SPRINT TRAINING?

Pick-up sprinting involves a gradual increase from a jog, to a striding pace, to a maximum effort sprint. A 1-1 ratio of the sprinting distance and the recovery walk that follows each repetition should be used. Thus, an athlete may jog 50 yards, stride 50, sprint 50, and terminate that repetition with a 50-yard walk. The walk or slow jog should allow near-complete recovery prior to performance of the next repetition. This jog-stride-sprint-recovery cycle tends to develop strength and speed and reduce the probability of muscle injuries in cold weather.

This 50-yard cycle is an example of early season training with the exact number of repetitions depending upon conditioning levels. As the degree of conditioning increases, the distance is lengthened, with late season pick-up sprints reaching segments of 120 yards. It is important to remember that complete recovery is desirable prior to sprinting each successive repetition. Distances beyond 120 yards make near-complete recovery extremely difficult. It is also important to note that use of 120-yard jog-stride-sprint-walk segments involves over-distance training for the indoor 60 and outdoor 100-yard dash. This type of training also develops anaerobic endurance or oxygen debt tolerance so vital to sprinters.

New Zealand athletes use a routine similar to pick-up sprints involving a series of four 50-yard sprints at near maximum speed (6–7 seconds) per 440-yard lap, jogging for 10 to 12 seconds after each sprint, and completing the 440-yard run in 64 to 76 seconds. According to Berben, New Zealand athletes have performed as many as 50 sprints (12½ × 440) with little reduction in speed on any of the repetitions. Since speed is not affected by fatigue products even with this high total running volume, it is apparent that recovery is near complete prior to each repetition and that oxygen debt tolerance is not improved. As the repetition distance approaches and exceeds 120 yards (120, 150, 220, 300, 440) anaerobic endurance or oxygen debt tolerance is improved. Use of these longer distances should occupy some of the training time for athletes in major sports competition.

WHAT IS HOLLOW SPRINT TRAINING?

Hollow sprints involve use of two sprints that are interrupted by a "hollow" period of recovery such as walking or jogging. One series might include a 60-yard sprint, 60-yard jog, 60-yard sprint, and a 60-yard walk for recovery. Similar segments of 120, 150, or 220 yards might be employed Since strength and speed are the primary objectives of this form of training, a near complete recovery is desirable prior to initiation of the next series.

The length of the training distance depends upon training objectives. Higher distances are most beneficial to 100-, 200-, and 400-yard dash athletes whereas shorter distances would be used by football, baseball, soccer, and rugby players desiring to improve speed of movement.

WHAT IS INTERVAL SPRINT TRAINING?

Interval training was derived from Fartlek running and has become, since the early 1950's, a popular approach to the training of middle distance runners, long distance runners, and sprinters. It involves three-quarter to maximum speed sprints mixed with carefully regulated recovery or rest periods.

The basic variables that must be carefully controlled are: frequency of training sessions, length and intensity of the work interval, and length and intensity of the rest interval.

Frequency of Training Sessions. Adequate recovery time is necessary prior to reconvening exercise if the body is to benefit from the previous workout. Most athletes train daily using 1 or 2 rest days at the end of the week or just prior to competition during the season.

Length and Intensity of the Work Interval. There is no magic formula for determining the number and length of repetitions. Training remains an individual matter with this prescription phase determined by the coach and athlete. It is not unreasonable, however, for an athlete to complete 15 to 50 repetitions of a distance, interspersed with walk-jog recovery.

The intensity of training (work per unit of time) is much more important than the duration of the work-out. In fact, when a plateau is reached, improvement only occurs by increasing the intensity of work and holding the length of the session constant.

Length and Intensity of the Rest Interval. It is during the rest interval that the heart adapts to the stress of exercise. The rest or recovery interval between repetitions allows the athlete to perform much more total exercise volume of high intensity than would normally be possible. This rest interval is vital to improved performance and must be carefully controlled.

A rest/work ratio of one for one is suggested between the repetition distance and the recovery walk or jog. For pure speed work (not anaerobic conditioning), a recovery period should allow a return to a fresh state. Training for this purpose (stride rate improvement) is discussed later in this chapter.

The Specificity of Interval Sprint Training. Both skill and performance are improved when work intensity and pace simulate competitive conditions. Sprint training should simulate the distances used in actual competition except when under and over-distance training is used.

WHAT IS FARTLEK TRAINING?

Fartlek training, which was developed in Sweden during the 1930's, consists of alternate fast-slow running over countryside, golf courses, farmland, or other soft, springy surfaces. It is important to note that the primary emphasis is on fast running, with training approached from a *time* rather than *distance* basis. Periodic walking/jogging is encouraged between bouts of vigorous activity. Fartlek should be used twice weekly in early training and once in competitive periods. When it is properly performed, both aerobic and anaerobic endurance are developed in near equal proportion.

Fartlek training is designed to eliminate boredom as well as to be a diversion from routine training. It has been successfully used by cross-country and distance runners for years. It is a personalized program that encourages the use of different competitive distances on the track. Both pace and terrain are constantly altered in one continuous workout, ranging from 20 minutes to three hours. Additional advantages include relaxation due to softer surfaces, necessity for self-reliance in planning each workout, and the flexibility to alter each training day to personal needs.

The obvious disadvantages of speed play are lack of control by a coach or instructor, limited opportunity for pace work, unsuitability for the extreme speeds acquired on a natural track, necessity for wooded areas and soft, springy surfaces not often found around schools and colleges, demand for a rather lengthy daily session, and the necessity to train alone.

DESCRIBE A SAMPLE FARTLEK WORKOUT

Short sprints, walking, incline running up stairs or hills, track running at meet pace or faster, backward running, and jogging are all used in combinations to provide individualized programs that are of a progressive nature. A sample workout is shown below: [2]

1. Jog ten minutes as a warm-up.
2. Five minutes of brisk calisthenics.
3. 1–2 × ¾ to ¼ mile at a fast, steady pace which might be described as three-fourths full speed. Walk five minutes after each.
4. 4–6 × 150-yard pick-up sprints (jog 50 yards, stride 50 yards, and sprint 50 yards, and walk 50 yards after each).
5. 4–6 × 440 yards at slightly faster than racing effort. Jog 440 yards after each.
6. Walk ten minutes.
7. Two miles of continuous slow running.
8. Walk five minutes.
9. 8–12 × 110 yards at 1½ to 2½ seconds slower than best effort, jogging 110 yards after each. Walk five minutes.
10. 4–6 × 60-yard sprints uphill, and walk back after each.
11. Jog one mile as a warm-down.

If you cannot punish yourself for a long period of time, Fartlek training is not your cup of tea.

WHAT CAN I DO TO IMPROVE MY STRIDE RATE?

Stride rate is the sum of the time for ground contact and time in the air. For top sprinters, this ratio is 2:1 at the start of the race and 1:1.3–1:1.5 at maximum speed later in the race. It is determined by speed, angle, height of release and air resistance in flight. Of these, release or ground reaction forces seem most important.

Females are about one second slower than males in the 100 meter dash due to slower stride rates. Ground reaction forces and power differences are the main cause. Also, children run with faster strides than adults. As height and leg length increases, stride rate decreases. The longer the lever, the more power required to move it at the same rate. Again, strength/power training surfaces.

In the past, the rate of stride frequency was considered an unalterable factor fixed at birth by the nervous and muscular systems' ability to produce rapid contraction and relaxation. There is now evidence to the contrary. Higher stride rates are possible in cycling (5.5–7.1/sec.) than sprinting (3.10–4.85/sec.), downhill running, and treadmill sprinting. The limiting factors are external (wind, surface conditions), and internal forces (strength/power ratio, muscle resistance, fat deposits between bundles of muscle fibers, and neurological muscular patterns). To improve stride rate then, you must concentrate on the *Sprint-assisted methods* to alter neurological patterns and *strength/power training* to improve the load/power ratio. Improving the load/power ratio is critical to taking faster steps. For female athletes, it may be the single most important factor. It serves to improve ground reaction forces and lessen the time for ground contact without loss of push-off power (see weight training program for sprinting improvement in this chapter).

Discussion of the sprint-assisted training methods (downhill running, towing, high speed treadmill sprinting, and pump and stride training) follow.

IS DOWNHILL RUNNING EFFECTIVE IN IMPROVING SPRINTING SPEED?

Yes. However, like all programs, it requires special control. Opponents of downhill running as a training device point out that the faster rate of leg movement is only imaginary and that the lead foot contacts the ground too far under the body, reducing stride length, limiting push off the track, and actually slowing the runner.

There is evidence supporting use of downhill running when the slope or incline is kept at 2.6 degrees or less. With greater slopes, the previous criticisms are valid. A program involving combined use of downhill-uphill sprinting is preferred. Running downhill attempts to increase rate of leg movement, develop speed, lengthen stride, and improve relaxation, while uphill running develops strength.

Downhill sprinting should occur early in the workout since maximum stride rate only occurs in the absence of fatigue.

IS TOWING EFFECTIVE IN IMPROVING SPRINTING SPEED?

Yes. In fact, results have been short of amazing. The most effectiive form of towing is performed with a *pacing machine* consisting of a tow bar and handle attached to the rear bumper of an automobile. This patented device (invented by Mark E. Shuttleworth) has been proven effective in improving stride length, increasing the rate of leg movement per second, and ultimately improving sprinting speed. Speeds faster than an 8.0 100-yard dash are possible using this apparatus, because of the pull and limited wind resistance. According to one user, subjects who regularly trained with the pacer improved their times in events from the 100-yard dash to the 880-yard run by much greater margins than those who did not use the apparatus. Sandwick[5] cites cases of sprinters reducing average times from 10.5 to 9.9 after five weeks of steady use. He offers additional support for its use, stating: "We feel it is an unquestionable aid in the development of any athlete where running speed is essential, as in the case of football, basketball, baseball and track."

Use of the pacer does fail to provide proper sprinting arm movement, since a two-handed grip on the bars is necessary for proper balance. Sprint-arm exercise while holding 2 to 5 pound dumbbells should therefore follow each session on the pacer.

After several years of using this apparatus, Sandwick has developed a scientifically sound program in regard to towing speed, repetitions, proper form, tow car operation, reducing injury, and efficient use of the apparatus. A summary of his conclusions follows:

Towing speed is dependent upon unaided 50-yard dash times with a running start. For maximum benefits, athletes are towed one-half second faster than their times in this test. Faster speeds have been shown to be less effective. The speeds increase as the subject improves the 50-yard dash time. The table below shows proper tow car speeds and corresponding total 100-yard dash and estimated 50-yard dash times (final 50 yards of the 100-yard dash). It is assumed that the final one-half of the 100-yard dash is covered faster than the first half. An individual who runs 100 yards in 11.0, then, is estimated as having covered the final 50 yards in five seconds. One-half second faster than this speed is then used as the towing pace (4.5). To adjust sprinters to the pacer, slower speeds of 16 to 18 mph are used prior to the faster runs.

UNAIDED AND ADJUSTED TOWING SPEEDS

100-yard Dash Time (total time)	Unaided First 50 Yards	Sprinter Last 50 Yards	Suggested 50-yard Time with Machine	Equivalent Tow Car Speed (mph)
13.0	7.0	6.0	5.5	18.6
12.0	6.5	5.5	5.0	20.5
11.0	6.0	5.0	4.5	22.7
10.0	5.5	4.5	4.0	25.6
9.0	5.0	4.0	3.5	29.2

Repetitions cover a maximum distance of 50 yards at the predetermined speeds and are preceded by thorough warm-up consisting of jogging, sprinting, and flexibility exercises. Four to six repetitions interrupted by a walk for complete recovery are used in preliminary workouts and systematically increased to eight runs by the fourth or fifth session. Two to three workouts weekly using the pacer are suggested. Runners accelerate gradually for the first 40 yards while holding the handles, reaching the desired speed at the first timing marker (flag), and continuing at that pace for 50 yards.

Running form is examined carefully in early runs at slower speeds. Emphasis is on a position close to the handles, a comfortable grip on the bars, proper toe-ground contact, proper shoulder and head alignment, and form commensurate with unaided sprinting. When proper form is evident and subject is accustomed to the apparatus, repetitions are initiated.

Tow car operation requires practice and follows specific rules. A 100-yard stretch of smooth, firm surface such as macadam, level grass, or cinder track is used; cinder track which is identical to competitive conditions, is strongly recommended. The car is accelerated gradually for the first 50 yards, reaching desired speeds at the first flag and holding that speed constant for the next 50 yards. The car is driven in low gear with no shifting allowed and gradually decelerated at the finish line (without using the brakes) by the drag of the engine.

The probability of injury using the pacer is low. Warm weather and adequate warm-up offer insurance against muscle injury. The inhalation of exhaust fumes apparently is not a problem since adequate air passes over the car roof. With proper tow-car operation, trial runs at a slow pace, and careful choice of firm, unobstructed surfaces, spills are avoided. Unless the pacer is used following heavy rains, there is also no track damage.

Efficient use of the pacer occurs when two bars are mounted on one vehicle to permit training in pairs. A motorcycle and rope can also be used.

One word of caution: unless your coach organizes a towing program, forget the idea. It is potentially dangerous without very careful control.

IS HIGH-SPEED TREADMILL SPRINTING EFFECTIVE IN IMPROVING SPRINTING SPEED?

Yes, although additional research is needed to uncover the most effective control of variables for such a supplementary training program.

Treadmill running is designed to gradually force the rate of leg movement per second to a speed beyond that capable in unaided running, by adjusting tread belt speed. The theory is that it will lead to improved speed on a flat surface. It has been shown that where daily use of a bicycle ergometer forced a more rapid rate of leg movement than that possible without aid of a motor, the benefit carried over to increased revolutions without motor assistance. Thus, the rate of leg movement in riding a bicycle was improved through forced techniques. Flat surface sprinting has also been improved through high-speed treadmill training.

A heavy-duty treadmill with speed adapter kit that provides speeds up to 26 mph must be used. Although the high-speed accuracy of a treadmill varies slightly with the weight of the individual, it is possible to determine a runner's maximum speed and then proceed slowly to increase the velocity beyond this point with or without the subject's knowledge. Maximum sprinting velocity can be determined in miles per hour using the test described earlier in this chapter, or determined on the treadmill, which is a more accurate method.

The following guidelines govern use of a high-speed treadmill training program:

1. Runners should use a standard warm-up procedure prior to entry on the treadmill:

    Running in place (high knee lift):

    > half speed–6 repetitions of 30 seconds each
    > three-quarter speed—2 repetitions of 15 seconds each
    > seven-eighths speed—2 repetitions of 8–10 seconds each
    > maximum speed—2 repetitions of 5–8 seconds each

2. A belt attached to the support rails, allowing free arm movement, balance, and safety, is needed for all high-speed work.

3. One spotter on each side of the treadmill will ensure safety should a runner slip or stumble.

4. A one-week acclimation period is needed to allow sprinters to adjust to treadmill sprinting.

5. Since the tread belt accelerates slowly and would introduce a fatigue factor if sprinters were required to jog at a slow pace and continue running until higher speeds are reached, tread belt speeds should be preset prior to entry. After a short acclimation period, entry at high speeds will be performed smoothly by all runners.

A sample program is shown below. Sprinters should be in an almost fully recovered state prior to each sprint since the objective is to improve the rate of leg movement per second and not to improve conditioning levels. A large wall clock (pool lap timer) can be used to time repetitions.

Keep in mind that the leg muscles will contract faster than ever before. To avoid injury under these conditions, both the warm-up and the acclimation period that slowly progresses to maximum and beyond maximum speeds are important.

Maximum Speed *I*	*1.5–2 mph Beyond* *Maximum Speed* *II*	*Support Running at Near-* *Maximum Tread Belt Speed* *III*
Subjects are tested weekly to determine maximum speed.	Speed adjusted 1.5–2 mph above maximum speed for that week.	Tread belt speed adjusted at maximum speed with which balance can be attained (24–26.5 mph).
1–3 repetitions for 3–5 seconds are given at maximum speed daily.	2–6 repetitions for 3–5 seconds daily.	2–5 repetitions for 3–5 seconds daily.
Free arm movement allowed with subjects in the belt.	Free arm movement allowed with subjects in the belt.	Free arm movement not permitted. Subjects grasp both rails and are required to maintain their grip and concentrate only on leg movement and keeping pace with the tread belt.

Proper running form is taught during several trial runs at slower speeds to allow the runner to adapt to treadmill use. Periodic pre- and post-testing in a 50-yard dash with a running start or the competitive 100-yard dash or 40-yard dash (football, basketball, baseball, soccer) is utilized to determine carry-over to unaided flat surface running.

Be extremely careful and *never* train alone. With a defective belt or a misplaced step at 25 mph, you could become a spot on a wall.

HOW DOES TREADMILL SPRINTING DIFFER FROM NORMAL SPRINTING ON A TRACK OR FIELD AREA?

In general, a sprinter is able to move faster on a treadmill. A treadmill also has some disadvantages that have a slowing effect; however, the aiding factors predominate and allow a faster rate of leg movement per second for most individuals, even without training.

The chart below points out the aiding and hindering factors and an explanation of why faster rates of speed occur in treadmill sprinting:

AIDING AND HINDERING FACTORS IN TREADMILL SPRINTING

+ FACTORS Aiding	Reasons for Greater Speed	− FACTORS Hindering
*Braking effect each time the lead foot touches the tread belt—belt speed is slowed at this point to obscure speedometer reading No wind resistance No unfavorable environmental conditions—temperature, inclimate weather Energy conservation—steady, unaltered pace, less knee lift, no acceleration—you accelerate fast or else	Less time on weight bearing foot Motorized belt forces a faster pace Stride length increased Challenging—pre-knowledge of belt speed Form improvement is possible; dialogue between coach and sprinter, immediate correction, high-speed filming	Limited push-off possible from weight bearing foot Form alteration required that affects positive transfer to flat-surface, un-aided sprinting

*The braking effect is greater in initial stages of treadmill running and tends to be eliminated as acclimation occurs and form instruction is given. At high speeds beyond one's maximum speed (in early use of treadmill), the braking effect almost reduces treadbelt speed to a sprinter's maximum speed. With continued training, this point is easily overcome.

Obviously, treadmill running is smoother and provides a feeling of complete mastery with little effort. Since it is an aided device, the total effort appears to be less although research indicates that oxygen uptake and energy expenditure are similar in treadmill and unaided running. The fact remains that form is altered, environment plays little influence, and a motorized belt assists one to contract and relax the muscles involved in sprinting faster than any other mode of training. It is also a quiet, safe, problem-free instrument.

Additional problems affecting treadmill sprinting include: (1) difficulty in determining belt speed. Accurate readings are possible up to 23.0 mph, while the speed adaptor kit permits speeds of 26.0 mph; thus a stopwatch or "surface speed indicator" is necessary for accurate readings in extreme speeds. (2) Adequate warm-up is needed prior to high-speed work. (3) The tread belt accelerates much more slowly than a sprinter, so an important training aspect is lost. (4) Speed increases are difficult to credit to a specific factor either on the treadmill or on flat surfaces; the degree to which faster rates of leg movement and/or increased stride length contribute is unknown.

WHAT IS PUMP AND STRIDE TRAINING?

After a thorough warm-up of jogging and flexibility exercises, the pump-and-stride method is used to improve stride rate. Runners execute three repetitions of 50 yards by bringing the knees toward the chest as far as possible in a stationary position and gradually moving forward for 50 yards. One hundred high knee pumps (20 every 10 yards) should be executed. A two minute walking rest interval is used between each repetition. Runners increase the distance to 75 and 100 yards over a 3 to 4 week period. Major emphasis is placed on rapid knee/arm pumping and high knee lifts.

WHAT ABOUT BODY FAT?

Resistance to rapid contraction within the muscle is provided by deposits of fat. Fat accumulates between bundles of muscle fibers and hinders their action. A reduction in total body fat would also reduce these deposits. For maximum speed, you should possess body fat of less than 10 percent of body weight. Since weight charts are grossly inadequate, even as an estimate of normal weight, the skinfold method should be used. Measurements at only two places (triceps, supra-iliac) are almost as reliable as use of the more complicated methods. Consult your coach for assistance in this area.

HOW IMPORTANT IS FAST-TWITCH FIBER?

It is a limiting factor for some athletes. People are born with differences in the properties of their skeletal muscle. The amount of sarcoplasm is more abundant in some individuals than others (also differs from muscle group to muscle group within the same individual). This sarcoplasm contains pigment granules giving it a redish appearance (red muscle); in other muscles where it is less abundant, muscle fibers are rather pale (white muscle). In many athletes, both types are present in every muscle group.

The important thing is that the white muscles (fast-twitch fibers) contract faster than the slower red muscles (slow-twitch fibers) which are geared more for endurance. In athletes where white fibers are plentiful in the muscles involved in sprinting, greater speed is possible. Hill running and sprinting activate and train existing fast-twitch fibers. There is also some indication that weight training can convert some of the red muscle to white muscle.

IS INCLINE RUNNING EFFECTIVE IN IMPROVING SPRINTING SPEED?

Training on uphill inclines is designed to increase leg strength, knee lift, cardiovascular/respiratory endurance, and speed endurance. It also trains the fast-twitch muscle fibers, although only limited research has been conducted in this area; opponents of uphill incline running contend that such training will shorten stride length and actually hinder sprinting speed. Advocates of uphill training counter by stating that since this method is combined with flat surface training, flexibility exercises, and stride training, it will not decrease stride length and can improve sprinting speed through improved strength. As indicated previously, the combined use of uphill-downhill-flat surface training appears to produce the most favorable results. The uphill slope should be no more than 3.4 degrees from the horizontal.

Staircase sprinting is also commonly used by football coaches as a means of improving leg strength. Keep in mind that any type of incline training program is a supplement to flat surface sprint training. An added advantage of uphill or staircase training is the caloric expenditure (considerably greater than expenditure in flat surface training) and the resultant strengthening of the knee ligaments. For the slightly overweight athlete and the participant in contact sports where the incidence of knee injuries is high, these are important factors.

IS THE USE OF WEIGHTED CLOTHING EFFECTIVE IN IMPROVING SPRINTING SPEED?

The use of ankle spats, heavy shoes, chest vests, and other items weighing from 2½ to 25 pounds as a means of improving sprinting speed must be evaluated from two approaches: (1) the immediate after effects of this increased resistance upon sprinting speed, and (2) the long-range effects upon strength and sprinting speed.

For immediate aftereffects, weighted clothing is worn for a period of 15 to 30 minutes and then removed just prior to actual competition to provide the initial feeling of lightfootedness. This feeling is provided by using one bat after swinging three, or using a weighted doughnut, or removing football gear, ankle spats, or heavy shoes. The important point is whether removal of this resistance results in improved performance. The following is a summary of the conflicting findings of past researchers:

1. Speed of throwing a baseball significantly increased, without hindering accuracy, following throws with a heavier ball.
2. Speed of swinging a bat increased significantly following use of a heavier object.
3. Use of a weighted vest prior to removal and testing in the vertical jump did not improve performance.
4. Preliminary use of a 16-pound shot reduced performance in the 12-pound shot.
5. Elbow flexion speed did not increase significantly following use of three levels of overload.
6. Neither foul shooting nor speed of riding a bicycle ergometer was affected by overload procedures.

It would appear also that this method is of questionable value in the improvement of sprinting speed.

Long-range use of weighted clothing is concerned with strength development and the subsequent effects upon sprinting speed. Additional research is needed to evaluate properly its long-term effects upon sprinting speed.

IS THERE AN IDEAL SPRINTING FORM?

No. Style varies from individual to individual with so-called correct form generally associated with championship sprinters. There just is no one perfect style for individuals of all body types and differences in strength, flexibility, explosive power, reflexes, reaction time, and endurance. There is also no one body type or build associated with sprinting speed. The one key factor is driving power, which can be present in any individual.

One researcher uncovered a range of factors among championship sprinters that may help somewhat. Few fell outside the realm of 130–170 pounds, 67–75 inches in height, or more than 25 years of age.

Since you are a unique individual, you must take the ideal form in theory and adapt it to your own personal traits. This will result in maximum efficiency for you.

Do not take form lightly. Running form is far from an unnatural act. Nine out of ten children from the elementary school through the college years possess faulty style. To eliminate faulty habits requires special attention.

WHAT ARE THE MOST IMPORTANT FACTORS IN GOOD SPRINTING FORM?

This is a good question, and the answer does not require great detail on the many different aspects of form. Researchers have associated numerous factors with successful sprinting:

1. A forceful push of the rear leg—kick action or driving power
2. High knee lift
3. Placement of the foot directly beneath the center of gravity
4. A long stride
5. Adequate upper and lower body strength
6. Proper body lean, and arm and leg movement

Keep in mind that sprinting is merely a series of jumps. If you run 100 meters in 12 seconds, for example, you have foot/ground contact for about 5 seconds and are in the air for 7 seconds. Unfortunately, straight running, rhythm, bounce, relaxation, smoothness, and mechanically sound upper and lower body movement are needed to take these jumps with maximum efficiency. You must master commonly accepted form from the start to the finish by studying, experimenting, and adapting to your body traits.

SO MANY CHILDREN AND ATHLETES RUN INCORRECTLY. WHAT ARE SOME OF THE COMMON MISTAKES AND HOW CAN THEY BE CORRECTED?

Running may be a basic fundamental movement, but it is far from a natural act. Anyone who observes the faulty styles at the preschool, elementary, high school, and college levels realizes how complex and difficult proper form is to master. Relays, team sports, and free play do little to improve form. Special attention is required at all school levels if faulty habits are to be eliminated early. The elementary schools are our only hope to develop proper form and correct errors before they are so deeply embedded that change is next to impossible.

COMMON ERRORS	CORRECTION
Arm Action	Practice loose, swinging movements from a standing position. Swing the entire arm from the shoulders. Thumbs should brush the thighs. Increase arm speed; elbows more flexed, hands loosely cupped and brushing against the side.
Hands too low	Place tape around the wrist and over the neck.
Hands moving too far forward	Swing arms to contact the hands of a partner standing behind the runner.
Hands outside line of elbows	Sprint while holding a stick in both hands with the proper spacing.
Body lean	Sprint with eye contact on a fixed spot, high or low, depending upon the problem.
Limited foot bounce	Walk forward high on toes using proper arm action, body weight low, bouncing the knee forward from the foot. Stand on one foot, bounce opposite foot up and down on the sole as rapidly as possible.
Unnecessary pounding into the ground	Practice running as lightly as possible
Incorrect knee-leg action	Practice running upstairs two-at-a-time and running along the beach in shallow water.
Striding: Overstriding	Same as above. Avoid placing the lead food beyond the center of gravity.
Understriding	Concentrate on complete extension of the hip and knee joint at ground contact and complete knee pickup of the recovery leg. Emphasize the push off with the contact foot.

Running is the basis for practically all sports activity. If it is done improperly, maximum speed for you is not reached. With one-tenth of a second making the difference in every sport, form becomes very critical. Devote at least ten minutes daily in your sport to form training.

WHAT DO YOU SUGGEST AS A YEAR-ROUND TRAINING PROGRAM FOR SPRINTERS?

The articulation of five basic programs are needed for optimum results: explosive power and strength training, flexibility training, form and stride training, reaction time training, and sprint training/sprint-assisted training. Fartlek training or a similar program is used periodically to assist in the development of aerobic and anaerobic endurance. Acquiring a high level of general conditioning (cardiovascular/respiratory and local muscular endurance) precedes use of specialized training programs.

Implementation of these programs on a year-round basis is shown in the chart below. Such a program is used by champion sprinters and it is felt that this is the only sound approach to becoming a champion athlete.

Following the competitive season, a modified three- to four-week rest period consisting of active games is desirable for both physical and mental relaxation without great physical deterioration. This post-season period utilizes a gradual conditioning process that progresses from light workouts to more intense training. Considerable attention is placed upon cardiovascular/respiratory training, strength training, explosive power training, form and stride training including practice in starting, and the elevation of the pain threshold through maximum effort drills.

The preseason period utilizes more intense training sessions as sprint training and supplementary programs strive for maximum improvement in strength, explosive power, flexibility, reaction time, and sprinting and starting form.

During the in-season period, strength and explosive power gains acquired during the off-season are maintained through one vigorous strength training session weekly (Wednesday following the normal practice routine). Such a maintenance approach is also desirable for athletes in football, basketball, soccer, and baseball during the in-season period. Daily stretching exercises and periodic form and stride training help maintain flexibility gains and continue to improve sprinting and starting form. The early in-season period is very intense, with large amounts of total sprinting and exercise volume incorporated into the daily schedule, tapering off as the competitive season approaches with longer recovery periods and intense training sessions, alternating with light workout days permitting complete recovery. Monday utilizes overdistance running at a slower pace, with the heaviest training day scheduled for Tuesday, strength/explosive power maintenance training held at the close of Wednesday's slightly lighter workout, followed by light workouts Thursday and Friday (practice run of Saturday's events), formal competition on Saturday, and a day of rest on Sunday.

This suggested weekly routine during the competitive season is relatively common; however, it is not the only routine in use among champion sprinters. Numerous other approaches may be equally effective.

During the late competitive season, practice intensity is again reduced. Periods of rest (one or two days in a seven-day period) are used throughout the off-season and in-season periods as needed by the individual.

MASTER SCHEDULE FOR A CONTINUOUS TRAINING PROGRAM.

SEASON	Approximate Time Period	Programs	Comments
In-Season	4–4½ months	Sprint training	Daily, including sprint-assisted training 2–3 times weekly prior to the competitive season or first contest.
		Form and stride training	2-3 times weekly including starting practice which occurs at the beginning of the practice session when athletes are fresh.
		Weight training	Training for strength maintenance, once weekly (middle of the week) using the basic program, 2–3 times weekly for additional strength and explosive power improvement prior to the first scheduled contest if needed. Follows sprint training.
		Flexibility training	Daily, prior to sprint training and following each weight training or isometric training session.

SEASON	Approximate Time Period	Programs	Comments
In-Season (Continued)		Maximum effort training	2–3 times weekly for 5–15 minutes following the sprint training session on days when weight training or isometrics are not scheduled. Used only 1–2 weeks prior to the first scheduled contest.
		Testing	50-yard dash with a flying start, once weekly.
Post-Season	4½–5 months	Sprint training	Alternate day program involving pickup sprints, hollow sprints, interval sprint training, and some speed play
		Form and stride training	Twice weekly. Includes starting practice.
		Weight training	Training for effect, 3 times weekly. Use basic program and concentrations stressing both strength and explosive power training. Great strength gains should occur during this period —to be maintained with one workout weekly during the in-season period.
		Flexibility training	Daily, prior to sprint training and following each weight-training session.
		Maximum effort training	Three times weekly using the basic program and concentrations.
Pre-Season	2–2½ months	Sprint training	Alternate-day program including sprint-assisted training (towing, downhill running, or treadmill running).
		Form and stride training	Three or four times weekly. Includes starting practice and concentration on weakness areas for perfection.

SEASON	Approximate Time Period	Programs	Comments
Pre-Season *(Continued)*		Weight training/ explosive power training	Alternate-day program when not engaged in sprint training. Explosive power training is oriented toward improved starting ability.
		Flexibility training	Daily, prior to sprint training and following each weight training session.
		Maximum effort training	Three times weekly following each sprint training session.
		Reaction time training	Twice weekly prior to sprint training sessions.

Football, basketball, soccer, and baseball players should also emphasize skill training in weakness areas during the post-season as a means of improving performance. Less attention should be given to skill areas where competence is already high.

From George D. Dintiman, *How to Run Faster: A Do-It-Yourself Book for Athletes in All Sports*. Champion Athlete Publishing Co., Box 2936, Richmond, Va., 23235. 1979.

IS RUNNING AT MAXIMUM SPEED AUTOMATIC OR IS IT NECESSARY TO CONCENTRATE DURING A CONTEST?

The mind can concentrate on only one act at a time. The athlete who is thinking about ways to elude a potential tackler or defensive player, about outside problems during a 100-yard dash, or whether the ball is going to be caught while he is running to first base, is distracting attention away from the important skill—the act of sprinting as fast as possible. You must concentrate hard on running, making an effort to accelerate and attain maximum speed. Failure to do so will result in sub-maximum speed. This explains why a fast runner is occasionally caught from behind by a slower player or why upsets occur in sprinting events. Sprinting with the step of the passer by the defensive halfback, lateral movement at top speed to maintain proper defensive position in guarding the dribbler, sprinting for a line drive, all require concentration on that act without distraction from outside phenomena.

Concentration is also important in the "start." Attention is focused upon the first muscular movement such as a fast arm action or quick, high knee lift rather than on the sound of the gun. If attention is placed on the gun, a slower reaction occurs, since you then must shift attention from sound to movement. A 22-caliber pistol about to go off 6 feet from your head will be heard. You need not listen for it.

In every sport, there are times when athletes are sprinting at 90 to 95 percent of their maximum speed. This is often interpreted as loafing when it may be only lack of concentration. Prove it to yourself. Time a 50-yard dash as you concentrate on a history exam, your arm movement, or length of your stride. Compare that time to one that involved total concentration on moving legs and arms at maximum speed. Sprinting cannot be combined with creative thinking.

HOW IMPORTANT IS SPEED IN MAKING A PROFESSIONAL FOOTBALL TEAM?

It is *the* most important factor for every position except quarterback. Professional football coaches use the 40-yard dash in full uniform as a test to determine the best position suited for the athlete, to evaluate the overall potential of an athlete for a specific position, and to determine overall football ability.

Failure to meet the 40-yard dash standards listed below make it difficult to become an excellent player for that position in professional football.

40-YARD DASH STANDARDS

Professional football—range of 6 teams surveyed

Offensive:		*Defensive:*	
Flanker	4.5–4.6	Cornerback	4.5–4.7
Halfback	4.6–4.8	Safety	4.7
Quarterback	4.7–4.8	Corner linebacker	5.0
Tight end	4.8–4.9	Middle linebacker	5.2
Fullback	4.8–5.0	End	5.0–5.2
Guard	5.1–5.2	Tackle	5.2–5.3
Center	5.4		
Tackle	5.4–5.5		

College football—range of 5 major teams surveyed

Backs	4.7–4.8	Defensive backs	4.8
Ends	4.8–4.9	Linebackers	5.2–5.3
Quarterbacks	4.9	Linemen	5.4–5.5

Ability, aggressiveness, stature, and weight can offset speed limitations at all positions. Rarely is a quarterback as fast as the standards listed. The cold fact remains, however, that you must possess above average speed to make it in the pros. Speed will not develop automatically. It takes hard work. Plan your long-term attack to improve speed and quickness.

WHAT CAN A TEAM SPORT COACH DO TO IMPROVE SPRINTING SPEED DURING THE IN-SEASON PERIOD?

Some adjustment and departure from the normal practice routine is necessary. It is recommended that you:

1. Commit a portion of each practice day and the major thrust of the off-season period to speed improvement.
2. Test at least twice per season using both a flying or running start and a stationary start, depending upon the sport and position.
3. Assign a sprint training coach specifically to this task. Elicit assistance from the track coach.
4. Change the proportion of anaerobic training to at least 75 percent.
5. Eliminate wind sprints from the program. Substitute with sprint training and sprint-assisted training that allow full recovery prior to each repetition.
6. Eliminate calisthenics from the beginning of each practice session. Replace with flexibility exercises, followed by sprint training.
7. Use explosive power/strength training (weight training) three times weekly following the practice session. Emphasize explosive movements that closely simulate the sprinting action.
8. Avoid use of isometric training. Static strength is of little use to the sprinter.
9. Have players trim off all excess fat.
10. Analyze each individual in an attempt to identify weaknesses that are restricting movement and preventing the player from reaching maximum speed potential.
11. Emphasize speed improvement through: increasing stride length, increasing rate of leg alternation per second, and improving acceleration to maximum speed.

Don't panic. These changes do not have to distract greatly from a normal practice routine.

Chapter References

CHAPTER ONE
[1]James H. Jordan, "Physiological and Anthropometrical Comparisons of Negroes and Whites," *JOPHER*, 40 (November–December 1969), 93–99.

CHAPTER FIVE
[1]American Association for Health, Physical Education, and Recreation, *Nutrition for Athletes*. Washington, D.C.
[2]Irwin M. Stillman and Samm S. Baker, *The Doctor's Quick Weight Loss Diet*. New York: Dell, 1967.

CHAPTER SEVEN
[1]Lynn Lashbrook, "Artificial Turf: The Facts about Fake Grass," *JOHPER*, 42 (November–December), 28–29.
[2]Fred L. Allman, Otho Davis, and Karl K. Klein, "Recommendation for the Cleating of Football Shoes," *The Journal of the National Athletic Trainers Association*, 6 (Fall 1971), 115–121.
[3]Karl K. Klein, *The Knees: Growth, Development and Activity Influences*. Greeloy: All American Productions and Publications, 1967.

CHAPTER EIGHT
[1]M. Ender, *Virginia Medical Monthly*, June 8, 1966.

CHAPTER ELEVEN
[1]George B. Dintiman, *How to Run Faster: A Do-It-Yourself Book for Athletes in All Sports*. (2nd ed.). Box 2936, Richmond Virginia: Champion Athlete Publishing Co., 1979.
[2]———. *Sprinting Speed: Its Improvement for Major Sports Competition*. Springfield, Illinois: Charles C. Thomas, Publisher, 1971.
[3]Lloyd C. Winter, *So You Want to Be a Sprinter?* Palo Alto, California: Fearon Publishers, 1956.
[4]Kenneth J. Doherty, *Modern Track and Field*. Englewood Cliffs, N.J.: Prentice-Hall, Inc., 1965.
[5]Sandwick, Charles M., "Pacing Machine" *Athletic Journal*. 47(1967), pp. 36–38.